Lecture Notes in Computer Science 9038

Commenced Publication in 1973
Founding and Former Series Editors:
Gerhard Goos, Juris Hartmanis, and Jan van Leeuwen

More information about this series at http://www.springer.com/series/7411

Alysson Bessani · Sara Bouchenak (Eds.)

Distributed Applications and Interoperable Systems

15th IFIP WG 6.1 International Conference, DAIS 2015
Held as Part of the 10th International Federated Conference
on Distributed Computing Techniques, DisCoTec 2015
Grenoble, France, June 2–4, 2015
Proceedings

 Springer

Editors
Alysson Bessani
Universidade de Lisboa
Lisbon
Portugal

Sara Bouchenak
INSA Lyon
Lyon
France

ISSN 0302-9743   ISSN 1611-3349   (electronic)
Lecture Notes in Computer Science
ISBN 978-3-319-19128-7   ISBN 978-3-319-19129-4   (eBook)
DOI 10.1007/978-3-319-19129-4

Library of Congress Control Number: 2015939270

LNCS Sublibrary: SL5 – Computer and Communication Networks and Telecommunications

Springer Cham Heidelberg New York Dordrecht London

Printed on acid-free paper

Springer International Publishing AG Switzerland is part of Springer Science+Business Media
(www.springer.com)

Foreword

The 10th International Federated Conference on Distributed Compting Techniques (DisCoTec) took place in Montbonnot, near Grenoble, France, during June 2–5, 2015. It was hosted and organized by Inria, the French National Research Institute in Computer Science and Control. The DisCoTec series is one of the major events sponsored by the International Federation for Information Processing (IFIP). It comprises three conferences:

- COORDINATION, the IFIP WG6.1 International Conference on Coordination Models and Languages.
- DAIS, the IFIP WG6.1 International Conference on Distributed Applications and Interoperable Systems.
- FORTE, the IFIP WG6.1 International Conference on Formal Techniques for Distributed Objects, Components and Systems.

Together, these conferences cover a broad spectrum of distributed computing subjects, ranging from theoretical foundations and formal description techniques to systems research issues.

Each day of the federated event began with a plenary keynote speaker nominated by one of the conferences. The three invited speakers were Alois Ferscha (Johannes Kepler Universität, Linz, Austria), Leslie Lamport (Microsoft Research, USA), and Willy Zwaenepoel (EPFL, Lausanne, Switzerland).

Associated with the federated event were also three satellite workshops, that took place on June 5, 2015:

- The 2nd International Workshop on Formal Reasoning in Distributed Algorithms (FRIDA), with a keynote speech by Leslie Lamport (Microsoft Research, USA).
- The 8th International Workshop on Interaction and Concurrency Experience (ICE), with keynote lectures by Jade Alglave (University College London, UK) and Steve Ross-Talbot (ZDLC, Cognizant Technology Solutions, London, UK).
- The 2nd International Workshop on Meta Models for Process Languages (MeMo).

Sincere thanks go to the chairs and members of the Program and Steering Committees of the involved conferences and workshops for their highly appreciated efforts. Organizing DisCoTec was only possible thanks to the dedicated work of the Organizing Committee from Inria Grenoble-Rhône-Alpes, including Sophie Azzaro, Vanessa Peregrin, Martine Consigney, Alain Kersaudy, Sophie Quinton, Jean-Bernard Stefani, and the excellent support from Catherine Nuel and the people at Insight Outside. Finally, many thanks go to IFIP WG6.1 for sponsoring this event, and to Inria Rhône-Alpes and his director Patrick Gros for their support and sponsorship.

Alain Girault
DisCoTec 2015 General Chair

DisCoTec Steering Committee

Preface

This volume contains the proceedings of the 15th IFIP International Conference on Distributed Applications and Interoperable Systems (IFIP DAIS 2015) held during June 2–4, 2015 in Grenoble. DAIS is one of the three conferecenes that form the DisCoTec 2015, the 10th International Federated Conference on Distributed Computing Techniques, together with COORDINATION and FORTE.

The proceedings volume includes 17 papers, among which 14 are full papers and 3 are short papers. The papers relate to areas such as fault tolerance, privacy, resource management, social recommenders, and cloud systems.

The program of the DisCoTec 2015 federated conference also includes invited talks by Alois Ferscha (Johannes Kepler Universität, Austria), Leslie Lamport (Microsoft Research, USA), and Willy Zwaenepoel (EPFL, Switzerland).

We would like to thank the Program Committee members for their effort in evaluating the submitted papers, and thank all the authors of submitted papers for considering DAIS for their work. Additionally, we would like to thank the DAIS Steering Committee for their support in organizing and setting up the conference. We also thank the developers and maintainers of the EasyChair conference management system for making their system available to the research community.

Finally, our thanks also go to IFIP, Inria, and Génération ROBOTS for their support for the DisCoTec 2015 federated conference.

April 2015

Alysson Bessani
Sara Bouchenak

Organization

DAIS Steering Committee

Jim Dowling	KTH Stockholm, Sweden
Frank Eliassen	University of Oslo, Norway
Pascal Felber	Université de Neuchâtel, Switzerland
Karl Goeschka	Vienna University of Technology, Austria
Seif Haridi	KTH, Stockholm, Sweden
Rüdiger Kapitza	Technische Universität Braunschweig, Germany
Kostas Magoutis	FORTH-ICS, Greece
Rui Oliveira	Universidade do Minho, Portugal (Chair)
Peter Pietzuch	Imperial College London, UK
Romain Rouvoy	Université Lille 1, France
Francois Taiani	University of Rennes 1, France

DAIS 2015 Program Committee

Program Committee Chairs

Alysson Bessani	Universidade de Lisboa, Portugal
Sara Bouchenak	INSA Lyon, France

Program Committee Members

Luciana Arantes	Université Pierre et Marie Curie-Paris 6, France
Carlos Baquero	HASLab, INESC TEC and Universidade do Minho, Portugal
Sonia Ben Mokhtar	LIRIS CNRS, France
Andrea Bondavalli	University of Florence, Italy
Rajkumar Buyya	University of Melbourne, Australia
Jian-Nong Cao	Hong Kong Polytechnic University, Hong Kong
Miguel Correia	IST/INESC-ID, Portugal
Wolfgang De Meuter	Vrije Universiteit Brussel, Belgium
Jim Dowling	Swedish Institute of Computer Science, Kista, Sweden
Frank Eliassen	University of Oslo, Norway
David Eyers	University of Otago, New Zealand
Pascal Felber	Université de Neuchâtel, Switzerland
Kurt Geihs	Universität Kassel, Germany
Karl M. Göschka	FH Technikum Wien, Austria
Fabíola Greve	Universidade Federal da Bahia, Brazil
Franz J. Hauck	University of Ulm, Germany

K.R. Jayaram	IBM Research, USA
Evangelia Kalyvianaki	City University London, UK
Rüdiger Kapitza	Technische Universität Braunschweig, Germany
Boris Koldehofe	University of Stuttgart, Germany
Benjamin Mandler	IBM Research, Israel
Rene Meier	Lucerne University of Applied Sciences, Switzerland
Alberto Montresor	University of Trento, Italy
Kiran-Kumar Muniswamy-Reddy	Harvard School of Engineering and Applied Sciences, USA
Marta Patino	Universidad Politécnica de Madrid, Spain
José Pereira	INESC TEC & Universidade do Minho, Portugal
Peter Pietzuch	Imperial College London, UK
Hans P. Reiser	University of Passau, Germany
Altair Santin	Pontifical Catholic University of Paraná, Brazil
Dilma Da Silva	Texas A&M University, USA
Spyros Voulgaris	VU University Amsterdam, The Netherlands

Additional Reviewers

Almeida, José Bacelar
Baraki, Harun
Barreto, Marcos
Bouchenak, Sara
Brandenburger, Marcus
Carlini, Emanuele
Cassens, Björn
Ceccarelli, Andrea
Ferreira, Pedro
Gonçalves, Ricardo
Li, Bijun
Lollini, Paolo
Martens, Arthur
Marynowski, João Eugenio
Mori, Marco
Myter, Florian
Nogueira, Andre

Pandey, Navneet Kumar
Petrucci, Vinicius
Pita, Robespierre
Regnier, Paul
Saey, Mathijs
Schiavoni, Valerio
Shoker, Ali
Stihler, Maicon
Sutra, Pierre
Swalens, Janwillem
Taherkordi, Amir
Taubmann, Benjamin
Tran Huu, Tam
Van de Water, Simon
Vandriessche, Yves
Witsch, Andreas

Contents

Fluidify: Decentralized Overlay Deployment in a Multi-cloud World

Ariyattu C. Resmi[1(✉)] and François Taiani[1,2]

[1] Université de Rennes 1 - IRISA, Rennes, France
[2] ESIR, Rennes, France
{rariyatt,francois.taiani}@irisa.fr

Abstract. As overlays get deployed in large, heterogeneous systems-of-systems with stringent performance constraints, their logical topology must exploit the locality present in the underlying physical network. In this paper, we propose a novel decentralized mechanism—Fluidify—for deploying an overlay network on top of a physical infrastructure while maximizing network locality. Fluidify uses a dual strategy that exploits both the logical links of an overlay and the physical topology of its underlying network. Simulation results show that in a network of 25,600 nodes, Fluidify is able to produce an overlay with links that are on average 94% shorter than that produced by a standard decentralized approach based on slicing, while demonstrating a sub-linear time complexity.

1 Introduction

Overlays are increasingly used as a fundamental building block of modern distributed systems, with numerous applications [15,5,8,11,22,25,13]. Unfortunately, many popular overlay construction protocols [10,27,1] do not usually take into account the underlying network infrastructure on which an overlay is deployed, and those that do tend to be limited to a narrow family of applications or overlays [30,29]. This is particularly true of systems running in multiple clouds, in which latency may vary greatly, and ignoring this heterogeneity can have stark implications in terms of performance and latency.

In the past, several works have sought to take into account the topology of the underlying infrastructure to realise network-aware overlays [30,29,28,21]. However, most of the proposed solutions are service-specific and they do not translate easily to other overlays. To address this lack, we propose a novel decentralized mechanism—called Fluidify—that seeks to maximize network locality when deploying an overlay network. Fluidify uses a dual strategy that exploits both the logical links of an overlay and the physical topology of its underlying infrastructure to progressively align one with the other. Our approach is fully decentralized and does not assume any global knowledge or central form of co-ordination.

The resulting protocol is generic, efficient, scalable. Simulation results show that in a network of 25,600 nodes, Fluidify is able to produce an overlay with links that are on average 94% shorter than that produced by a standard decentralized

© IFIP International Federation for Information Processing 2015
A. Bessani and S. Bouchenak (Eds.): DAIS 2015, LNCS 9038, pp. 1–15, 2015.
DOI: 10.1007/978-3-319-19129-4_1

approach based on slicing, while converging to a stable configuration in a time that is sub-linear ($\approx O(n^{0.6})$) in the size of the system.

The remainder of the paper is organized as follows. We first present the problem we address and our intuition (Sec. 2). We then present our algorithm (Sec. 3), and its evaluation (Sec. 4). We finally discuss related work (Sec. 5), and conclude (Sec. 6).

2 Background, Problem, and Intuition

Overlay networks organize peers in logical topologies on top of an existing network to extend its capabilities, with application to storage [22,25], routing [8,11], recommendation [27,1], and streaming [15,5]. Although overlays were originally proposed in the context of peer-to-peer (P2P) systems, their application today encompasses wireless sensor networks [7] and cloud computing [3,13].

2.1 The Problem: Building Network-Aware Overlays

One of the challenges when using overlays, in particular structured ones, is to maintain desirable properties within the topology, in spite of failures, churn, and request for horizontal scaling. This challenge can be addressed through decentralized topology construction protocols [10,27,17,14], which are scalable and highly flexible. Unfortunately, such topology construction solutions are not usually designed to take into account the infrastructure on which an overlay is deployed. This brings clear advantages in terms of fault-tolerance, but is problematic from a performance perspective, as overlay links may in fact connect hosts that are far away in the physical topology. This is particularly likely to happen in heterogeneous systems, such as multi-cloud deployment, in which latency values might vary greatly depending on the location of individual nodes.

For instance, Fig. 1(a) depicts a randomly connected overlay deployed over two cloud providers (rounded rectangles). All overlay links cross the two providers, which is highly inefficient. By contrast, in Fig. 1(b), the same logical overlay only uses two distant links, and thus minimizes latency and network costs.

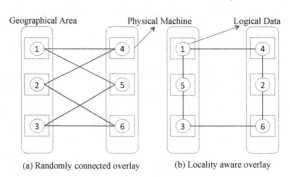

(a) Randomly connected overlay   (b) Locality aware overlay

Fig. 1. Illustration of a randomly connected overlay and a network-aware overlay

This problem has been explored in the past [30,29,28,21,20], but most of the proposed solutions are either tied to a particular service or topology, or limited to unstructured overlays, and therefore cannot translate to the type of systems we have just mentioned, which is exactly where the work we present comes in.

2.2   Our Intuition: A Dual Approach

Our proposal, Fluidify, uses a dual strategy that exploits both an overlay's logical links and its physical topology to incrementally optimize its deployment.

We model a deployed overlay as follows: each node possesses a physical index, representing the physical machine on which it runs, and a logical index, representing its logical position in the overlay. Each node also has a physical and logical neighbourhood: the physical neighbors of a node are its d closest neighbors in the physical infrastructure, according to some distance function $d_{net}()$ that captures the cost of communication between nodes. The logical neighbors of a node are the node's neighbors in the overlay being deployed. For simplicity's sake, we model the physical topology as an explicit undirected graph between nodes, with a fixed degree. We take d to be the fixed degree of the graph, and the distance function to be the number of hops in this topology.

Fig. 2(a) shows an initial configuration in which the overlay has been deployed without taking into account the underlying physical infrastructure. In this example, both the overlay (solid line) and the physical infrastructure (represented by the nodes' positions) are assumed to be rings. The two logical indices 0 and 1 are neighbors in the overlay, but are diametrically placed in the underlying infrastructure. By contrast Fig. 2(c) shows an optimal deployment in which the logical and physical links overlap.

Our intuition, in Fluidify, consists of exploiting both the logical and physical neighbors of individual nodes, in a manner inspired from epidemic protocols, to move from the configuration of Fig. 2(a) to that of Fig. 2(c). Our basic algorithm is organized in asynchronous rounds and implements a greedy approach as follows: in each round, each node n randomly selects one of its *logical* neighbors (noted p) and considers the *physical* neighbor of p (noted q) that is closest to itself. n evaluates the overall benefit of exchanging its logical index with that of q. If positive, the exchange occurs (Fig. 2(b) and then Fig. 2(c)).

Being a greedy algorithm, this basic strategy carries the risk of ending in a local minimum (Fig.3). To mitigate such situations, we use simulated annealing

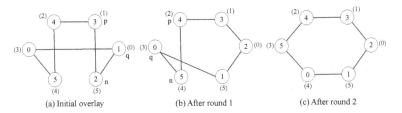

(a) Initial overlay   (b) After round 1   (c) After round 2

Fig. 2. Example of basic Fluidify approach on a system with $n=6$ and $d=2$

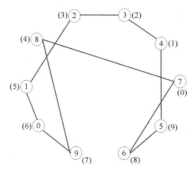

Fig. 3. Example of local minimum of a system with $n=10$ and $d=2$

(taking inspiration from recent works on epidemic slicing[19]), resulting in a decentralized protocol for the deployment of overlay networks that is generic, efficient and scalable.

3   The Fluidify Algorithm

3.1   System Model

We consider a set of nodes $N = \{n_1, n_2, .., n_N\}$ in a message passing system. Each node n possesses a physical (n.net) and a logical index (n.data). n.net represents the machine on which a node is deployed. n.data represents the role n plays in the overlay, e.g. a starting key in a Chord ring [17,25].

Table 1 summarizes the notations we use. We model the physical infrastructure as an undirected graph $\mathcal{G}_{\text{net}} = (N, E_{\text{net}})$, and capture the proximity of nodes in this physical infrastructure through the distance function $\mathsf{d}_{\text{net}}()$. In a first approximation, we use the hop distance between two nodes in $\mathcal{G}_{\text{net}}$ for $\mathsf{d}_{\text{net}}()$, but any other distance would work. Similarly, we model the overlay being deployed as an undirected graph $\mathcal{G}_{\text{data}} = (N, E_{\text{data}})$ over the nodes N.

Our algorithms use the k-NN neighborhood of a node n in a graph $\mathcal{G}_x$, i.e. the k nodes closest to n in hop distance in $\mathcal{G}_x$, which we note as $\Gamma_x^k(n)$. We assume that these k-NN neighborhoods are maintained with the help of a topology construction protocol [10,27,1]. In the rest of the paper, we discuss and evaluate our approach independently of the topology construction used, to clearly isolate its workings and benefits. Under the above model, finding a good deployment of $\mathcal{G}_{\text{data}}$ onto $\mathcal{G}_{\text{net}}$ can be seen as a graph mapping problem, in which one seeks to optimize the cost function $\sum_{(n,m)\in E_{\text{data}}} \mathsf{d}_{\text{net}}(n, m)$.

3.2   Fluidify

The basic version of Fluidiy (termed Fluidify (basic)) directly implements the ideas discussed in Sec. 2.2 (Fig. 4): each node n first chooses a random *logical* neighbor (noted p, line 2), and then searches for the *physical* neighbor of p

Table 1. Notations and Entities

$n.\text{net}$	physical index of node n
$n.\text{data}$	logical index of node n
d_{net}	distance function to calculate the distance between two nodes in physical space
$\mathcal{G}_{\text{net}}$	the physical graph (N, E_{net})
$\mathcal{G}_{\text{data}}$	the logical graph (N, E_{data})
$\Gamma_{\text{net}}^k(n)$	k closest nodes to n in $\mathcal{G}_{\text{net}}$, in hop distance
$\Gamma_{\text{data}}^k(n)$	k closest nodes to n in $\mathcal{G}_{\text{data}}$, in hop distance

Table 2. Parameters of Fluidify

k_{net}	size of the physical neighborhood explored by Fluidify
k_{data}	size of the logical neighborhood explored by Fluidify
K_0	initial threshold value for simulated annealing
r_{max}	fade-off period for simulated annealing (# rounds)

```
 1: In round(r) do
 2:     p ← random node from Γ_data^{k_data}(n)
 3:     q ← argmin_{u∈Γ_net^{k_net}(p)} Δ(n, u)

 4:     conditional_swap(n, q, 0)

 5: Procedure Δ(n, u)
 6:     δ_n ← Σ_{(n,r)∈E_data} d_net(u, r) − Σ_{(n,r)∈E_data} d_net(n, r)

 7:     δ_u ← Σ_{(u,r)∈E_data} d_net(n, r) − Σ_{(u,r)∈E_data} d_net(u, r)

 8:     return δ_n + δ_u
 9: Procedure conditional_swap(n, q, δ_lim)
10:     if Δ(n, q) < δ_lim then
11:         swap n.data and q.data
12:         swap Γ_data^{k_data}(n) and Γ_data^{k_data}(q)
13:     end if
```

Fig. 4. Fluidify (basic)

(noted q) that offers the best reduction in cost (argmin operator at line 3)[1]. The code shown slightly generalises the principles presented in Sec. 2, in that the nodes p and q are chosen beyond the 1-hop neighborhood of n and p (lines 2 and 3), and consider nodes that are k_{data} and k_{net} hops away, respectively.

The potential cost reduction is computed by the procedure $\Delta(n, u)$ (lines 5-8), which returns the cost variation if n and u were to exchange their roles in the overlay. The decision whether to swap is made in conditional_swap$(n, q, \delta_{\text{lim}})$ (with $\delta_{\text{lim}} = 0$ in Fluidify Basic).

To mitigate the risk of local minimums, we extend it with simulated annealing [19], which allows two nodes to be swapped even if there is an increase in the cost function. We call the resulting protocol Fluidify (SA), shown in Figure 5. In this version, we swap nodes if the change in the cost function is less than a

---

[1] $\text{argmin}_{x \in S}\big(f(x)\big)$ returns one of the x in S that minimizes $f(x)$.

```
1: In round(r) do
2:      p ← random node from Γ_data^{k_data}(n)
3:      q ← argmin_{u∈Γ_net^{k_net}(p)} Δ(n, u)

4:      conditional_swap(n, q, Δ_limit(r))

5: Procedure Δ_limit(r)
6:      return max(0, K_0 × (1 − r/r_max))
```

Fig. 5. Fluidify (SA)

limit, $\Delta_{\text{limit}}(r)$, that gradually decreases to zero as the rounds progress (line 4). $\Delta_{\text{limit}}(r)$ is controlled by two parameters, K_0 which is the initial threshold value, and r_{max} which is the number of rounds in which it is decreased to 0. In the remainder of this paper, we use Fluidify to mean Fluidify (SA).

4   Evaluation

4.1   Experimental Setting and Metrics

Unless otherwise indicated, we use rings for both infrastructure graph $\mathcal{G}_{\text{net}}$ and overlay graph $\mathcal{G}_{\text{data}}$. We assume that the system has converged when the system remains stable for 10 rounds.

The default simulation scenario is one in which the system consists of 3200 nodes, and use 16-NN logical and physical neighborhoods ($k_{\text{net}} = k_{\text{data}} = 16$) when selecting p and q. The initial threshold value for simulated annealing (K_0) is taken as $|N|$. r_{max} is taken as $|N|^{0.6}$ where 0.6 was chosen based on the analysis of the number of rounds Fluidify (basic) takes to converge.

We assess the protocols using two metrics:

- Proximity - captures the quality of the overlay constructed by the topology construction algorithm. Lower value denotes a better quality.
- Convergence time - measures the number of rounds taken by the system to converge.

Proximity is defined as the average network distance of logical links normalized by the diameter of the network graph $\mathcal{G}_{\text{net}}$:

$$proximity = \frac{\underset{(n,m)\in E_{\text{data}}}{\mathbb{E}}\ \mathrm{d}_{\text{net}}(n, m)}{\text{diameter}(\mathcal{G}_{\text{net}})} \tag{1}$$

where $\mathbb{E}$ represents the expectation operator, i.e. the mean of a value over a given domain, and *diameter*() returns the longest shortest path between pairs of vertices in a graph, i.e. its diameter. In a ring, it is equal to $N/2$.

4.2   Baselines

The performance of our approach is compared against three other approaches. One is Randomized (SA) (Fig. 6) where each node considers a set of random nodes from N for a possible swap. The other is inspired from epidemic

```
1: In round(r) do
2:     S ← k_net random nodes from N
3:     q ← argmin_{u∈S} Δ(n,u)
4:     conditional_swap(n, q, Δ_limit(r))
```

Fig. 6. Randomized (SA)

```
1: In round(r) do
2:     S ← Γ_data^{k_data}(n)
3:     q ← argmin_{u∈S} Δ(n,u)
4:     conditional_swap(n,q,0)
```

Fig. 7. PROP-G

```
1: In round(r) do
2:     q ←    argmin    Δ(n,u)
             u∈Γ_net^{k_net}(n)
3:     conditional_swap(n, q, Δ_limit(r))
```

Fig. 8. Slicing (SA)

```
1: In round(r) do
2:     p ← random node from Γ_data^{k_data}(n)
3:     S ← Γ_net^{k_net/2}(p) ∪ Γ_net^{k_net/2}(n)
4:     q ← argmin_{u∈S} Δ(n,u)
5:     conditional_swap(n,q,0)
```

Fig. 9. Data-Net & Net

```
1: In round(r) do
2:     p ← random node from Γ_data^{k_data}(n)
3:     S ← Γ_net^{k_net/2}(p) ∪ { k_net/2 rand. nodes ∈ N \ Γ_net^{k_net/2}(p) }
4:     q ← argmin_{u∈S} Δ(n,u)
5:     conditional_swap(n,q,0)
```

Fig. 10. Data-Net & R

slicing[19,9], and only considers the physical neighbors of a node n for a possible swap (Slicing (SA), in Figure. 8). The third approach is similar to PROP-G[20], and it only considers logical neighbours of a node n for a possible swap (PROP-G (SA), in Figure. 7). In all these approaches simulated annealing is used as indicated by (SA). The only difference between the above four approaches is the way in which the swap candidates are taken.

To provide further comparison points, we also experimented with some combinations of the above approaches. Fig. 9 (termed *Data-Net & Net*) is a combination of Fluidify (basic) with Slicing (SA). Fig. 10 (termed *Data-Net & R*) is a combination of Fluidify (basic) with Randomized (SA). We also tried a final variant, *combination-R*, in which once the system has converged using Fluidify (basic) (no more changes are detected for a pre-determined number of rounds), nodes look for random swap candidates like we did in Fig. 6.

4.3   Results

All the results (Figs. 11-18 and Tables 3-5) are computed with Peersim [18] and are averaged over 30 experiments. The source code is made available in http://armi.in/resmi/fluidify.zip. When shown, intervals of confidence are computed at 95% confidence level using a student t-distribution.

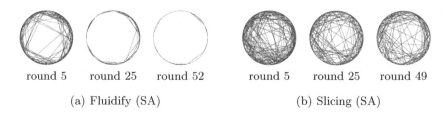

round 5   round 25   round 52   round 5   round 25   round 49

(a) Fluidify (SA)   (b) Slicing (SA)

Fig. 11. Illustrating the convergence of Fluidify (SA) & Slicing (SA) on a ring/ring topology. The converged state is on the right. ($N = K_0 = 400$, $k_{net} = k_{data} = 16$)

Table 3. Performance of Fluidify against various baselines

Nodes	Proximity(%)				Convergence (rounds)			
	Fluid(SA)	Slicing(SA)	Rand(SA)	PROP-G(SA)	Fluid(SA)	Slicing(SA)	Rand(SA)	PROP-G(SA)
100	4.06	10.46	7.70	13.88	18.10	17.16	23.80	17.03
200	2.70	10.12	6.27	12.99	28.50	26.33	43.43	25.13
400	1.71	9.76	5.35	12.65	42.50	39.20	85.36	38.06
800	1.26	9.34	4.83	12.14	64.13	58.93	136.76	57.16
1,600	0.86	8.80	4.41	11.57	96.80	90.56	198.03	85.13
3,200	0.69	8.47	3.82	11.31	144.40	138.20	274.80	128.14
6,400	0.51	8.13	3.07	11.27	216.10	203.40	382.10	198.24
12,800	0.46	7.66	2.28	11.01	324.00	292.10	533.67	263.32
25,600	0.43	6.99	1.79	10.02	485.00	418.60	762.13	392.81

Evaluation of Fluidify (SA). The results obtained by Fluidify (SA) and the three baselines on a ring/ring topology are given in Table 3 and charted in Figs. 12 and 13. In addition, Fig. 11 illustrate some of the rounds that Fluidify (SA) and Slicing (SA) perform. Fig. 12 shows that Fluidify clearly outperforms the other three approaches in terms of proximity over a wide range of network sizes.

Fig 13 charts the convergence time against network size in loglog scale for Fluidify and its competitors. Interestingly all approaches show *a polynomial convergence time*. This shows the scalability of Fluidify even for very large networks. If we turn to Tab. 3, it is evident that as the network size increases, the time taken for the system to converge also increases. Both Fluidify and Slicing (SA) converges around the same time with Slicing (SA) converging a bit faster than Fluidify. Randomized (SA) takes much longer (almost twice as many rounds). PROP-G (SA) converges faster in comparison to all other approaches. The better convergence of PROP-G (SA) and Slicing (SA) can be explained by the fact that both approaches run out of interesting swap candidates more rapidly than Fluidify. It is important to note that all approaches are calibrated to consider the same number of candidates per round. This suggests that PROP-G (SA) and Slicing (SA) runs out of potential swap candidates because they consider candidates of lesser quality, rather than considering more candidates faster.

Fig. 14 shows how the proximity varies with round for our default system settings. Initial avg. link distance was around $N/4$ where N is the network size and this is expected as the input graphs are randomly generated. So the initial proximity was approximately equal to 50%. Fluidify was able to bring down

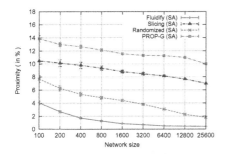
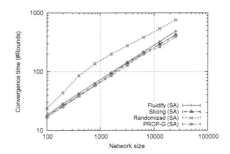

Fig. 12. Proximity. Lower is better. Fluidify (SA) clearly outperforms the baselines in terms of deployment quality.

Fig. 13. Convergence time. All three approaches have a sublinear convergence ($\approx 1.237 \times |N|^{0.589}$ for Fluidify).

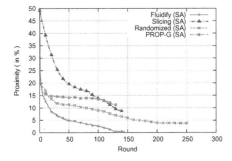
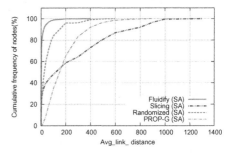

Fig. 14. Proximity over time ($N = K_0 = 3200$, $k_{net} = k_{data} = 16$). Fluidify (SA)'s optimization is more aggressive than those of the other baselines.

Fig. 15. Average link distances in converged state ($N = K_0 = 3200$, $k_{net} = k_{data} = 16$). Fluidify (SA)'s links are both shorter and more homogeneous.

the proximity from 50% to 0.7%. A steep decrease in proximity was observed in initial rounds and later it decreases at a lower pace and finally settles to a proximity value of 0.7% as shown in Fig 14. Randomized (SA) and PROP-G (SA) were able to perform well in the initial stages but later on the gain in proximity decreases. Slicing (SA) is unable to get much gain in proximity from the start itself and converges to a proximity value of 8.4%. Cumulative distribution of nodes based on the avg. link distance in a converged system for all the three approaches is depicted in Fig. 15. It is interesting to see that nearly 83% of the nodes are having an average link distance less than 10 and 37% were having an average link distance of 1 in the case of Fluidify. But for Slicing (SA) even after convergence, a lot of nodes are having an average link distance greater than 200. Slicing (SA) clearly fails in improving the system beyond a limit.

The maximum, minimum and the mean gain obtained per swap in a default system setting using Fluidify is shown in Fig. 16(a). As the simulation progresses the maximum, minimum and the mean value of the cost function per swap in

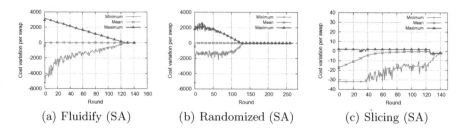

(a) Fluidify (SA)   (b) Randomized (SA)   (c) Slicing (SA)

Fig. 16. Variation of the cost function per swap over time. Lower is better. ($N = K_0 = 3200$, $k_{\text{net}} = k_{\text{data}} = 16$, note the different scales) Fluidify (SA) shows the highest amplitude of variations, and fully exploits simulated annealing, which is less the case for Randomized (SA), and not at all for slicing.

each round starts getting closer and closer and finally becomes equal on convergence. Maximum gain per swap (negative cost) is obtained in the initial rounds of the simulation. Maximum value obtained by the cost function is expected to gradually decrease from a value less than or equal to 3200, which is the initial threshold value for simulated annealing, to 0. Variation of cost function for Randomized (SA) (Fig. 16(b)) and PROP-G (SA) also shows a similar behaviour where the system progresses with a very small gain for a long period of time. The most interesting behaviour is that of Slicing (SA) (Fig.16(c)) which does not benefit much with the use of simulated annealing. The maximum gain that can be obtained per swap is 32 and the maximum negative gain is 2. This is because only the physically closer nodes of a given node are considered for a swap and the swap is done with the best possible candidate.

The *message cost* per round per node will be equal to the amount of data that a node exchanges with another node. In our approach the nodes exchange their logical index and the logical neighbourhood. We assume that each index value amounts to 1 unit of data. So the message cost will be $1 + k_{\text{data}}$ which will be 17 in default case. The *communication overhead* in the network per cycle will be equal to the average number of swaps occurring per round times the amount of data exchanged per swap. A single message costs 17 units. So a swap will cost 34 units. In default setting, an average of 2819 swaps happen per round and this amounts to around 95846 units of data per round.

All the four approaches that we presented here are generic and can be used for any topologies. Table. 4 shows how the three approaches fares for various topologies in a default setting. Fluidify clearly out performs the other approaches.

Effects of Variants. Figure. 17 shows that compared to its variants like Fluidify (basic), combination-R, Data-Net & Net (Fig. 9), Data-Net & R (Fig. 10), Fluidify (SA) is far ahead in quality of convergence. Here also we consider a ring/ring topology with default setting. The convergence time taken by Fluidify is slightly higher compared to its variants as shown in Fig. 18.

Table 5 shows how varying the initial threshold value for Fluidify affects its performance. From the table it is clear that as the initial threshold value

Table 4. Performance on various topologies

Approach	Physical topology	Logical topology	Proximity(%)	Convergence(#Rounds)
Fluidify(SA)	torus	torus	2.4(±0.05)	162(±2.34)
Fluidify(SA)	torus	ring	2.6(±0.03)	171(±3.6)
Fluidify(SA)	ring	torus	1.8(±0.06)	156(±2.36)
Slicing(SA)	torus	torus	4.5(±0.05)	130(±2.16)
Slicing(SA)	torus	ring	5.2(±0.02)	128(±3.26)
Slicing(SA)	ring	torus	9.5(±0.08)	143(±4.1)
Randomized(SA)	torus	torus	3.82(±0.08)	423(±2.41)
Randomized(SA)	torus	ring	4.05(±0.04)	464(±3.28)
Randomized(SA)	ring	torus	2.7(±0.05)	442(±3.82)
PROP-G(SA)	torus	torus	4.6(±0.05)	132(±2.34)
PROP-G(SA)	torus	ring	5.6(±0.03)	130(±3.6)
PROP-G(SA)	ring	torus	10.1(±0.06)	128(±2.36)

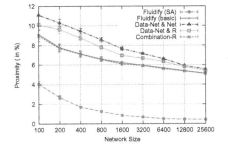

Fig. 17. Comparison of different variants of Fluidify - Proximity

Fig. 18. Comparison of different variants of Fluidify - Convergence

Table 5. Impact of K_0 on Fluidify (SA)

K_0	Proximity (%)	Convergence (rounds)
320	2.4	156
640	1.6	145
1600	1.1	146
3200	0.7	144

increases the proximity that we obtain also become better and better. With a higher threshold value, more swaps will occur and therefore there is a higher chance of getting closer to the global minimum. The threshold value that gives the best performance is used for all our simulations.

5   Related Work

Fully decentralized systems are being extensively studied by many researchers. Many well known and widely used P2P systems are unstructured. However, there are several overlay networks in which the node locality is taken into account. Structured P2P overlays, such as CAN [22], Chord [25], Pastry [24], and Tapestry [31], are designed to enhance the searching performance by giving some importance to node placement. But, as pointed out in [23], structured designs are likely to be less resilient, because it is hard to maintain the structure required for routing to function efficiently when hosts are joining and leaving at a high rate. Chord in its original design, does not consider network proximity at all. Some modification to CAN, Pastry, and Tapestry are made to provide locality to some extent. However, these results come at the expense of a significantly more expensive overlay maintenance protocol.

One of the general approaches used to bridge the gap between physical and overlay node proximity is landmark clustering. Ratnasamy et al. [21] use landmark clustering in an approach to build a topology-aware CAN [22] overlay network. Although the efficiency can be improved, this solution needs extra deployment of landmarks and produces some hotspots in the underlying network when the overlay is heterogeneous and large. Some [30] [29] have proposed methods to fine tune the landmark clustering for overlay creation. The main disadvantage with landmark system is that there needs to be a reliable infrastructure to offer these landmarks at high availability. Application layer multicast algorithms construct a special overlay network that exploits network proximity. The protocol they use are often based on a tree or mesh structure. Although they are highly efficient for small overlays, they are not scalable and creates hotspots in the network as a node failure can make the system unstable and difficult to recover. Later proximity neighbour selection [2] was tried to organise and maintain the overlay network which improved the routing speed and load balancing. Waldvogel and Rinaldi [12][28] propose an overlay network(Mithos) that focuses on reducing routing table sizes. It is a bit expensive and only very small overlay networks are used for simulations and the impact of network digression is not considered.

Network aware overlays are used to increase the efficiency of network services like routing, resource allocation and data dissemination. Works like [16] and [4] combines the robustness of epidemics with the efficiency of structured approaches in order to improve the data dissemination capabilities of the system. Gossip protocols which are scalable and inherent to network dynamics can do efficient data dissemination. Frey et al.[5] uses gossip protocols to create a system where nodes dynamically adapt their contribution to the gossip dissemination according to the network characteristics like bandwidth and delay. Kermarrec et al. [6] use gossip protocols for renaming and sorting. Here nodes are given id values and numerical input values. Nodes exchange these input values so that in the end the input of rank k is located at the node with id k. Slicing method [19][9] was made use of in resource allocation. Specific attributes of network(memory, bandwidth, computation power) are taken into account to partition the network into slices. Network aware overlays can be used in cloud infrastructure [26] to provide efficient data dissemination.

Most of the works on topology aware overlays are aimed at improving a particular service such as routing, resource allocation or data dissemination. What we are proposing is a generalized approach for overlay creation giving importance to data placement in the system. It has higher scalability and robustness and less maintenance cost compared to other approaches. The simulated annealing and slicing approach is motivated mainly by the works [19],[6],[9]. But these works concentrated mainly on improving a single network service while we concentrate on a generalized solution that can significantly improve all the network services.

6 Conclusion and Future Work

In this paper, we present–Fluidify–a novel decentralized mechanism for overlay deployment. Fluidify works by exploiting both the logical links of an overlay and the physical topology of its underlying network to progressively align one with the other and thereby maximizing the network locality. The proposed approach can be used in combination with any topology construction algorithm. The resulting protocol is generic, efficient, scalable and can substantially improve network overheads and latency in overlay based-systems. Simulation results show that in a ring/ring network of 25,600 nodes, Fluidify is able to produce an overlay with links that are on average 94% shorter than that produced by a standard decentralized approach based on slicing.

One aspect we would like to explore in future is to deploy Fluidify in a real system and see how it fares. A thorough analytical study of the behaviour of our approach is also intended.

Acknowledgments. This work was partially funded by the DeSceNt project granted by the Labex CominLabs excellence laboratory of the French Agence Nationale de la Recherche (ANR- 10-LABX-07-01).

References

1. Bertier, M., Frey, D., Guerraoui, R., Kermarrec, A.-M., Leroy, V.: The gossple anonymous social network. In: Gupta, I., Mascolo, C. (eds.) Middleware 2010. LNCS, vol. 6452, pp. 191–211. Springer, Heidelberg (2010)
2. Druschel, P., Hu, Y.C., Rowstron, A.: Topology-aware routing in structured peer-to-peer overlay networks. In: Schiper, A., Shvartsman, M.M.A.A., Weatherspoon, H., Zhao, B.Y. (eds.) Future Directions in DC 2002. LNCS, vol. 2584, pp. 103–107. Springer, Heidelberg (2003)
3. DeCandia, G., Hastorun, D., Jampani, M., Kakulapati, G., Lakshman, A., Pilchin, A., Sivasubramanian, S., Vosshall, P., Vogels, W.: Dynamo: Amazon's highly available key-value store. In: SOSP 2007 (2007)
4. Doerr, B., Elsässer, R., Fraigniaud, P.: Epidemic algorithms and processes: From theory to applications. Dagstuhl Reports 3(1), 94–110 (2013)
5. Frey, D., Guerraoui, R., Kermarrec, A.-M., Koldehofe, B., Mogensen, M., Monod, M., Quéma, V.: Heterogeneous gossip. In: Bacon, J.M., Cooper, B.F. (eds.) Middleware 2009. LNCS, vol. 5896, pp. 42–61. Springer, Heidelberg (2009)

6. Giakkoupis, G., Kermarrec, A.-M., Woelfel, P.: Gossip protocols for renaming and sorting. In: Afek, Y. (ed.) DISC 2013. LNCS, vol. 8205, pp. 194–208. Springer, Heidelberg (2013)
7. Grace, P., Hughes, D., Porter, B., Blair, G.S., Coulson, G., Taiani, F.: Experiences with open overlays: A middleware approach to network heterogeneity. In: Eurosys 2008 (2008)
8. Gupta, A., Sahin, O.D., Agrawal, D., Abbadi, A.E.: Meghdoot: content-based publish/subscribe over p2p networks. In: Jacobsen, H.-A. (ed.) Middleware 2004. LNCS, vol. 3231, pp. 254–273. Springer, Heidelberg (2004)
9. Jelasity, M., Kermarrec, A.M.: Ordered slicing of very large-scale overlay networks. In: P2P 2006 (2006)
10. Jelasity, M., Montresor, A., Babaoglu, O.: T-man: Gossip-based fast overlay topology construction. Comput. Netw. 53(13), 2321–2339 (2009)
11. Kermarrec, A.M., Triantafillou, P.: Xl peer-to-peer pub/sub systems. ACM Computing Surveys (CSUR) 46(2) (2013)
12. Krishnamurthy, B., Wang, J.: On network-aware clustering of web clients. In: SIGCOMM 2000, pp. 97–110. ACM (2000)
13. Lakshman, A., Malik, P.: Cassandra: A decentralized structured storage system. SIGOPS Oper. Syst. Rev. 44(2) (2010)
14. Leitao, J., Pereira, J., Rodrigues, L.: Epidemic broadcast trees. In: SRDS 2007 (2007)
15. Li, B., Xie, S., Qu, Y., Keung, G.Y., Lin, C., Liu, J., Zhang, X.: Inside the new coolstreaming: Principles, measurements and performance implications. In: IEEE INFOCOM 2008 (2008)
16. Matos, M., Schiavoni, V., Felber, P., Oliveira, R., Rivière, E.: Lightweight, efficient, robust epidemic dissemination. J. Parallel Distrib. Comput. 73(7), 987–999 (2013)
17. Montresor, A., Jelasity, M., Babaoglu, O.: Chord on demand. In: P2P 2005 (2005)
18. Montresor, A., Jelasity, M.: Peersim: A scalable p2p simulator. In: P2P 2009 (2009)
19. Pasquet, M., Maia, F., Rivière, E., Schiavoni, V.: Autonomous multi-dimensional slicing for large-scale distributed systems. In: Magoutis, K., Pietzuch, P. (eds.) DAIS 2014. LNCS, vol. 8460, pp. 141–155. Springer, Heidelberg (2014)
20. Qiu, T., Chen, G., Ye, M., Chan, E., Zhao, B.Y.: Towards location-aware topology in both unstructured and structured p2p systems. In: ICPP, p. 30. IEEE Computer Society (2007)
21. Ratnasamy, S., Handley, M., Karp, R., Shenker, S.: Topologically-aware overlay construction and server selection. In: INFOCOM 2002, vol. 3, pp. 1190–1199 (2002)
22. Ratnasamy, S., Francis, P., Handley, M., Karp, R., Shenker, S.: A scalable content-addressable network. SIGCOMM Comput. Commun. Rev. 31(4), 161–172 (2001)
23. Lv, Q., Ratnasamy, S., Shenker, S.: Can heterogeneity make gnutella scalable? In: Druschel, P., Kaashoek, F., Rowstron, A. (eds.) IPTPS 2002. LNCS, vol. 2429, pp. 94–103. Springer, Heidelberg (2002)
24. Rowstron, A., Druschel, P.: Pastry: Scalable, decentralized object location, and routing for large-scale peer-to-peer systems. In: Guerraoui, R. (ed.) Middleware 2001. LNCS, vol. 2218, pp. 329–350. Springer, Heidelberg (2001)
25. Stoica, I., Morris, R., Karger, D., Kaashoek, M.F., Balakrishnan, H.: Chord: A scalable peer-to-peer lookup service for internet applications. In: SIGCOMM 2001 (2001)
26. Tudoran, R., Costan, A., Wang, R., Bougé, L., Antoniu, G.: Bridging Data in the Clouds: An Environment-Aware System for Geographically Distributed Data Transfers. In: IEEE/ACM CCGrid, Chicago (May 2014)

27. Voulgaris, S., van Steen, M.: Epidemic-style management of semantic overlays for content-based searching. In: Cunha, J.C., Medeiros, P.D. (eds.) Euro-Par 2005. LNCS, vol. 3648, pp. 1143–1152. Springer, Heidelberg (2005)
28. Waldvogel, M., Rinaldi, R.: Efficient topology-aware overlay network. In: SIG-COMM/CCR 2003 (2003)
29. Xu, Z., Tang, C., Zhang, Z.: Building topology-aware overlays using global soft-state. In: ICDSC 2003 (May 2003)
30. Zhang, X.Y., Zhang, Q., Zhang, Z., Song, G., Zhu, W.: A construction of locality-aware overlay network: moverlay and its performance. IEEE J. Sel. A. Commun. 22(1), 18–28 (2006)
31. Zhao, B.Y., Kubiatowicz, J., Joseph, A.D.: Tapestry: An infrastructure for fault-tolerant wide-area location and routing. Computer 74 (2001)

MERCi-MIsS: Should I Turn off My Servers?

Mar Callau-Zori[1]([✉]), Luciana Arantes[2], Julien Sopena[2], and Pierre Sens[2]

[1] IRISA, Université de Rennes 1 - France
mar.callau-zori@irisa.fr
[2] Sorbonne Universités, UPMC Univ Paris 06, CNRS, Inria, LIP6 - France
{Luciana.Arantes,julien.sopena,Pierre.Sens}@lip6.fr

Abstract. In recent years, the electrical consumption of data centers has increased considerably leading to a rise in the expenditure bill and in greenhouse gas emissions. Several existing *on/off algorithms* reduce energy consumption in data centers or Clouds by turning off unused (idle) machines. However, the turning off/on of servers consumes a certain amount of energy and also induces the wear and tear of disks. Based on the data streaming paradigm which deals with large amount of data on-line, we present in this paper MERCi-MIsS, a proposal whose aim is to save energy in data centers and Clouds and tackle the above tradeoff problems without degrading, as much as possible, the quality of services of the system. MERCi-MIsS dynamically estimates the future workload based on the recent past workload, deciding if servers should then be turned either on or off. We have implemented MERCi-MIsS on top of Twitter Storm. Evaluation results from experiments using real traces from Grid'5000 confirm the effectiveness and efficiency of MERCi-MIsS algorithm to save energy and avoid disk damage while the quality of service is only slightly degraded.

1 Introduction

In a Cloud environment, the provider renders available a great number of resources for clients to perform their tasks. Cloud computing has been presented as a green approach in front of traditional data centers since their resources are shared by a huge number of users, optimizing, thus, the use of the resources.

Although Cloud computing seems the correct approach for saving energy, more effort must be made in order to design efficient Cloud data centers [1]. In the Cloud, clients and providers have different responsibilities: the client is responsible for his/her application while the provider is interested in adopting energy-aware and cost effective policies. Furthermore, providers' energy-aware solutions should deal with a large number of applications. Therefore, based on a global view of the system, providers have to apply energy saving techniques which will not interfere in aspects which are responsibility of the clients.

One well-known approach to reduce energy consumption, called *on/off algorithm*, consists in turning off unused (idle) machines [2, 3], since the power of idle machines is estimated between 25-60% of the peak power [4, 5]. However, such an algorithm entails some negative impacts. Firstly, the turning off/on of

© IFIP International Federation for Information Processing 2015
A. Bessani and S. Bouchenak (Eds.): DAIS 2015, LNCS 9038, pp. 16–29, 2015.
DOI: 10.1007/978-3-319-19129-4_2

servers consumes energy. Hence, a server should stay off during a minimum time period (called *critical time*) which compensates the energy in rebooting it when compared with the energy of keeping it idle [3, 6]. A second negative impact is that the reduction of the number of available resources can degrade the quality of service (QoS) engaged by the provider through the Service Level Agreement (SLA), i.e., an agreement between the provider and the client which sets up the QoS that the provider should guarantee. The non satisfaction of SLAs could result in penalization to the provider. In this paper, we consider that the violation of SLA leads to monetary charges to the provider, i.e., the latter must reimburse the client if some service does not satisfy the SLA requirements. Finally, booting affects disk lifetime, i.e., the probability of disk damage, and thus replacement, increases with the number of boots [2, 7–11]. Thus, an energy saving solution should take into account the costs of the wear and tear of disks.

Considering the above discussed points, this paper presents MERCi-MIsS [1], a streaming-based algorithm which dynamically decides the number of servers to turn on/off. MERCi-MIsS proposes an energy saving strategy taking into account energy cost and disk wear-and-tear cost. MERCi-MIsS exploits a streaming model which is able to process great volume of data and, thus, decides on the fly about the number of servers to turn on/off. It exploits global system information, in terms of the number of required working, idle, off, turning on, and turning off servers. It also dynamically estimates the minimum number of idle servers which the system must keep in order to provide energy saving while ensuring the execution of unexpected works. We have also extended the *critical time* in order to take into account the wear and tear related to disk ignitions.

Performance evaluation experiments were conducted over traces concerning the usage of French Grid'5000 platform (a scientific experiment-driven research environment: www.grid5000.fr). Results confirm that MERCi-MIsS outperforms some energy saving algorithms found in the literature. It also provides shorter average time delay for processing clients' works than these algorithms.

Roadmap. Firstly, in Sec. 2, we discuss the minimum time that a server must be off in order to save energy boot. In Sec. 3, we present MERCi-MIsS, how it predicts the workload, computes both the monetary cost of non-working servers and of disk wear-and-tear. Evaluation is presented in Sec. 4. Sec. 5 discusses some related work. Finally, Sec. 6 concludes and proposes some future work.

2   Minimal Period of Time for off Servers

The turning off and on of servers induces energy consumption. If we decide to turn off a server, it must be off for at least a minimum period of time which compensates the energy spent in rebooting it. In [3], the authors denote such a period of time the *critical time* (T_S). They also propose how to evaluate it.

Considering the parameters given in Table 1, the critical time T_S is the minimum period of time that a server is turning off which renders the energy spent

---

[1] Maximizing Energy and disk ReplaCement saving — MInimizing SLA penalties.

Table 1. Event parameters for a single server

$E_{on \to off}$	energy cost of turning off (J)	P_{idle}	energy power of an idle server (W)
$E_{off \to on}$	energy cost of turning on (J)	P_{off}	energy power of an off server (W)
$\delta_{on \to off}$	time spent in turning off (sec)	δ_{tot}	time spent in turning off&on (sec)
$\delta_{off \to on}$	time spent in turning on (sec)		$\delta_{tot} = \delta_{on \to off} + \delta_{off \to on}$
$\$_E$	cost of the energy ($ / J)	$\$_B$	cost of a boot ($)

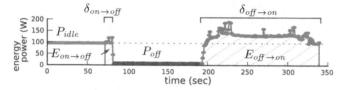

Fig. 1. Energy consumption of different states. Real experiment in Grid'5000.

in booting a server equals to the energy in keeping it idle, i.e., T_S such that $E_{idle}(T_S) = E_{reboot}(T_S)$, where the energy spent in T_S seconds of an idle server is $E_{idle}(T_S) = P_{idle} \times T_S$ while the energy for rebooting the server for the same period is $E_{reboot}(T_S) = E_{on \to off} + P_{off} \times (T_S - \delta_{tot}) + E_{off \to on}$, (the energy spent for both turning off and on the server plus the energy to keep it off). Hence, the critical time T_S is $\frac{E_{on \to off} + E_{off \to on} - P_{off} \times \delta_{tot}}{P_{idle} - P_{off}}$.

For instance, Fig. 1 shows an energy experiment conducted on a Dell Power Edge R720 server. The energy spent in turning on and off the server (green area in Fig. 1) is $E_{off \to on} + E_{on \to off} = 19,749J$, which respectively takes $\delta_{off \to on} + \delta_{on \to off} = 158$ seconds. Considering the average power of an off server and idle is $P_{off} = 8W$ and $P_{idle} = 97W$ resp., a power off server consumes in T_S seconds $E_{reboot}(T_S) = 19,749 + 8(T_S - 158)$ and an idle one consumes $E_{idle}(T_S) = 97T_S$. Hence, if the server keeps off at least $T_S = 208sec.$, the decision of turning it off is an efficient one; otherwise, it is not worthwhile turning it off.

In the same paper, the authors argue that a T_S must be increased with the T_r factor which is related to the wear and tear with regard to the disk ignitions. However, they do not explain how to compute T_r.

We propose, therefore, in this article, an estimation for T_r. To this end, we add to $E_{reboot}(T_S)$ the energy cost (in Joules) associated with disk damage due to ignitions. Considering the cost of a new disk device (in money units) and the number of ignitions that a disk supports [8], the disk-cost of a boot (in money units) is estimated as $\$_B$. By dividing it by the cost of the energy $\$_E$, ($\$_B$ / $\$_E$), it is possible to estimate the energy spent in Joules due to disk damage. We have, then $E_{reboot}(t) = E_{on \to off} + P_{off} \times (t - \delta_{tot}) + E_{off \to on} + \$_B / \$_E$. Thus, the *minimum critical time* T_S is:

$$T_S = \frac{E_{on \to off} + E_{off \to on} - P_{off} \times \delta_{tot}}{P_{idle} - P_{off}} + \frac{\$_B}{\$_E (P_{idle} - P_{off})} \qquad (1)$$

In conclusion, an on/off algorithm must ensure this minimum critical time is used in order to both save energy and the cost of disk replacement.

3   MERCi-MIsS

MERCi-MIsS is an on/off algorithm based on streaming over sliding window model. That is, data are processed on-the-fly, continuously producing an output. We describe the MERCi-MIsS architecture in Section 3.1. On/Off algorithms turn on and off servers according to the needs of the system and prediction of future workload. Usually, algorithms estimate future workload based on previous one aiming at minimizing energy consumption as well as satisfying unexpected works, i.e., works that arrive when the system has not enough available servers. Thus, having a *minimum number of idle servers* helps to solve some unexpected situations. We denote m_0 such a minimum number of idle servers. In this case, at every time, the system can always process a new work that needs at most m_0 servers. Considering m_0 idle servers and the prediction of future workload based on the past workload, MERCi-MIsS decides about the number of servers to turn off or on at a given time. Section 3.2 describes how MERCi-MIsS takes decisions. In Section 3.3 we present how we evaluate the service maintainability cost associated with the energy spent in turn on/off servers and disk replacement.

3.1   MERCi-MIsS Architecture

We consider that time is discretized in seconds, i.e., at every second it is possible to obtain the state of each server. At any time t, MERCi-MIsS needs the information about the current number of required servers and the current state of the system. While the former can be inferred from the workload with which the scheduler has to deal, the latter depends on the current processing works and might be affected by energy-aware policies. Figure 2 presents the architecture.

The number of required servers is predicted by MERCi-MIsS based on the history of clients' requests sent to the scheduler. Upon receiving a request, the scheduler decides when to execute the work. Notice, that, in some cases, clients must wait for their requests to be serviced (e.g., the system has not enough available servers). Hence, at any time t, the scheduler deduces the number of required servers to satisfy clients requests and providing the history of such a number to MERCi-MIsS, which stores it to predict future requirements.

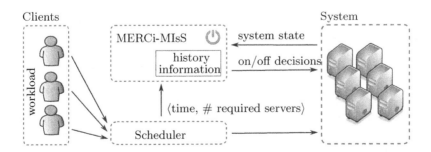

Fig. 2. MERCi-MIsS interaction with scheduler and system

Concerning the system state, MERCi-MIsS continuously receives information about it (the current number of working servers, idle servers, and off servers), producing as output the decisions about how many servers to turn off and on.

3.2   MERCi-MIsS Turn on/off Decisions

MERCi-MIsS exploits stream processing over sliding windows. As we have already discussed, the number of current required servers can be deduced by the scheduler workload. To this end, it keeps a window $\mathcal{W}$ with the most recent number of required servers, informed by the scheduler. Concerning the state of the system, at t, MERCi-MIsS receives as input $\langle n_w(t), n_{idle}(t), n_{off}(t)\rangle$ and produces as output the decisions about how many servers to turn off $d_{on \to off}(t)$ and how many servers to turn on $d_{off \to on}(t)$. Tab. 2 summarizes our notations.

One of the aims of MERCi-MIsS is to guarantee a minimum number, m_0, of idle servers at any time t. If some clients request more than m_0 servers, some servers must be turned on. On the other hand, when MERCi-MIsS decides to turn off some servers, it ensures that at least m_0 idle servers are on.

MERCi-MIsS, which decides either to turn on or off some servers, is described in Algorithm 1. We point out that both actions can not be taken at the same time since they are contradictory. If the system does not have a minimum of m_0 idle servers (lines 1-3), a number of servers will be turned on in order to ensure m_0 idle servers (at most we can turn on $n_{off}(t)$ servers). Otherwise, MERCi-MIsS tries to turn off some servers (lines 4-9), aiming at saving energy.

According to the critical time T_S, we can turn off all the servers which will not be used in the next T_S seconds (i.e. we need to estimate the maximum number of working servers in the next T_S seconds). However, the future workload is not known. Hence, MERCi-MIsS exploits the outliers border given in boxplot. The latter is a statistics graph where several descriptive values of a sample are represented. It shows five values from a data set: the upper and lower extremes, the upper and lower hinges (quartiles), and the median [12]. Values of the data set greater than the upper extreme are considered outliers. Hence, we can view the upper extreme UE, as a "normal" maximum bound of the data set. MERCi-MIsS estimates the future maximum number of working servers as the upper extreme value related to the number of working servers over the past history.

When the system has at least m_0 idle nodes MERCi-MIsS algorithm calculates the number of servers to turn off (lines 4-9). To energy efficiency, the number of servers to turn off is the number of servers not used within at least the next T_S seconds. In the current time t, the maximum number of servers to be used in

Table 2. Servers type and decisions at time t

$n_w(t)$	nb. of working servers at t	$n_{on \to off}(t)$	nb. of servers turning off at t
$n_{idle}(t)$	nb. of idle servers at t	$n_{off \to on}(t)$	nb. of servers turning on at t
$n_{on}(t)$	nb. of power on servers at t	$d_{on \to off}(t)$	decision about the number of
	$n_{on}(t) = n_w(t) + n_{idle}(t)$		servers to turn off at t
$n_{off}(t)$	nb. of power off servers at t	$d_{off \to on}(t)$	decision about the number of
			servers to turn on at t

Algorithm 1. MERCi-MIsS algorithm

Parameters: m_0, minimum number of idle servers;
$\quad\quad\quad\quad$ w, whisker length;
$\quad\quad\quad\quad$ $\delta_{off\to on}$, the time spends in turn on
Input: $\langle n_w(t), n_{idle}(t), n_{off}(t)\rangle$, system state
Output: $d_{on\to off}(t)$, number of servers to turn off;
$\quad\quad\quad\quad$ $d_{off\to on}(t)$, number of servers to turn on

1 **if** $n_{idle}(t) < m_0$ **then**
2 $\quad$ $d_{on\to off}(t) = 0$
3 $\quad$ $d_{off\to on}(t) = \min\{n_{off}(t), m_0 - n_{idle}(t)\}$

4 **else**
5 $\quad$ $Q1 \leftarrow$ quartile$(1, \mathcal{W})$
6 $\quad$ $Q3 \leftarrow$ quartile$(3, \mathcal{W})$
7 $\quad$ $UE = Q3 + w\,(Q3 - Q1)$
8 $\quad$ $d_{on\to off}(t) = \max\{0, \min\{n_{on}(t) - UE,$
$\quad\quad\quad\quad\quad\quad$ $n_{idle}(t) + d_{off\to on}(t - \delta_{off\to on}) - m_0\}\}$
9 $\quad$ $d_{off\to on}(t) = 0$

---

the next T_S seconds is given by $n_m(t) = \max\{n_w(s) : s \in [t + 1, t + T_S]\}$. Thus, we can turn off all the other servers which are on, i.e., $n_{on}(t) - n_m(t)$.

Note that we are considering that the number of future required servers, $n_m(t)$, is known at t and, in this case, $n_{on}(t) - n_m(t)$ represents the most efficient energy saving. However, this is not a realistic assumption since we can not foresee the future. Therefore, it is necessary to estimate $n_m(t)$ based on previous history of working servers. One first idea would be to use the maximum number of these servers in the recent history. Nevertheless, such an approach could induce a bad estimation if an unusual situation with high number of servers took place in recent history. In order to avoid such a mistake, MERCi-MIsS uses UE, the upper extreme value of boxplot, to estimate the number of working servers and the decision about the servers to turn off is (1) $d_{on\to off}(t) = n_{on}(t) - UE$. The upper extreme value UE is based on the first and third quartile[2] (respectively, $Q1$ and $Q3$) as well as a parameter w, called whisker length (usually $w = 1.5$). The upper extreme value is, thus, computed as $UE = Q3 + w\,(Q3 - Q1)$. Note that MERCi-MIsS computes quartiles over the sliding window $\mathcal{W}$ related to the number of required servers.

On the other hand, in order to ensure m_0 number of idle servers at time $t + 1$, the maximum number of servers to turn off at time t should be equal to $n_{idle}(t+1) - m_0$. However, since $n_{idle}(t+1)$ is unknown, MERCi-MIsS estimates the number of idle servers at time $t+1$ as the number of current idle servers plus the number of servers that MERCi-MIsS decides to turn on at time $t - \delta_{off\to on}$, i.e., such servers will be on at time $t + 1$. Hence, for guaranteeing m_0 idle servers

---

[2] Quartiles are ranked statistics which split data set into four equal groups. First quartile, Q1, is a value that is (equal or) greater that the 25% of the data values (resp. Q3 is equal or greater that the 75%).

at $t+1$, we have that the number of servers to turn off satisfies (2) $d_{on \to off}(t) = n_{idle} + d_{off \to on}(t - \delta_{off \to on}) - m_0$.

Taking into account both conditions, i.e., the number of servers not used within at least the next T_S seconds and m_0 idle servers at time $t+1$, the number of nodes to turn off at t is equal to the minimum of (1) and (2) (line 8).

Exploiting System Information. In the estimation of m_0 at $t+1$, MERCi-MIsS considers that the number of working servers at time $t+1$ is the same as the current number of working servers at t. However, there exist some cases where the system could give more information about the number of working servers and MERCi-MIsS could exploit it. For instance, if the workload was stored in a queue that MERCi-MIsS could have access to, the number of working servers at time $t+1$ could be inferred (provided that the workload queue is not empty).

3.3 Service Maintainability Cost

Service cost is composed of two costs: the *service performance cost*, associated with the clients' works execution, and the *service maintainability cost* related to the energy spent in turning on/off servers as well as disk replacement. One of the main goal of on/off algorithms is to reduce service maintainability cost as much as possible without degrading the QoS for the clients.

Service performance cost is related to the energy consumed by working servers. It is well-known that the energy spent by working servers depends on the work that must be executed, i.e., the clients' requests [13]. Estimating this energy consumption is not a trivial task. However, we can consider that a server which executes a given work spends the same energy regardless when the work is executed. In other words, the energy consumed by working servers to process a fixed workload is the same independently on the work that each server performs. Consequently, the service performance cost does not depend on the energy-aware policy. However, the turning on and off of servers introduces different energy consumption and disk replacements. The cost associated with them depends on the energy-aware policy and is considered as service maintainability cost. In this section, we focus in describe the service maintainability cost.

Service maintainability cost, $maintenance_\$$, has two parts: 1) $energy_{\neg w}$, monetary cost of energy of non-working servers (idle servers, off servers, and turning on and off actions); and 2) the monetary cost to replace disks.

$$maintenance_\$ = \$_E \times energy_{\neg w} + \$_{replacement_{disk}} \qquad (2)$$

At time t, the system has $n_w(t)$ working servers, $n_{idle}(t)$ servers, (i.e., $n_{on}(t) = n_w(t) + n_{idle}(t)$), $n_{off}(t)$ off servers, turning off servers ($d_{on \to off}(t)$), and turning on servers ($d_{off \to on}(t)$). Note that even if these values are related to time t, the evaluation of energy consumption concerns the whole period of time during which the system is running. In the cost of $energy_{\neg w}$, both idle and off states are quite stable in terms of energy consumption. It is then possible to have representative average consumption values: P_{idle} and P_{off} power (Joules / sec) for idle and off servers respectively while the energy cost to turn on (respectively, off) a server is $E_{on \to off}$ (respectively, $E_{off \to on}$). Based on the energy parameters of Table 1 and the notations of Table 2, the energy consumed by non working servers, $energy_{\neg w}$, for the whole execution period of the system is given by:

$$energy_{\neg w} = \sum_t \left(P_{idle} \times n_{idle}(t) + P_{off} \times n_{off}(t) + \right.$$
$$\left. + E_{on \to off} \times d_{on \to off}(t) + E_{off \to on} \times d_{off \to on}(t) \right) \tag{3}$$

The money cost associated with disk damage has a direct relation with the number of boots. As a boot is a turning off which will be eventually followed by a turning on, we cannot consider $n_{on \to off}(\cdot) + n_{off \to on}(\cdot)$ as the number of boots, otherwise, in the whole execution of the system, we would sum twice the number of boots. As a consequence, we consider the number of boots as the number of turning off $n_{on \to off}(\cdot)$ (eventually turning off servers will be power on). Hence, the disk money cost (in $) is given by Equation 4.

$$\$replacement_{disk} = \sum_t \$_B \times n_{on \to off}(t) \tag{4}$$

In Sec. 2, we defined T_S as the minimal critical time for saving energy which also includes the energy associated with disk replacement. Therefore, if T_S is respected, $maintenance_\$$ represents the minimum service maintainability cost.

Besides the monetary cost, $maintenance_\$$, we must consider the time delay to attend clients' requests which affects the quality of service. We propose a tradeoff metric based on the Energy-Delay product (EDP) [14], where the energy-performance tradeoff is evaluated by multiplying the energy by the time delay. To capture the disk damage we propose Energy&Disk-Delay product (EDDP) in Eq. 5 as the product of the energy consumed in the whole experiment (energy of non working servers plus disk replacement) by the average time delay to attend to clients' requests. Minimizing EDDP is equivalent to maximizing its inverse which represents the "performance-per-cost", where performance is the inverse of average time delay (service has low performance, if the time delay is high).

$$EDDP = \left(energy_{\neg w} + \frac{\$remplacement_{disk}}{\$_E} \right) \times time_{delay} \tag{5}$$

$maintenance_\$$ estimation and EDDP concern all servers in the system during the whole experiment. However, considering just one server, we know that if it stays off at least T_S seconds, some energy is saved when compared to keeping it idle. In fact, the longer the period of time the server is off, the higher the energy saved. Hence, if a server keeps off Δt time, the service maintainability saved cost, denoted $savings_\$$, is given by Equation 6, where $E_{tot} = E_{on \to off} + E_{off \to on}$.

$$savings_\$(\Delta t) = \$_E \times \left((P_{idle} - P_{off}) \times \Delta t - E_{tot} + P_{off} \times \delta_{tot} \right) - \$_B \tag{6}$$

The minimum $savings_\$$ takes place at $T_S + 1$, i.e., $savings_\$(T_S + 1) = \$_E \times (P_{idle} - P_{off})$. Notice that, if a server is off $T_S + a$, the service maintainability saving is $savings_\$(T_S + a) = a \times \$_E \times (P_{idle} - P_{off})$.

4   Evaluation

In this section we firstly present the evaluation environment and input traces. Then we give a brief description of some algorithms with which we compared MERCi-MIsS, and finally, some comparative evaluation results are presented.

4.1   Evaluation Setup

MERCi-MIsS input (i.e., number of working servers) can be obtained by monitoring the states of the nodes or by inferring from users' reservation traces. We used real traces from [15] corresponding to 6 months (from 1st Feb. 2009 to 27 February 2010) related to reservations in Grid'5000 (12,948 reservations). Users made resource reservations indicating the submission time, the number of requested nodes, and the maximum duration of the reservations (however, users can cancel reservations before the ending time). Using the number of requested servers, the starting time, and the ending time, the number of working servers can be inferred. Assuming that the number of servers reserved by the users is the number of working servers, although users cannot use some of them, we assume that all the reserved servers must be on. Unfortunately, in the original traces, the actual ending time is not provided. Hence, we simulate this value considering the maximum duration as the actual duration. Energy values, cost, and duration are summarizing in Tab. 3. $E_{off \to on}$, $E_{on \to off}$, $\delta_{off \to on}$, $\delta_{on \to off}$, P_{off}, and P_{idle} are obtained from a real experiment where 20 Grid'5000 servers of the Lyon site, which represent more than 20% of servers of the site, were booted 50 times (the Lyon site has electrical consuming monitoring). The obtained results are similar to the ones presented in [3]. The costs of a boot $B_\$$ and the cost of energy $E_\$$ are taken from [8]. According to Sec. 2, the critical time T_S=1457 sec.

Table 3. MERCi model parameters

$E_{off \to on}$ 24,536.04J	$E_{on \to off}$ 1,501J	P_{off} 9.58W	P_{idle} 150.16W
$\delta_{off \to on}$ 120sec	$\delta_{on \to off}$ 10sec	$\$_B$ 0.5 cents/boot	$\$_E$ 10 cents/KWH

MERCi-MIsS evaluation experiments were conducted using Petrel-Storm on Grid'5000 platform. Storm [16] is an event processor to streams and Petrel-Storm is a tool for writing, submitting, debugging, and monitoring Storm topologies in Python [17]. By exploiting Grid'5000 traces, the input stream $S = \{R_t\}_t$ corresponds to a set of reservations R at time t. In the simulation, the interaction with the system which provides information about the system state (Sec. 3.1) does not take place. Instead, Storm operator maintains itself the system state $(n_w(t), n_{idle}(t), n_{off}(t))$. Hence, for each time t, the operator produces the decision about turning on $d_{off \to on}(t)$ or off $d_{on \to off}(t)$. Using the stream approach, we have implemented:

Perfect Prediction. An ideal on/off algorithm which always has enough available servers and ensures the minimum *maintenance*$_\$$ cost. Thus, every arriving work immediately starts executing without any delay. However, the perfect prediction is only feasible provided the future workload is known.

Turn-Off Algorithm. In this algorithm, idle servers are always turned off. However, the algorithm does not ensure that a server stays off T_S seconds. Furthermore, the average time delay to satisfy clients' requests can be greater compared to other algorithms since the probability of having unexpected works which can not be immediately executed is higher than in an algorithm which always keeps some idle available servers.

EARI [3]. An on/off algorithm for reservation-based systems (users reserve resources for a fixed time). EARI relies on the prediction of the next reservations. It estimates the number of servers to turn off whenever there are no waiting reservation requests to be scheduled. Nevertheless, no policy about turning on servers is described. Given M possible servers to turn off, EARI estimates the next reservation R with arrival time t using n servers. If R arrives before T_S seconds, then n servers stay on during T_S and $M - n$ servers are turned off. If after T_S seconds no reservation arrives, the above n servers are released, i.e., they will be considered to belong to the pool of possible servers to turn off. The estimation of reservation values (starting time t and number of servers n) is based on the history of previous reservations. Basically, the predicted value is the mean of the previous values $(mean(N))$ corrected with the mean of the previous errors $(mean(\mathcal{E}_N))$. Basically, the predicted value is the mean of the 5 previous values corrected with the mean of the 3 previous errors.

MERCi-MIsS. For performance evaluation, we consider a time-based sliding window of size 5min, slide of 3min, and the whisker length $w = 1.5$. While MERCi-MIsS bases its estimation on recent time (the last 5 minutes), EARI uses the last (5) reservation values. Notice that we could consider a longer time interval (till 3h) in EARI which would correspond to a much higher number of reservations. However, the risk of loosing the correlation between time and the number of reservations could greatly increase.

4.2　Evaluation Results

In this section, we present a comparative by evaluating: 1) the tradeoff between the service maintainability cost and the average time delay to attend clients's requests; 2) the service maintainability cost; 3) the impact on the time delay and the number of delayed reservations; and 4) the processing time to take decisions.

Tradeoff Between Maintainability Cost and Time Delay. Energy-aware policies must try to reduce service maintainability cost without increasing time delay for processing clients' work which degrades QoS. Fig. 3a shows the average time delay versus the service maintainability cost. The closer to the point (0,0), the lower the time delay and the service maintainability cost (better energy-aware policy). EARI has higher service maintainability cost and time delay than MERCi-MIsS. MERCi-MIsS has also a lower time delay than the Turn-Off policy. However, MERCi-MIsS has a slightly higher service maintainability cost than

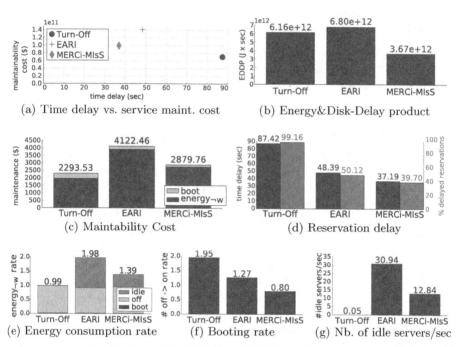

Fig. 3. Turn Off, EARI and MERCi-MIsS performace

the latter. The results of Fig. 3b also confirm that MERCi-MIsS presents the smallest EDDP (see Sec. 3.3). From both results, MERCi-MIsS has the best tradeoff between energy of non working servers, disk replacement, and time delay.

Service Maintainability Cost. Fig. 3c shows such a cost ($) for each algorithm. Blue and green portions of the bars are, resp., the cost related to the energy spent by non-working servers $energy_{\neg w}$ and disk replacement. Turn-Off is the best for monetary cost, but, it degrades the time delay as discussed later. In order to understand more deeply the service maintainability cost, we show different aspects: (1) Fig. 3e concerns the energy consumption of non working servers; (2) Fig. 3f is related to the number of boots (disk damage); and, (3) Fig. 3g shows the average number of idle servers per second. The energy bars in Fig. 3e are the energy consumed in the service maintainability divided by the energy in the perfect prediction algorithm. Three different colors make distinguishable the fraction of energy spent in different states (boot, off, and idle). As expected, Turn-Off algorithm consumes less energy in idle servers (the number of idle servers is close to 0 in Figure 3g). It is, thus, the best algorithm for saving energy. Notice that the number of idle servers in the perfect prediction is very low (0.62 server per second in average). On the other hand, MERCi-MIsS consumes 29% less energy than EARI. Fig. 3g confirms that such a reduction is due to idle servers. Bars in Fig. 3f represent the number of boots with regard to the perfect prediction. As expected, Turn-off performs the greatest number of boots which is almost twice the number in perfect prediction algorithm. In both Turn-off and EARI, the boot rate is higher than in the perfect prediction algorithm, contrarily to MERCi-MIsS, which presents lower boot rate than the latter (the ratio is smaller than 1). Fig. 3g, which shows the average number of idle servers per second, allows a better understanding of the different energy-aware policies. Turn-Off has a number of idle servers per second close to 0 (not 0 because a server must be in idle state to be turned off) while EARI has higher number of idle servers per second than MERCi-MIsS (2.4 times). Observing Fig. 3e-3g, we conclude that, during some periods, EARI maintains a large number of idle servers which are not required (EARI fails in the future workload prediction).

Reservation Delay. Keeping servers in the off state has an impact on the QoS. Fig. 3d shows two results: 1) in the left side (blue), the average time delay for reservation; and 2) in the right side (green), the percent of delayed reservations. As expected, Turn-Off has a large number of delayed reservations (almost the whole reservation set) and the largest time delay. The impact of off servers on the QoS in the MERCi-MIsS is lower than in the EARI (shorter time delay and smaller number of delayed reservations). Therefore, in MERCi-MIsS, the number of off servers induces less degradation of the QoS than in the other algorithms. Such a result strengthens the previous one which concludes that MERCi-MIsS provides a better prediction of the future workload than the other algorithms. Comparing to the latter, it presents shorter time delay while using fewer resources. Hence, it has lower service maintainability cost.

Time for Decision Processing. On/Off algorithms should present a performance which allows the respective implementation in real environments. Tab. 4 summarizes the time spent to decide about the turn on/off actions. Obviously, the Turn-Off is the fastest one since no information is processed to take such a decision. EARI has a time processing close to Turn-Off due to the size of the processed information which is quite small (the last 5 reservations). MERCi-MIsS has the largest time processing because it considers the number of working servers of the last 5 minutes. However, we should emphasize that MERCi-MIsS time processing is feasible, i.e., 197 micro-sec while the time step is 1 sec. Hence, the three policies have time processing which are suitable for real environments.

Table 4. Decision time processing in microseconds

Turn-off	EARI	MERCi-MIsS
3.09	5.22	169.91

5   Related Work

In [18], authors present a survey on techniques for improving the energy efficiency of large-scale distributed systems. A taxonomy and survey of energy-efficient data centers and cloud computing systems can be found in [19].

The first on/off algorithm which considers disk damage was proposed in [2] where authors presented Muse, an operating system for a hosting center.

The prediction approach focuses on estimating the resource demand of each customer considering her/his current request load level, contrarily to MERCi-MIsS algorithm, which characterizes the system load based on client demands, being, thus, more suitable for environments with a huge number of clients or with a dynamic set of users.

The concept of critical time, the minimum period of time which a server must be off to save energy, was introduced in [3]. The article then proposes the EARI algorithm for reservations-based environments such as Grid'5000, on top of which they conducted some evaluation experiments. We have extended their critical time concept with the time corresponding to the fraction that must be added to the former in order to consider the energy spent due to disk damage.

[20] presents two algorithms (online and offline) to turn off content delivery networks during periods of low load. The algorithms have three goals: maximize energy reduction, minimize the impact on client-perceived service availability, and reduce the wear-and-tear on hardware reliability. However, they have been designed to content delivery networks which operate as application service providers and can not be applied in other context such as infrastructure as a software (IaaS) or software as a service (SaaS).

The article [11] presents an online algorithm based on the number of active servers x_t at any time t. It uses a cost function to minimize some costs such as energy cost, cost related with network delay, and the cost of booting (including delay, mitigation, and disk damage). Nevertheless, as we have discussed in previous sections, the number of active working servers are not sufficient to compute the total energy cost because turning on and off servers consumes energy (analogous situation for power off servers). Therefore, an energy cost function must consider other server states than just active state. Concretely, the cost related to the disk damage is a linear function of the difference in consecutive times $x_t - x_{t-1}$. Hence, it is not fair to take into account just active servers such as in scenarios where, whenever one server concludes its turning on, the system decides to turn off one server. In this case, the number of active servers is always $x_t - x_{t-1} = 0$ and the model does not consider any disk damage.

A different approach of on/off algorithms is based on processor dynamic voltage/frequency scaling [8, 21]. However, processors consist of a small fraction of the total server power [22], entailing a moderate energy savings [13]. In [8], the authors consider disk damage to the dynamic voltage/frequency scaling strategy.

6   Conclusions and Future Work

We have presented MERCi-MIsS whose aim is to reduce energy consumption in data centers without degrading the provided quality of services. MERCi-MIsS takes into account the energy spent by servers and disk damage due to wear-and-tear of ignitions and continuously decides how many servers to power off or on. We have conducted some simulation experiments based on real traces. The results related to the Energy&Disk-Delay product (EDDP) metric, which expresses the above three aspects, confirm that MERCi-MIsS reduces in more than 39% the value of this metric when compared to the other algorithms.

As future work, we plan to evaluate heterogeneous systems by grouping servers according to their respective critical time and then applying MERCi-MIsS on each group. We will also evaluate the performance over other workloads.

Acknowledgements. This research is founding by the French National Agency for Research, ANR-10-SEGI-0009.

References

1. Cook: How clean is your cloud? Greenpace (2012)
2. Chase, J.S., Anderson, D.C., Thakar, P.N., Vahdat, A.M., Doyle, R.P.: Managing energy and server resources in hosting centres. In: SOSP 2001 (2001)
3. Orgerie, A.C., Lefévre, L., Gelas, J.P.: Chasing gaps between bursts: Towards energy efficient large scale experimental grids. In: PDCAT 2008 (2008)
4. Fu, Y., Lu, C., Wang, H.: Robust control-theoretic thermal balancing for server clusters. In: IPDPS 2010 (2010)
5. Gulati, A., et al.: VMware Distributed Resource Management: Design, Implementation, and Lessons Learned (2012)
6. Benini, L., Bogliolo, A., De Micheli, G.: A survey of design techniques for system-level dynamic power management. In: VLSI 2000 (2000)
7. Elerath, J.G.: Specifying reliability in the disk drive industry: No more MTBF's. In: RAMS 2000 (2000)
8. Chen, Y., Das, A., Qin, W., Sivasubramaniam, A., Wang, Q., Gautam, N.: Managing server energy and operational costs in hosting centers. In: SIGMETRICS 2005 (2005)
9. Bisson, T., Brandt, S.C., Long, D.D.E.: A hybrid disk-aware spin-down algorithm with I/O subsystem support. In: IPCCC 2007 (2007)
10. Chen, S., Hu, Y., Peng, L.: Optimization of electricity and server maintenance costs in hybrid cooling data centers. In: CLOUD 2013 (2013)
11. Lin, M., Wierman, A., Andrew, L.L.H., Thereska, E.: Dynamic right-sizing for power-proportional data centers. IEEE/ACM Trans. Netw. (2013)
12. McGill, R., et al.: Variations of box plots. The American Statistician (1978)
13. Fan, X., Weber, W.D., Barroso, L.A.: Power provisioning for a warehouse-sized computer. In: ISCA 2007 (2007)
14. Gandhi, A., Gupta, V., Harchol-Balter, M., Kozuch, M.A.: Optimality analysis of energyperformance trade-off for server farm management. Perf. Eval. (2010)
15. www.ens-lyon.fr/LIP/RESO/ict-energy-logs/index.html
16. Storm, storm-project.net, Petrel: github.com/AirSage/Petrel
17. https://github.com/AirSage/Petrel
18. Orgerie, A.C., et al.: A survey on techniques for improving the energy efficiency of large-scale distributed systems. ACM Comput. Surv. (2013)
19. Beloglazov, A., et al.: A taxonomy and survey of energy-efficient data centers and cloud computing systems. Advances in Computers (2011)
20. Mathew, V., Sitaraman, R., Shenoy, P.: Energy-aware load balancing in content delivery networks. In: INFOCOM 2012 (2012)
21. Hotta, Y., Sato, M., Kimura, H., Matsuoka, S., Boku, T., Takahashi, D.: Profile-based optimization of power performance by using dynamic voltage scaling on a pc cluster. In: IPDPS 2006 (2006)
22. Meisner, D., Gold, B.T., Wenisch, T.F.: Powernap: Eliminating server idle power. In: ASPLOS 2009 (2009)

Fully Distributed Privacy Preserving Mini-batch Gradient Descent Learning

Gábor Danner$^{(\boxtimes)}$ and Márk Jelasity

University of Szeged, and MTA-SZTE Research Group on AI, Szeged, Hungary
{danner,jelasity}@inf.u-szeged.hu

Abstract. In fully distributed machine learning, privacy and security are important issues. These issues are often dealt with using secure multiparty computation (MPC). However, in our application domain, known MPC algorithms are not scalable or not robust enough. We propose a light-weight protocol to quickly and securely compute the sum of the inputs of a subset of participants assuming a semi-honest adversary. During the computation the participants learn no individual values. We apply this protocol to efficiently calculate the sum of gradients as part of a fully distributed mini-batch stochastic gradient descent algorithm. The protocol achieves scalability and robustness by exploiting the fact that in this application domain a "quick and dirty" sum computation is acceptable. In other words, speed and robustness takes precedence over precision. We analyze the protocol theoretically as well as experimentally based on churn statistics from a real smartphone trace. We derive a sufficient condition for preventing the leakage of an individual value, and we demonstrate the feasibility of the overhead of the protocol.

Keywords: Fully distributed learning · Mini-batch stochastic gradient descent · P2P smartphone networks · Secure sum

1 Introduction

Our long-term research objective is to design fully distributed machine learning algorithms for various distributed systems including networks of smartphones, smart meters, or embedded devices. The main motivation for a distributed solution in our cloud-based era is to preserve privacy by avoiding the central collection of any personal data. Another advantage of distributed processing is that this way we can make full use of all the local personal data, which is impossible in cloud-based or private centralized data silos that store only specific subsets of the data.

In our previous work we proposed several distributed machine learning algorithms in a framework called gossip learning. In this framework models perform random walks over the network and are trained using stochastic gradient descent [18] (see Section 4). This involves an update step in which nodes use their local data to improve each model they receive, and then forward the updated model along the next step of the random walk. Assuming the random walk is secure—which in itself is a research problem on its own, see e.g. [13]—it is hard for an

© IFIP International Federation for Information Processing 2015
A. Bessani and S. Bouchenak (Eds.): DAIS 2015, LNCS 9038, pp. 30–44, 2015.
DOI: 10.1007/978-3-319-19129-4_3

adversary to obtain the two versions of the model right before and right after the local update step at any given node. This provides reasonable protection against uncovering private data.

However, this method is susceptible to collusion. If the nodes before and after an update in the random walk collude they can recover private data. In this paper we address this problem, and improve gossip learning so that it can tolerate a much higher proportion of honest but curious (or semi-honest) adversaries. The key idea behind the approach is that in each step of the random walk we form groups of peers that securely compute the sum of their gradients, and the model update step is performed using this aggregated gradient. In machine learning this is called mini-batch learning, which—apart from increasing the resistance to collusion—is known to often speed up the learning algorithm as well (see, for example, [8]).

It might seem attractive to run a secure multiparty computation (MPC) algorithm within the mini-batch to compute the sum of the gradients. The goal of MPC is to compute a function of the private inputs of the parties in such a way that at the end of the computation, no party knows anything except what can be determined from the result and its own input [24]. Secure sum computation is an important application of secure MPC [7].

However, we do not only require our algorithm to be secure but also fast, lightweight, and robust, since the participating nodes may go offline at any time [2] and they might have limited resources. One key observation is that for the mini-batch algorithm we do not need a precise sum; in fact, the sum over any group that is large enough to protect privacy will do. At the same time, it is unlikely that all the nodes will stay online until the end of the computation. We propose a protocol that—using a tree topology and homomorphic encryption—can produce a "quick and dirty" partial sum even in the event of failures, has adjustable capability of resisting collusion, and can be completed in logarithmic time.

2   Related Work

There are many approaches that have goals similar to ours, that is, to perform computations over a large and highly distributed database or network in a secure and privacy preserving way. Our work touches upon several fields of research including machine learning, distributed systems and algorithms, secure multiparty computation and privacy. Our contribution lies in the intersection of these areas. Here we focus only on related work that is directly relevant to our present contributions.

Algorithms exist for completely generic secure computations, Saia and Zamani give a comprehensive overview with a focus on scalability [22]. However, due to their focus on generic computations, these approaches are relatively complex and in the context of our application they still do not scale well enough, and do not tolerate dynamic membership either.

Approaches targeted at specific problems are more promising. Clifton et al. propose, among other things, an algorithm to compute a sum [7]. This algorithm requires linear time in the network size and it does not tolerate node failure either.

Bickson et al. focus on a class of computations over graphs, where the computation is performed in an iterative manner through a series of local updates [3]. They introduce a secure algorithm to compute local sums over neighboring nodes based on secret sharing. Unfortunately, this model of computation does not cover our problem as we want to compute mini-batches of a size independent of the size of the direct neighborhood, and the proposed approach does not scale well in that sense. Besides, the robustness of the method is not satisfactory either [17]. Han et al. address stochastic gradient search explicitly [12]. However, they assume that the parties involved have large portions of the database, so their solution is not applicable in our scenario.

The algorithm of Ahmad and Khokhar is similar to ours [1]. They also use a tree to aggregate values using homomorphic encryption. In their solution all the nodes have the same public key and the private key is distributed over a subset of elite nodes using secret sharing. The problem with this approach in our application is that for each mini-batch a new key set has to be generated for the group, which requires frequent access to a trusted server, otherwise the method is highly vulnerable in the key generation phase.

We need to mention the area of differential privacy [9], which is concerned with the the problem that the (perhaps securely computed) output itself might contain information about individual records. The approach is that a carefully designed noise term is added to the output. Gradient search has been addressed in this framework (for example, [20]). In our distributed setup, this noise term can be computed in a distributed and secure way [10].

3   Model

Communication. We model our system as a very large set of nodes that communicate via message passing. At every point in time each node has a set of neighbors forming a connected network. The neighbor set can change over time, but nodes can send messages only to their current neighbors. Nodes can leave the network or fail at any time. We model leaving the network as a node failure. Messages can be delayed up to a maximum delay. Messages cannot be dropped, so communication fails only if the target node fails before receiving the message.

The set of neighbors is either hard-wired, or given by other physical constraints (for example, proximity), or set by an overlay service. Such overlay services are widely available in the literature and are out of the scope of our present discussion. It is not strictly required that the set of neighbors are random, however, we will assume this for the sake of simplicity. If the set is not random, then implementing a random walk with a uniform stationary distribution requires additional well-proven techniques such as Metropolis-Hastings sampling or structured routing [23].

Data Distribution. We assume a horizontal distribution, which means that each node has full data records. We are most interested in the extreme case when each node has only a single record. The database that we wish to perform data mining over is given by the union of the records stored by the nodes.

Adversarial Model. We assume that the adversaries are honest but curious (or semi-honest). That is, nodes corrupted by an adversary will follow the protocol but the adversary can see the internal state of the node as well as the plaintext of the messages that the node receives or sends. The goal of the adversary is to learn about the private data of other nodes (note that the adversary can obviously see the private data on the node it observes directly).

We assume a static adversarial model, which means that the corrupted nodes are picked a priori, independently of the state of the protocol or the network. As of the number of corrupted nodes, we will consider the threshold model, in which at most a given number of nodes are corrupted, as well as a probabilistic model, in which any node can be corrupted with a given constant probability [16].

Wiretapping is assumed to be impossible. In other words, communication channels are assumed to be secure. This can easily be implemented if there is a public key infrastructure in place.

We also assume that adversaries are not able to manipulate the set of neighbors. In each application domain this assumption translates to different requirements. For example, if an overlay service is used to maintain the neighbors then this service has to be secure itself.

4   Background on Gossip Learning

Although not strictly required for understanding our key contribution, it is important to briefly overview the basic concepts of stochastic gradient descent search, and our gossip learning framework (GOLF) [18].

The basic problem of *supervised binary classification* can be defined as follows. Let us assume that we are given a labeled database in the form of pairs of feature vectors and their correct classification, i.e. $z_1 = (x_1, y_1), \dots, z_n = (x_n, y_n)$, where $x_i \in \mathbb{R}^d$, and $y_i \in \{-1, 1\}$. The constant d is the *dimension* of the problem (the number of features). We are looking for a *model* $f_w : \mathbb{R}^d \to \{-1, 1\}$ parameterized by a vector w that correctly classifies the available feature vectors, and that can also *generalize* well; that is, which can classify unseen examples too.

Supervised learning can be thought of as an optimization problem, where we want to minimize the empirical risk

$$E_n(w) = \frac{1}{n} \sum_{i=1}^{n} Q(z_i, w) = \frac{1}{n} \sum_{i=1}^{n} \ell(f_w(x_i), y_i) \tag{1}$$

where function $Q(z_i, w) = \ell(f_w(x_i), y_i)$ is a loss function capturing the prediction error on example z_i.

Training algorithms that iterate over available training data, or process a continuous stream of data records, and evolve a model by updating it for each individual data record according to some update rule are called *online learning algorithms*. Gossip learning relies on this type of learning algorithms. Ma et al. provide a nice summary of online learning for large scale data [15].

Stochastic gradient search [5,6] is a generic algorithmic family for implementing online learning methods. The basic idea is that we iterate over the training examples in a random order repeatedly, and for each training example z_t we calculate the gradient of the error function (which describes classification error), and modify the model along this gradient to reduce the error on this particular example according to the rule

$$w_{t+1} = w_t - \gamma_t \nabla_w Q(z_t, w_t) \tag{2}$$

where γ_t is the learning rate at step t that often decreases as t increases.

A popular way to accelerate the convergence is the use of mini-batches, that is, to update the model with the gradient of the sum of the loss functions of a few training examples (instead of only one) in each iteration. This allows for fast distributed implementations as well [11].

In gossip learning, models perform random walks on the network and are trained on the local data using stochastic gradient descent. Besides, several models can perform random walks at the same time, and these models can be combined time-to-time to accelerate convergence. Our approach here will be based on this scheme, replacing the local update step with a mini-batch approach.

5   Our Solution

Based on the assumptions in Section 3 and building on the GOLF framework outlined in Section 4 we now present our algorithm for computing a mini-batch gradient in a single step of the mini-batch gradient descent algorithm. First of all, recall that models perform random walks over the nodes in the network. At each step, when a node receives a model to update, it will first create a mini-batch group by building a rooted tree. According to our assumptions adversaries cannot manipulate the neighborhood and they do not corrupt the protocol execution, so this can be achieved via simple local flooding algorithms.

Let us now describe what kind of tree is needed exactly. The basic version of our algorithm will require a *trunked tree*.

Definition 1 (Trunked Tree). *Any rooted tree is* 1*-trunked. For* $k > 1$*, a rooted tree is* k*-trunked if the root has exactly one child node, and the corresponding subtree is a* $(k-1)$*-trunked tree.*

Let N denote the intended size of the mini-batch group. We assume that N is significantly less than the network size. Let S be a parameter that determines the desired security level ($N \geq S \geq 2$). We can now state that we require an *S-trunked tree* rooted at the node that is being visited by gossip learning.

This tree can be constructed on an overlay network by taking $S - 1$ random steps, and then performing a flooding algorithm with appropriately set time-to-live and branching parameters. The exact algorithm for this is not very interesting, mostly because it can be very simple. The reason is that when building the tree, no attention needs to be paid to reliability. We generate the tree quickly and use it only once quickly. Normally, some subtrees will be lost in the process but our algorithm is designed to tolerate this.

The effect of certain parameters, such as the branching factor and node failures, will be discussed later in the evaluation. In rare cases, when the neighborhood size is too small or when there are many cycles in the network, it could be hard to achieve the desired branching factor, which can result in a deeper tree than desired resulting in an increased time-complexity. Apart from this performance issue, the algorithm will function correctly even in these cases. From now on, for simplicity, we assume that the desired branching factor can be achieved.

The sum we want to calculate is over vectors of real numbers. We discuss the one-dimensional gradient from now on for simplicity. Homomorphic encryption works over integers, to be precise, over the set of residue classes $\mathbb{Z}_n$ for some large n. For this reason we need to discretize the real interval that includes all possible sums we might calculate, and we need to map the resulting discrete intervals to residue classes in $\mathbb{Z}_M$ where M defines the granularity of the resolution of the discretization. This mapping is natural, we do not go into details here. Since the gradient of the loss function for most learning algorithms is bounded, this is not a practical limitation.

The basic idea of the algorithm is to divide the local value into S shares, encrypt these with asymmetric additively homomorphic encryption (such as the Paillier cryptosystem), and send them to the root via the chain of ancestors. Although the shares travel together, they are encrypted with the public keys of different ancestors. Along the route, the arrays of shares are aggregated, and periodically re-encrypted. Finally, the root calculates the sum.

The algorithm consists of three procedures, shown in Algorithm 1. These are run locally on the individual nodes. Procedure INIT is called once after the node becomes part of the tree. Procedure ONMESSAGERECEIVED is called whenever a message is received by the node. A message contains an array of dimension S that contains shares encoded for S ancestors. The first element msg[1] is encrypted for the current node, so it can decrypt it. The rest of the shares are shifted down by one position and added (with homomorphic encryption) to the local array of shares to be sent. After all the messages have been processed, the ith element ($1 \leq i \leq S-1$) of the array SHARES is now encrypted with the public key of the ith ancestor of the current node and contains a share of the sum of the subtree except the local value of the current node. The Sth element is stored unencrypted in variable KNOWN-SHARE.

Procedure ONNOMOREMESSAGESEXPECTED is called when the node has received a message from all of its children, or when the remaining children are considered to be dead by a failure detector. The timeout used here has to take into account the depth of the given subtree and the maximal delay of a message. In the case of leaf nodes, this procedure is called right after INIT.

The function call ANCESTOR(i) returns the descriptor of the ith ancestor of the current node that contains the necessary public keys as well. During tree building this information can be given to each node. For the purposes of this function, the parent of the root is defined to be itself. Function ENCRYPT(x, y) encrypts the integer x with the public key of node y using an asymmetric additively homomorphic cryptosystem. DECRYPT(x) decrypts x with the private key of the current node.

Algorithm 1.

---

  procedure INIT
    shares ← new array$[1..S]$
    for i ← 1 **to** S **do**
      shares$[i]$ ← Encrypt$(0,$ Ancestor$(i))$
    end for
    knownShare ← 0
  end procedure

  procedure ONMESSAGERECEIVED(msg)
    for i ← 1 **to** $S - 1$ **do**
      shares$[i]$ ← shares$[i]$ ⊕ msg$[i + 1]$
    end for
    knownShare ← knownShare + Decrypt(msg$[1]$)
  end procedure

  procedure ONNOMOREMESSAGESEXPECTED
    if IAmTheRoot() **then**
      for i ← 1 **to** $S - 1$ **do**
        knownShare ← knownShare + Decrypt(shares$[i]$)
      end for
      Publish((knownShare + localValue) mod M)
    else
      randSum ← 0
      for i ← 1 **to** $S - 1$ **do**
        rand ← Random(M)
        randSum ← randSum + rand
        shares$[i]$ ← shares$[i]$ ⊕ Encrypt(rand, Ancestor$(i))$
      end for
      knownShare ← knownShare + localValue − randSum
      shares$[S]$ ← Encrypt(knownShare mod M, Ancestor$(S))$
      SendToParent(shares)
    end if
  end procedure

Operation $a \oplus b$ performs the homomorphic addition of the two encrypted integers a and b to get the encrypted form of the sum of these integers. Function RANDOM(x) returns a uniformly distributed random integer in the range $[0, x - 1]$.

If the current node is the root, then the elements of the received array are decrypted and summed. The root can decrypt all the elements because it is the parent of itself, so all the elements are encrypted for the root when the message reaches it. If the current node is not the root then the local value has to be added, and the Sth element of the array has to be filled. First, the local value is split into S shares according to the S-out-of-S secret-sharing scheme discussed in [16]: $S - 1$ out of the S shares are uniformly distributed random integers between 0 and $M - 1$. The last share is the difference between the local value and the sum of the random numbers (mod M). This way, the sum of shares equals the local value (mod M).

Also, the sum of any non-empty proper subset of these shares is uniformly distributed, therefore nothing can be learned about the local value without knowing all the shares.

The shares calculated this way can be encrypted and added to the corresponding shares, and finally the remaining Sth share is re-encrypted with the public key of the Sth ancestor and put into the end of the array. When this array is sent to the parent, it contains the S shares of the partial sum corresponding to the full sub-tree.

We note here that if during the algorithm a child node never responds, then its subtree will be essentially missing (will have a sum of zero) but other than that the algorithm will terminate normally. This is acceptable in our application, because for a mini-batch we simply need the sum of any number of gradients, this will not threaten the convergence of the gradient descent algorithm.

6 Discussion

6.1 Security

To steal information, that is, to learn the sum over a subtree, the adversary needs to catch and decrypt all the S shares of the corresponding message that was sent by the root of the subtree in question. Recall that if the adversary decrypts less than S shares from any message, it still has only a uniform random value due to our construction. To be more precise, to completely decrypt a message sent to node c_1, the adversary needs to corrupt c_1 and all its $S - 1$ closest ancestors, denoted by $c_2, .., c_S$, so he can obtain the necessary private keys.

The only situation when the shares of a message are not encrypted with the public keys of S *different* nodes—and hence when less than S nodes are sufficient to be corrupted—is when the distance of the sender from the root is less than S. In this case, the sender node is located in the trunk of the tree. However, decrypting such a message does not yield any more information than what can be calculated from the (public) result of the protocol and the local values (gradients) of the nodes needed to be corrupted for the decryption. This is because in the trunk the sender of the message in question is surely the only child of the first corrupted node, and the message represents the sum of the local values of all the nodes, except for the ones needed to be corrupted. To put it in a different way, corrupting less than S nodes never gives more leverage than learning the private data of the corrupted nodes only.

Therefore, the only way to steal extra information (other than the local values of the corrupted nodes) is to form a continuous chain of corrupted nodes $c_1, .., c_S$ towards the root, where c_{i+1} is the parent of c_i. This makes it possible to steal the partial sums of the subtrees rooted at the children of c_1. For this reason we now focus only on the $N - S$ vulnerable subtrees not rooted in the trunk.

As a consequence, a threshold adversary cannot steal information if he corrupts at most $S - 1$ nodes. A probabilistic adversary that corrupts each node with probability p can steal the exact partial sum of a given subtree whose root is not corrupted with probability p^S.

Even if the sum of a given subtree is not stolen, some information can be learned about it by stealing the sums of other subtrees. However, this information is limited, as demonstrated by the following theorem.

Theorem 1. *The private value of a node that is not corrupted cannot be exactly determined by the adversary as long as at least one of the S closest ancestors of the node is not corrupted.*

Proof. Let us denote by t the target node, and by u the closest ancestor of t that is not corrupted. The message sent by t cannot be decrypted by the adversary, because one of its shares is encrypted to u (because u is one of the S closest ancestors of t). The same holds for all the nodes between t and u. Therefore the smallest subtree that contains t and whose sum can be stolen also contains u. Due to the nested nature of subtrees, bigger subtrees that contains t also contains u as well. Also, any subtree that contains u also contains t (since t is the descendant of u). Therefore u and t cannot be separated. Even if every other node is corrupted in the subtree whose sum is stolen, only the sum of the private values of u and t can be determined.

Therefore p^S is also an upper bound on the probability of stealing the exact private value of a given node that is not corrupted.

6.2   Complexity

In a tree with a maximal branching factor of B each node sends only one message, and receives at most B. The length of a message is $\mathcal{O}(SC)$, an array of S encrypted integers, where C is the length of the encrypted form of an integer. Let us now elaborate on C. First, as stated before, the sum of the gradients is represented on $\mathcal{O}(\log M)$ bits, where M is a design choice defining the precision of the fixed point representation of the real gradient. Let us assume for now that we use the Paillier cryptosystem [19]. In this case, we need to set the parameters of our cryptosystem in such a way that the largest number it can represent is no less than $n = \min(B^S M, NM)$, which is the upper bound of any share being computed by the algorithm (assuming $B \geq 2$). In the Paillier cryptosystem the ciphertext for this parameter setting has an upper bound of $\mathcal{O}(n^2)$ for a single share. Since

$$S \log n^2 = S \log \min(B^S M, NM)^2 \leq 2(S^2 \log B + S \log M), \qquad (3)$$

the number of bits required is $\mathcal{O}(S^2 \log B + S \log M)$.

The computational complexity is $\mathcal{O}(BSE)$ per node, where E is the cost of encryption, decryption, or homomorphic addition. All these three operations boil down to one or two exponentiations in modular arithmetic in the Paillier cryptosystem. Note that this is independent of N.

The time complexity of the protocol is proportional to the depth of the tree. If the tree is balanced, this results in $S + \mathcal{O}(logN)$ steps altogether.

6.3   Robustness

As mentioned before, if a node failure occurs then the subtree rooted at that node is left out of the sum. In our application this does not render the output useless, since in mini-batch methods one can apply mini-batches of varying size.

Let us take a closer look at the possible effect of node failure. From the point of starting to build the tree until the root computes the end result a certain number of nodes might fail at random. The worst-case scenario is when all these nodes fail right after the construction of the tree but before starting to propagate shares upwards.

We have conducted experiments to assess the robustness of the trees under various parameter settings. In the initialization step, a random graph of 1,000,000 nodes is generated in the following way: 20% percent of the nodes are marked public and then each node gets 20 links to random public nodes. These links represent bidirectional communication channels. It has been argued that such a construction is a viable approach in the presence of NAT devices on the open Internet [21]. Also, recently Berta et al. [2] estimated that the NAT types of about 20% of smartphones are either open access or full cone. Thus, the parameter setting and the overlay above is a good representation of one application domain: smartphone networks.

After this, random trees are generated with a depth of D and a maximal branching factor of B, in the following way: a root is chosen randomly, which selects B of its neighbors as children, then each of them, in turn, selects B of their respective neighbors, and so on, until depth D is reached. No node selects its parent, but multiple nodes may try to select the same node, in which case it becomes the child of only one of them. Therefore nodes can have less than B children, but this happens infrequently, if the graph is large enough compared to the tree. These trees are used to calculate the expected value of the ratio of the nodes that are reachable from the root via a chain of available nodes, assuming a given chance for node failure, in the worst case scenario we outlined above. If the probability of node failure is f, a node located at level d of the tree (the root has level 0) will successfully contribute its local value to the sum with probability $(1 - f)^{(d+1)}$.) The results are shown in Figure 1. Each curve represents a given setting of B and D. Each point is based on 50 different random trees.

To provide an indication of feasible failure rates in an actual network, we analyzed the trace collected by Berta et al. [2]. In this trace a node was defined to be available when it had network connectivity and when it was on a charger at the same time. Figure 2 shows statistics about smartphone availability. For each hour, we calculated the probability that a node that has been online for at least a minute remains online for 1, 5 or 10 more minutes. As the figure illustrates, these probabilities are rather high even for a 10 minute extra time, which is certainly sufficient to complete a mini-batch for any reasonable batch size, given that the time complexity is logarithmic in size. Comparing this with Figure 1, under these realistic failure rates the resulting computation will cover a large subset of the intended mini-batch.

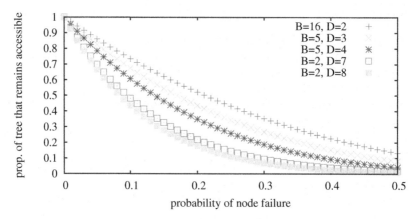

Fig. 1. The expected value of the ratio of nodes that successfully contribute to the computation, plotted as a function of the probability of node failure. B denotes maximal branching factor and D denotes depth. (An isolated node has depth 0.)

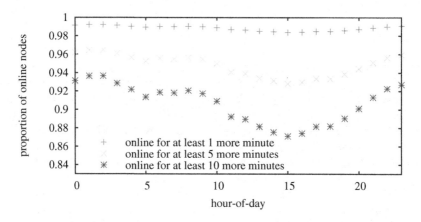

Fig. 2. Expected availability of smartphones that have been online for at least a minute. Hour-of-day is in UTC.

7   Variations

Although the robustness of the algorithm is useful, we have to be careful when publishing a sum based on too few participants. The algorithm can be modified to address this issue. Let us denote by R the minimal required number of actual participants ($S \leq R \leq N$). Each message is padded with an (unencrypted) integer n indicating the number of nodes its data is based on. When the node exactly $S-1$ steps away from the root (thus in the trunk) is about to send its message, it checks whether $n + S - 1 \geq R$ holds (since the remaining nodes towards the root have no children except the one on this path). If not, it sends a failure message instead.

The nodes fewer than $S - 1$ steps away from the root transmit a failure message if they receive one, or if they fail to receive any messages.

One can ask the question whether the trunk is needed, as the protocol can be executed on any tree unmodified. However, having no trunk makes it easier to steal information about subtrees close to the root. If the tree is well-balanced and the probability of failure is small, these subtrees can be large enough for the stolen partial sums to not pose a practical privacy problem in certain applications. The advantages include a simpler topology, a faster running time, and increased robustness.

Another option is to replace the top $S - 1$ nodes with a central server. To be more precise, we can have a server simulate the top $S - 1$ nodes with the local values of these nodes set to zero. This server acts as the root of a 2-trunked tree. From a security point of view, if the server is corrupted by a semi-honest adversary, we have the same situation when the top $S - 1$ nodes are corrupted by the same adversary. As we have shown in Section 6.1, one needs to corrupt at least S nodes in a chain to gain any extra advantage, so on its own the server is not able to obtain extra information other than the global sum. Also, the server does not need more computational capacity or bandwidth than the other nodes. This variation can be combined with the size propagation technique described above. Here, the child of the server can check whether $n \geq R$ holds.

8   Evaluation of Convergence Speed

Here, we illustrate the cost of using mini-batch learning instead of stochastic gradient descent, and we also illustrate the overhead of our cryptographic techniques on the mini-batch algorithm.

We simulated our algorithm over the Spambase binary classification data set from the UCI repository[14], which consists of 4601 records, 39.4% of which are positive. 10% of the records were reserved for testing. Each node had one record resulting in a network size of 4601. The trees we tested had a trunk length of S with D additional levels below the trunk with a branching factor of B. Each node stays alive during the calculation of the batch-sum with probability P resulting in E nodes (E is a random variable) that end up participating in the computation (see Figure 1).

The learning method we used was logistic regression [4]. We used the L2-regularized logistic regression online update rule

$$w \leftarrow \frac{t}{t+1}w + \frac{\eta}{t+1}(y - p)x$$

where w is the weight vector of the model, t is the number of samples seen by the model (not including the new one), x is the feature vector of the training example, y is the correct label (1 or 0), p is the prediction of the model (probability of the label being 1), and η is the learning parameter. We generalize this rule to mini-batches of size E as follows:

$$w \leftarrow \frac{t}{t+E}w + \left(\frac{1}{E}\sum_{i=1}^{E}\frac{\eta}{t+i}\right)\sum_{i=1}^{E}(y_i - p_i)x_i$$

where $(y_i - p_i)x_i$ is supposed to be calculated by the individual nodes, and summed using Algorithm 1. After the update, t is increased by E instead of 1. η was set to 1000.

Our baseline is the case when one instance of stochastic gradient descent (SGD) is started by each node and the nodes immediately forward all received models after updating it, thereby utilizing all the available bandwidth (in practice users can set upper bounds on this utilization, we assumed the maximal bandwidth is the same at all the nodes). We run mini-batch with and without cryptography (secure mini-batch and mini-batch). The number of instances we start of these mini-batch variants are chosen so that they use the same bandwidth as SGD. With cryptography we use Algorithm 1 to compute the gradient sum. Without cryptography we use the same tree but we do not encode the messages. Instead, we propagate the plain partial sum instead of S different encoded shares. Note that mini-batch with and without cryptography is in fact identical except that with cryptography all the messages are at most about $2S$ times larger and thus they take this much longer to transmit (see Section 6.2).

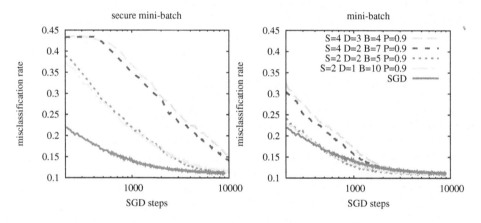

Fig. 3. Misclassification rate (zero-one error) of secure mini-batch (left) and mini-batch (right) averaged over the nodes and over 1000 different runs as a function of time (measured in SGD steps).

Figure 3 shows our results. Clearly, mini-batch gradient does not result in serious performance loss in itself. Cryptography does add overhead that is linearly proportional to the parameter S, since the message size includes the factor of S due to sending this number of shares.

9   Conclusion

We proposed a secure sum protocol to prevent the collusion attack in gossip learning. The main idea is that instead of SGD we implement a mini-batch method and the sum within the mini-batch is calculated using our novel secure algorithm. We can achieve very high levels of robustness and very good scalability through exploiting the fact that the mini-batch gradient algorithm does not require the sum to be precise. The algorithm runs in logarithmic time and it is designed to calculate a partial sum in case of node failures. It can tolerate collusion unless there are S consecutive colluding nodes on any path to the root of the aggregation tree, where S is a free parameter. Under practical parameter settings the communication complexity of the secure mini-batch algorithm is only approximately a constant factor of $2S$ larger than that of the plain mini-batch algorithm.

References

1. Ahmad, W., Khokhar, A.: Secure aggregation in large scale overlay networks. In: IEEE Global Telecommunications Conference (GLOBECOM 2006) (2006)
2. Berta, Á., Bilicki, V., Jelasity, M.: Defining and understanding smartphone churn over the internet: A measurement study. In: Proceedings of the 14th IEEE International Conference on Peer-to-Peer Computing (P2P 2014). IEEE (2014)
3. Bickson, D., Reinman, T., Dolev, D., Pinkas, B.: Peer-to-peer secure multi-party numerical computation facing malicious adversaries. Peer-to-Peer Networking and Applications 3(2), 129–144 (2010)
4. Bishop, C.M.: Pattern Recognition and Machine Learning. Springer (2006)
5. Bottou, L.: Stochastic gradient descent tricks. In: Montavon, G., Orr, G.B., Müller, K.-R. (eds.) Neural Networks: Tricks of the Trade, 2nd edn. LNCS, vol. 7700, pp. 421–436. Springer, Heidelberg (2012)
6. Bottou, L., LeCun, Y.: Large scale online learning. In: Thrun, S., Saul, L., Schölkopf, B. (eds.) Advances in Neural Information Processing Systems 16, MIT Press, Cambridge (2004)
7. Clifton, C., Kantarcioglu, M., Vaidya, J., Lin, X., Zhu, M.Y.: Tools for privacy preserving distributed data mining. SIGKDD Explor. Newsl. 4(2), 28–34 (2002)
8. Dekel, O., Gilad-Bachrach, R., Shamir, O., Xiao, L.: Optimal distributed online prediction using mini-batches. J. Mach. Learn. Res. 13(1), 165–202 (2012)
9. Dwork, C.: A firm foundation for private data analysis. Commun. ACM 54(1), 86–95 (2011)
10. Dwork, C., Kenthapadi, K., McSherry, F., Mironov, I., Naor, M.: Our data, ourselves: Privacy via distributed noise generation. In: Vaudenay, S. (ed.) EUROCRYPT 2006. LNCS, vol. 4004, pp. 486–503. Springer, Heidelberg (2006)
11. Gimpel, K., Das, D., Smith, N.A.: Distributed asynchronous online learning for natural language processing. In: Proceedings of the Fourteenth Conference on Computational Natural Language Learning (CoNLL 2010), pp. 213–222. Association for Computational Linguistics, Stroudsburg (2010)
12. Han, S., Ng, W.K., Wan, L., Lee, V.C.S.: Privacy-preserving gradient-descent methods. IEEE Transactions on Knowledge and Data Engineering 22(6), 884–899 (2010)
13. Jesi, G.P., Montresor, A., van Steen, M.: Secure peer sampling. Computer Networks 54(12), 2086–2098 (2010)
14. Lichman, M.: UCI machine learning repository (2013), http://archive.ics.uci.edu/ml
15. Ma, J., Saul, L.K., Savage, S., Voelker, G.M.: Identifying suspicious URLs: an application of large-scale online learning. In: Proceedings of the 26th Annual International Conference on Machine Learning (ICML 2009), pp. 681–688. ACM, New York (2009)

16. Maurer, U.: Secure multi-party computation made simple. Discrete Applied Mathematics 154(2), 370–381 (2006)

17. Naranjo, J.A.M., Casado, L.G., Jelasity, M.: Asynchronous privacy-preserving iterative computation on peer-to-peer networks. Computing 94(8-10), 763–782 (2012)

18. Ormándi, R., Hegedűs, I., Jelasity, M.: Gossip learning with linear models on fully distributed data. Concurrency and Computation: Practice and Experience 25(4), 556–571 (2013)

19. Paillier, P.: Public-key cryptosystems based on composite degree residuosity classes. In: Stern, J. (ed.) EUROCRYPT 1999. LNCS, vol. 1592, pp. 223–238. Springer, Heidelberg (1999)

20. Rajkumar, A., Agarwal, S.: A differentially private stochastic gradient descent algorithm for multiparty classification. In: JMLR Workshop and Conference Proceedings of AISTATS 2012, vol. 22, pp. 933–941 (2012)

21. Roverso, R., Dowling, J., Jelasity, M.: Through the wormhole: Low cost, fresh peer sampling for the internet. In: Proceedings of the 13th IEEE International Conference on Peer-to-Peer Computing (P2P 2013). IEEE (2013)

22. Saia, J., Zamani, M.: Recent results in scalable multi-party computation. In: Italiano, G.F., Margaria-Steffen, T., Pokorný, J., Quisquater, J.-J., Wattenhofer, R. (eds.) SOFSEM 2015. LNCS, vol. 8939, pp. 24–44. Springer, Heidelberg (2015)

23. Stutzbach, D., Rejaie, R., Duffield, N., Sen, S., Willinger, W.: On unbiased sampling for unstructured peer-to-peer networks. IEEE/ACM Transactions on Networking 17(2), 377–390 (2009)

24. Yao, A.C.: Protocols for secure computations. In: Proceedings of the 23rd Annual Symposium on Foundations of Computer Science (FOCS), pp. 160–164 (1982)

Incentivising Resource Sharing
in Federated Clouds

Eduardo de Lucena Falcão$^{(\boxtimes)}$, Francisco Brasileiro, Andrey Brito,
and José Luis Vivas

Department of Computing and Systems,
Federal University of Campina Grande, Campina Grande, Brazil
{eduardolfalcao,jlvivas}@lsd.ufcg.edu.br
{fubica,andrey}@computacao.ufcg.edu.br

Abstract. An important cloud federation enabler is the development of suitable business models, which has so far received relatively little attention from investigators. Few efforts have been dedicated to investigation of business models for enabling cloud federations, especially with regard to distribution issues, in which centralized solutions are usually preferred. Hence, in our work we focus on the use of fully decentralized mechanisms supporting federation of private clouds based on barter mechanisms. We analyze the adaptation of fully decentralized incentive mechanisms previously used in the context of P2P desktop grids, and show that they are not suitable for federated cloud systems because fairness cannot always be guaranteed. We show initial results concerning the use of a mechanism intended to guarantee a higher level of fairness and thereby to promote voluntary participation in a decentralized federation without any central or trusted enforcing authority.

Keywords: Cloud and grid computing · Cooperation incentives and fairness · Peer to peer computing

1 Introduction

Organizations with variable and peaky demand patterns often turn to public clouds (cf. "cloud bursting" [4]) in order to meet unexpected or short-term needs. However, during off-peak times resources might become idle, which constitutes an efficiency loss for the organization. An alternative for cloud providers is to participate in a federation for exchanging idle resources. In particular private cloud providers, due to the usually limited amount of owned resources, would greatly benefit from this [2].

From the architectural perspective, cloud federations can be either centralized or Peer-to-Peer (P2P) [3]. In centralized architectures, resource allocation is typically performed by a trusted central entity that is able to prevent free riding and to perform the best matching of consumers and providers. In P2P federations, on the other hand, participants must communicate and negotiate directly with each other. The advantages of decentralized topologies include extensibility, deployment, management, use and growth. The drawbacks, however,

© IFIP International Federation for Information Processing 2015
A. Bessani and S. Bouchenak (Eds.): DAIS 2015, LNCS 9038, pp. 45–50, 2015.
DOI: 10.1007/978-3-319-19129-4_4

include difficulties in discovery, routing, security, and the fact that participants are mostly unknown to each other and cannot be assumed to be trustworthy or collaborative. Moreover, peers should be assumed to be selfish and to have an economic incentive to become free riders.

Similarly, from a market perspective cloud federations can be also classified as centralized or decentralized. In a centralized market system, bids and requests are collected by a central entity or market auctioneer that matches them and decide the best matching of buyers and sellers. In decentralized markets, on the other hand, buyers and sellers must explore the market by themselves and bargain directly with each other. Participants may provide resources in exchange for payment or by bartering. Payment schemes would require the introduction of complex management mechanisms and procedures, whereas bartering schemes can be implemented e.g. in the shape of flexible credit and debit local annotations. The latter would be very suitable for the federation of private clouds, since it is a wholly money-less and distributed scheme that can do without any trusted centralized entities. Obviously, there is a close relation between the architecture and the market structures of private cloud federations. In this work, we propose a lightweight P2P cloud federation infrastructure implementing a decentralized market system.

An important challenge concerns the promotion of cooperation among rational selfish individuals in a decentralized context with no central and trusted enforcing authority. In this kind of system, participants are usually left to themselves and only with limited information about the actual behavior or intention of other actors, may not keep promises, and must rely solely on their own experience, acquired through interactions with each other, in order to decide to what extent they should trust other partners. It is therefore natural to expect that, at first hand, participants will prefer to act as free riders. Moreover, collaborative partners may defect from the federation if they are not satisfied with the results of participation. Some form of individual incentives must therefore be enforced in order to ensure sustained voluntary participation. Our aim is to propose one such mechanism enabling the collaborative peer to make efficient decisions that guarantees both its satisfaction, defined as the ratio between received and requested resources (which should ideally be one), and fairness, defined as the ratio between the amount of resources obtained and the amount of resources provided (which should ideally be approximately one on the long run). The challenge is to find a scheme that guarantees that the levels of both fairness and satisfaction are good enough to ensure that most participants will not defect and free riders will be isolated or kept with a low degree of satisfaction.

For the reasons explained above, incentives or punishment procedures must exist in order to promote cooperation and keep the federation alive. The scheme we propose in this paper leverages the notion of the Network of Favors (NoF) [1], an incentive mechanism for resource sharing in P2P opportunistic desktop grids. In NoF, each peer uses only its own locally stored interaction history with other peers, which is basically the balance of favors exchanged (total amount of favors a peer A consumed from peer B minus total amount of favors a peer A donated to peer B), in order to decide which ones will be given priority in resource requests. We call this notion of NoF the *Satisfaction-Driven* NoF (SD-NoF). In the SD-NoF a collaborator always supply all of its idle resources to the federation, with the expectation of accumulating credits with other peers, which may be converted to favors in the future. This ensures the best possible levels of satisfaction to collaborators, independently of the level of resource contention. This scheme is suitable for opportunistic desktop grids, since the costs of providing resources, which are intended primarily for in-house consumption, are assumed to be so low that collaborators may disregard fairness and focus only on maximizing satisfaction. However, in the case of private and P2P federated clouds, resources are dedicated, and the associated overhead costs (management staff, energy and space) may not be negligible. Fairness may thus become an important goal, which may be achieved by limiting the amount of supplied resources, thereby isolating free riders more efficiently specially in scenarios with low resource contention. To this end, we introduce a feedback control loop mechanism regulating the amount of supplied resources. Briefly, in order to reward cooperative actors and isolate free riders, a peer in the federation will draw upon its current assessment of fairness in order to define the amount of offered resources, even if it would have at any given moment more idle resources than those offered. By contrast to the SD-NoF, we call this new scheme *Fairness-Driven* NoF (FD-NoF).

The outcome is a mechanism that more closely conforms to the game theoretical results derived from the notion of reciprocal altruism [5], which shows how selection can operate against cheaters or non-reciprocators (the free riders in the NoF). Altruistic behavior is defined as a behavior that benefits another unrelated individual at a certain cost for the contributing individual. Selection would seem to favor "cheaters", i.e. those individuals that fail to reciprocate favors. However, selection might also discriminate against cheaters if the altruist is able to curtail future altruistic gestures to those individuals, assuming that the sum of the benefits for the altruist of those lost acts outweighs their cost. As a result, the altruist will prefer to exchange altruistic acts with other altruist individuals, not with cheaters.

2   Feedback Control Loop Mechanism

Andrade *et al.* [1] proved that whenever there is resource contention[1] between collaborators (κ), the SD-NoF works well and prioritizes collaborators before free riders. However, only prioritizing collaborators is not enough in scenarios with low resource contention ($\kappa < 1$), since in this case all the surplus resources will nevertheless be offered, thus benefiting free riders. To avoid this, collaborators could try to regulate the amount of resources provided, thereby indirectly increasing the value of κ. Collaborators are not able to directly control the value of κ in a decentralized P2P system, and may not even have an interest in doing it. However,

---

[1] Contention is a metric that characterizes the degree of competition for offered resources, defined as the ratio of requested resources by provided resources.

contention may be indirectly increased when collaborators try to balance their level of fairness. The simplest way to do it is by decreasing the amount of provided resources. If fairness is close to 1 for each collaborator, the value of contention will also be close to 1. However, the overall level of satisfaction may decrease thereby, and affect not only free riders but collaborators as well.

Each collaborator is then equipped with the feedback control loop mechanism and must define on its own a threshold value τ for the desired minimum level of fairness. The mechanism enhances fairness by controlling the amount of provided resources until its value becomes higher than τ; once the desired level of fairness has been achieved, the algorithm will instead focus on enhancing satisfaction by increasing the amount of resources provided. Roughly, the feedback control loop mechanism decides whether to decrease or increase the amount of resources provided by a fixed value at each step of the simulation, in this work chosen to be 5% of the total resources capacity, in order to achieve the desired levels of both fairness and satisfaction. By this mechanism, a collaborator could momentarily "leave" the federation, by supplying no resources, until it receives again some favors.

2.1   Simulation Model

To assess the behavior of the participants in the FD-NoF, we have built a simulator for a simplified model of a resource sharing P2P federation of cloud providers. The federation consists of a community of n peers, with $(1 - f) \cdot n$ collaborators and $f \cdot n$ free riders, $0 \leq f \leq 1$. We are interested in understanding how the set of collaborators perform in relation to the set of free riders. Thus, to eliminate the influence that different kinds of participants might have in the results, we assume that all collaborators have the same capacity and needs, and free riders the same needs. The simulation proceeds in steps. At each step each collaborator can be in a consumer state with probability of π or in a provider state with probability $1 - \pi$. Each collaborator is assumed to have a total resource capacity of C, and the amount of demand requested by any consuming collaborator is $D \cdot C$, where $D \geq 0$. In the SD-NoF, when in a provider state a collaborator will always offer all of its resources, i.e. C. At each step, the resources are given to one or more peers selected from the set of consuming peers according to the balance of favors exchanged (more details of NoF in [1]). Free riders, in contrast, never provide resources and are always in a consumer state, each one requesting $D \cdot C$ resources at every step.

2.2   Scenarios

Our goal is to understand the behavior of the peers in scenarios with low, moderate and high levels of κ, with values ranging over the set $\{0.5, 1.0, 2.0, 4.0\}$.

We are interested in the scenarios in which the amount of free riders may seriously affect the level of fairness for collaborators. The higher the percentage of free riders in the system, the more resources, which are provided solely by collaborators, they will collectively consume in total, thereby affecting negatively the level of fairness for collaborators. Thus, we chose $f = 0.75$ for all scenarios.

The larger the number of participants in the federation, the worse will be the situation to the free riders, even with constant f. This is because the larger the total amount of collaborators, the less will be at each step the deviation from the expected value of the total amount of providers, and hence the probability that a significant amount of resources will be available to free riders, which would imply that the number of providers is a bit higher than average. Then, we fix n to 100 in all scenarios.

Finally, for simplicity we consider $C = 1$. In summary, our design of experiments will have three parameters with constant values, $n = 100$, $f = 0.75$ and $C = 1$, and two variables with changing values: D and π — which both generates the different levels of κ. We run the simulations in 4000 steps, sufficient for ensuring that the fairness of collaborators achieves stability.

3   Results and Analysis

In order to evaluate the Feedback Control Loop we simulated the scenarios presented in section 2.2 in both SD-NoF and FD-NoF. Figure 1 shows the average fairness of collaborators (lines) and the individual fairness of each one of them (circles) along the four κ values, at the last step of the simulation in both SD-NoF and FD-NoF, the latter with $\tau \in \{0.8, 0.95\}$.

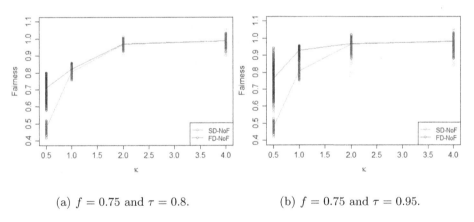

(a) $f = 0.75$ and $\tau = 0.8$.   (b) $f = 0.75$ and $\tau = 0.95$.

Fig. 1. Average and density of fairness to collaborators along $\kappa \in \{0.5, 1, 2, 4\}$ with SD-NoF and FD-NoF.

From Figure 1 we may observe that the Feedback Control Loop Mechanism was able to increase the values of fairness in low and moderate κ scenarios. Because f is high (75%), although free rider's individual satisfaction tends to be low (due to the high resource contention between themselves), their collective action strongly affects the fairness of collaborators in SD-NoF, which is on average 0.48 and 0.81 for contention values of 0.5 and 1, respectively (see yellow line on Figures 1a and 1b). In this case, FD-NoF increased the fairness of collaborators on average by 60% and 15%, respectively, when τ was set to 0.95, and by 48% and 3%, respectively, when τ was set to 0.8.

Moreover, in scenarios with high values of κ, FD-NoF behaves similarly to SD-NoF, regardless the high f value and τ, which is good since SD-NoF already works fine in these scenarios. One can also notice that the higher is the value of τ, the tougher is the task of the controller. Thus, not surprisingly, when we used $\tau = 0.95$, only few collaborators could indeed approach it when $\kappa = 0.5$. Obviously, as κ increases, the Feedback Control Loop Mechanism gets more efficient. Also, smaller values of τ lead to less variability among collaborators.

In summary, FD-NoF achieves its goal: collaborators improve their level of fairness by controlling the amount of supplied resources.

4   Conclusions and Future Works

In our work we introduce the FD-NoF, an enhancement of the NoF [1], by defining a Feedback Control Loop mechanism to regulate the amount of resources provided. With the aid of this mechanism collaborators may achieve greater levels of fairness by indirectly increasing the levels of resource contention. FD-NoF behaves similarly to SD-NoF in high resource contention scenarios, which is a positive result since SD-NoF by itself already provides good values of fairness.

As future work, we will implement the FD-NoF as part of the middleware[2], and deploy and evaluate the performance of the FD-NoF on the federated cloud that comprises the computing infrastructure of the EUBrazilCC project[3]. Moreover, we will refine the FD-NoF in order to accelerate convergence by introducing delegation schemes enabling the donation of services on behalf of a third agent.

References

1. Andrade, N., Brasileiro, F., Cirne, W., Mowbray, M.: Discouraging free riding in a peer-to-peer cpu-sharing grid. In: Proceedings of 13th IEEE International Symposium on High performance Distributed Computing 2004, pp. 129–137 (June 2004)
2. Gomes, E.R., Vo, Q.B., Kowalczyk, R.: Pure exchange markets for resource sharing in federated clouds. Concurrency and Computation: Practice and Experience 24(9), 977–991 (2012)
3. Grozev, N., Buyya, R.: Inter-cloud architectures and application brokering: taxonomy and survey. Software: Practice and Experience 44(3), 369–390 (2014)
4. Marshall, P., Keahey, K., Freeman, T.: Elastic site: Using clouds to elastically extend site resources. In: Conference on Cluster, Cloud, and Grid Computing (CC-GRID), pp. 43–52 (May 2010)
5. Trivers, R.L.: The evolution of reciprocal altruism. The Quarterly Review of Biology 46(1), 35–57 (1971)

---

[2] http://fogbowcloud.org/
[3] http://eubrazilcloudconnect.eu/

Similitude: Decentralised Adaptation in Large-Scale P2P Recommenders

Davide Frey[1], Anne-Marie Kermarrec[1], Christopher Maddock[2],
Andreas Mauthe[2], Pierre-Louis Roman[3(✉)], and François Taïani[3]

[1] Inria, Rennes, France
{davide.frey,anne-marie.kermarrec}@inria.fr
[2] School of Computing and Communications,
Lancaster University, Lancaster, UK
{c.maddock1,a.mauthe}@lancaster.ac.uk
[3] Université de Rennes 1, IRISA – ESIR, Rennes, France
{pierre-louis.roman,francois.taiani}@irisa.fr

Abstract. Decentralised recommenders have been proposed to deliver privacy-preserving, personalised and highly scalable on-line recommendations. Current implementations tend, however, to rely on a hard-wired similarity metric that cannot adapt. This constitutes a strong limitation in the face of evolving needs. In this paper, we propose a framework to develop dynamically adaptive decentralised recommendation systems. Our proposal supports a *decentralised* form of adaptation, in which individual nodes can independently select, and update their own recommendation algorithm, while still collectively contributing to the overall system's mission.

Keywords: Distributed Computing · Decentralised Systems · Collaborative Filtering · Recommendation Systems · Adaptation

1 Introduction

With the growth of the modern web, recommendation has emerged as a key service to help users navigate today's on-line content. Designing highly scalable and privacy-preserving recommenders is hard, and one promising approach consists in exploiting fully decentralised mechanisms such as gossip [21,5], or DHTs [29]. These decentralised recommenders, however, have so far used a mostly homogeneous design. They typically rely on one similarity metric [30] to self-organise large numbers of users in implicit communities and offer powerful means to compute personalised recommendations. Figuring out the right similarity metric that best fits the needs of a large collection of users is, however, highly challenging.

To address this challenge, we explore, in this paper, how dynamic adaptation can be applied to large-scale decentralised recommenders by allowing each individual node to choose autonomously between different similarity metrics. Extending on earlier works in the field [19,12], we propose several adaptation variants, and show how small changes in adaptation decisions can drastically impact a recommender's overall performance, while demonstrating the feasibility of decentralised self-adaptation in peer-to-peer recommender systems.

© IFIP International Federation for Information Processing 2015
A. Bessani and S. Bouchenak (Eds.): DAIS 2015, LNCS 9038, pp. 51–65, 2015.
DOI: 10.1007/978-3-319-19129-4_5

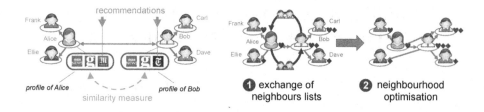

Fig. 1. Implicit overlay   **Fig. 2.** Refining neighbourhoods

In the following, we motivate and present our work (Sec. 2 and 3), evaluate it (Sec. 4 and 5), before discussing related work (Sec. 6), and concluding (Sec. 7).

2   Background

Modern on-line recommenders [20,11,28,22,9] remain, in their vast majority, based around centralised designs. Centralisation comes, however, with two critical drawbacks. It first raises the spectre of a *big-brother* society, in which a few powerful players are able to analyse large swaths of personal data under little oversight. It also leads to a *data siloing* effect. A user's personal information becomes scattered across many competing services, which makes it very difficult for users themselves to exploit their data without intermediaries [31].

These crucial limitations have motivated research on decentralised recommendation systems [5,7,4,25], in particular based on implicit interest-based *overlays* [30]. These overlays organise users (represented by their machines, also called *nodes*) into implicit communities to compute recommendations in a fully decentralised manner.

2.1   Interest-Based Implicit Overlays

More precisely, these overlays seek to connect users[1] with their k most similar other users (where k is small) according to a predefined *similarity metric*. The resulting *k-nearest-neighbour* graph or *k*nn is used to deliver personalised recommendations in a scalable on-line manner. For instance, in Figure 1, *Alice* has been found to be most similar to *Frank, Ellie*, and *Bob*, based on their browsing histories; and *Bob* to *Carl, Dave*, and *Alice*.

Although *Bob* and *Alice* have been detected to be very similar, their browsing histories are not identical: *Bob* has not visited *Le Monde*, but has read the *New York Times*, which Alice has not. The system can use this information to recommend the *New York Times* to *Alice*, and reciprocally recommend *Le Monde* to Bob, thus providing a form of decentralised collaborative filtering [13].

Gossip algorithms based on asynchronous rounds [10,30] turn out to be particularly useful in building such interest-based overlays. Users typically start with a random neighbourhood, provided by a random peer sampling service [17].

---

[1] In the following we will use *user* and *node* interchangeably.

They then repeatedly exchange information with their neighbours, in order to improve their neighbourhood in terms of similarity. This greedy sampling procedure is usually complemented by considering a few random peers (returned by a decentralised *peer sampling service* [17]) to escape local minima.

For instance, in Figure 2, *Alice* is interested in hearts, and is currently connected to *Frank*, and to *Ellie*. After exchanging her neighbour list with *Bob*, she finds out about *Carl*, who appears to be a better neighbour than *Ellie*. As such, *Alice* replaces *Ellie* with *Carl* in her neighbourhood.

2.2   Self-Adaptive Implicit Overlays

The overall performance of a service using a $k$nn overlay critically depends on the similarity metric it uses. Unfortunately, deciding at design time which similarity metric will work best is highly challenging. The same metric might not work equally well for all users [19]. Further, user behaviour might evolve over time, thereby rendering a good initial static choice sub-efficient.

Instead of selecting a static metrics at design time, as most decentralised recommenders do [5,3,4], we propose to investigate whether each node can identify an optimal metric dynamically, *during* the recommendation process. Adapting a node's similarity metric is, however, difficult for at least three reasons. First, nodes only possess a limited view of the whole system (their *neighbourhood*) to make adaptation decisions. Second, there is a circular dependency between the information available to nodes for adaptation decisions and the actual decision taken. A node must rely on its neighbourhood to decide whether to switch to a new metric. But this neighbourhood depends on the actual metric being used by the node, adding further instability to the adaptation. Finally, because of the decentralised nature of these systems, nodes should adapt independently of each other, in order to limit synchronisation and maximise scalability.

3   Decentralised Adaptation

We assume a peer-to-peer system in which each node p possesses a set of *items*, items(p), and maintains a set of k neighbours ($k = 10$ in our evaluation). p's neighbours are noted $\Gamma(p)$, and by extension, $\Gamma^2(p)$ are p's neighbours' neighbours. Each node p is associated with a similarity metric, noted p.sim, which takes two sets of items and returns a similarity value.

The main loop of our algorithm (dubbed SIMILITUDE) is shown in Alg. 1 (when executed by node p). Ignoring line 3 for the moment, lines 2-4 implement the greedy $k$nn mechanism presented in Section 2. At line 4, **argtop**^{k} selects the k nodes of *cand* (the candidate nodes that may become p's new neighbours) that maximise the similarity expression p.sim$\big(\text{items}(p), \text{items}(q)\big)$.

Recommendations are generated at lines 5-6 from the set it_Γ of items of all users in p's neighbourhood (noted items($\Gamma(p)$)). Recommendations are ranked using the function SCORE at line 8, with the similarity score of the user(s) they

Algorithm 1. SIMILITUDE

1: **in every round do**
2:   $cand \leftarrow \Gamma(p) \cup \Gamma^2(p) \cup 1$ random node
3:   ADAPTSIM($cand$)
4:   $\Gamma(p) \leftarrow$
       $\underset{q \in cand}{\textbf{argtop}^k} \left(p.\text{sim}\left(\text{items}(p), \text{items}(q)\right) \right)$
5:   $it_\Gamma \leftarrow \text{items}\left(\Gamma(p)\right) \setminus \text{items}(p)$
6:   $rec \leftarrow$
       $\underset{i \in it_\Gamma}{\textbf{argtop}^m} \left(\text{SCORE}(i, p.\text{sim}, \text{items}(p), \Gamma(p)) \right)$
7: **end round**
8: **function** SCORE($i, sim, items, \Gamma$)
9:   **return** $\sum\limits_{q \in \Gamma | i \in \text{items}(q)} sim(items, \text{items}(q))$
10: **end function**

Algorithm 2. ADAPTSIM

1: **function** ADAPTSIM($cand$)
2:   $top\_sims \leftarrow$
       $\underset{s \in SIM}{\textbf{argmax}} \left(\textbf{avg}_4 \left(\text{EVAL\_SIM}(s, cand)\right) \right)$
3:   **if** $p.\text{sim} \notin top\_sims$ **then**
4:     $p.\text{sim} \leftarrow$ random element from top_sims
5:   **end if**
6: **end function**

7: **function** EVAL_SIM($s, cand$)
8:   $hidden_f \leftarrow$ proportion f of items(p)
9:   $visible_f \leftarrow$ items(p) $\setminus hidden_f$
10:   $\Gamma_f \leftarrow \underset{q \in cand}{\textbf{argtop}^k} \left(s(visible_f, \text{items}(q)) \right)$
11:   $it_f \leftarrow \text{items}(\Gamma_f) \setminus visible_f$
12:   $rec_f \leftarrow$
       $\underset{i \in it_f}{\textbf{argtop}^m} \left(\text{SCORE}(i, s, visible_f, \Gamma_f) \right)$
13:   **return** $S = \dfrac{|rec_f \cap hidden_f|}{|rec_f|}$
14: **end function**

are sourced from. Recommendations suggested by multiple users take the sum of all relevant scores. The top m recommendations from it_Γ (line 6) are suggested to the user (or all of them if there are less than m).

3.1   Dynamic Adaptation of Similarity

The adaptation mechanism we propose (ADAPTSIM) is called at line 3 of Alg. 1, and is shown in Alg. 2. A node p estimates the potential of each available metric ($s \in SIM$, line 2) using the function EVAL_SIM(s). In EVAL_SIM(s), p hides a fraction f of its own items (lines 8-9) and creates a 'temporary potential neighbourhood' Γ_f for each similarity metric available (line 10, $f = 20\%$ in our evaluation). From each temporary neighbourhood, p generates a set of recommendations (lines 11-12) and evaluates them against the fraction f of internally hidden items, resulting in a score S for each similarity s (its *precision* (Figure 5)).

This evaluation is repeated four times and averaged to yield a set of the highest-achieving metrics (*top_sims*) (note that multiple metrics may achieve the same score). If the current metric-in-use $p.\text{sim}$ is not in *top_sims*, p switches to a random metric from *top_sims* (lines 3-4).

After selecting a new metric, a node suspends the metric-selection process for two rounds during which it only refines its neighbours. This *cool-off* period allows the newly selected metric to start building a stable neighbourhood thereby limiting oscillation and instability.

3.2   Enhancements to Adaptation Process

We now extend the basic adaptation mechanism presented in Section 3.1 with three additional *modifiers* that seek to improve the benefit estimation, and limit instability and bias: *detCurrAlgo*, *incPrevRounds* and *incSimNodes*.

detCurrAlgo (short for "detriment current algorithm") slightly detracts from the score of the current metric in use. This modifier tries to compensate for the fact that metrics will always perform better in neighbourhoods they have built up themselves. In our implementation, the score of the current metric in use is reduced by 10%.

incPrevRounds (short for "incorporate previous rounds") takes into consideration the scores S_{r-i} obtained by a metric in previous rounds to compute a metric's actual score in round r, $S_r^{\star}$ (Figure 3). In doing so, it aims at reducing the bias towards the current environment, thereby creating a more stable network with respect to metric switching.

incSimNodes (short for "incorporate similar nodes") prompts a node to refer to the metric choice of the most similar nodes it is aware of in the system. This is based on the knowledge that similar metrics are preferable for nodes with similar profiles, and thus if one node has discovered a metric which it finds to produce highly effective results, this could be of significant interest to other similar nodes. The modifier works by building up an additional score for each metric, based on the number of nodes using the same metric in the neighbourhood. This additional score is then balanced with the average of the different metrics' score (Figure 4).

4   Evaluation Approach

We validate our adaptation strategies by simulation. In this section, we describe our evaluation protocol; we then present our results in Section 5.

4.1   Data Sets

We evaluate SIMILITUDE on two datasets: Twitter, and MovieLens. The former contains the feed subscriptions of 5,000 similarly-geolocated Twitter users, randomly selected from the larger dataset presented in [8][2]. Each user has a profile containing each of her Twitter subscriptions, i.e., each subscribed feed counts as a positive rating. The MovieLens dataset [1] contains 1 million movie ratings from 6038 users, each consisting of an integer value from 1 to 5. We count values 3 and above as positive ratings. We pre-process each dataset by first removing the items with less than 20 positive ratings because they are of little interest to the recommendation process. Then, we discard the users with less than five remaining ratings. After pre-processing, the Twitter dataset contains 4569 users with a mean of 105 ratings per user, while the MovieLens dataset contains 6017 users with a mean of 68 ratings per user.

---

[2] An anonymised version of this dataset is available at
http://ftaiani.ouvaton.org/ressources/onlyBayLocsAnonymised_21_Oct_2011.tgz

$$S_r^\star = S_r + \sum_{i=1}^{5}(0.5 - \tfrac{i}{10}) \times S_{r-i}^\star \qquad S_{r,sim}^\star = S_{r,sim} + \underset{x \in SIM}{avg}(S_{r,x}) \times \frac{|sim \ in \ \Gamma(p)|}{|\Gamma(p)|}$$

Fig. 3. Incorporating previous rounds   **Fig. 4.** Incorporating similar nodes

$$Precision(u_i \in users) = \frac{|rec_i \cap hidden_i|}{|rec_i|}$$
$$Recall(u_i \in users) = \frac{|rec_i \cap hidden_i|}{|hidden_i|}$$

$$Overlap(u_i, u_j) = |items_i \cap items_j|$$
$$Big(u_i, u_j) = |items_j|$$
$$OverBig(u_i, u_j) = Overlap(u_i, u_j) + Big(u_i, u_j)$$
$$Jaccard(u_i, u_j) = \frac{Overlap(u_i, u_j)}{items_i \cup items_j}$$

Fig. 5. Precision and recall   **Fig. 6.** The four similarity metrics used

4.2 Evaluation Metrics

We evaluate recommendation quality using precision and recall (Figure 5). *Precision* measures the ability to return few incorrect recommendations, while *recall* measures the ability to return many correct recommendations. In addition, we evaluate specific aspects of our protocol. First, we count how many nodes reach their *optimal* similarity metrics—we define more precisely what we understand by *optimal* in Section 4.5. Finally, we observe the level of instability within the system, by recording the number of nodes that switch metric during each round.

4.3 Simulator and Cross Validation

We measure recommendation quality using a cross-validation approach. We split the profile of each user into a visible item set containing 80% of its items, and a hidden item set containing the remaining 20%. We use the visible item set to construct the similarity-based overlay and as a data source to generate recommendations as described in Section 3. We then consider a recommendation as successful if the hidden item set contains a corresponding item.

In terms of protocol parameters, we randomly associate each node with an initial neighbourhood of 10 nodes, as well as with a randomly selected similarity metric to start the refinement process. At each round, the protocol provides each node with a number of suggestions equal to the average number of items per user. We use these suggestions to compute precision and recall. Each simulation runs for 100 rounds; we repeat each run 10 times and average the results. Finally, we use two rounds of cool-off by default.

4.4 Similarity Metrics

We consider four similarity metrics: *Overlap, Big, OverBig* and, *Jaccard* [19], shown in Figure 6. These metrics are sufficiently different to represent distinct similarity choices for each node, and offer a representative adaptation scenario.

Overlap counts the items shared by a user and its neighbour. As such, it tends to favour users with a large number of items. *Big* simply counts the number of items of the neighbour, presuming that the greater the number of items available, the more likely a match is to be found somewhere in the list. This likewise favours users with a larger number of items. *OverBig* works by combining *Big* and *Overlap*—thereby discrediting the least similar high-item users. Finally *Jaccard* normalises the overlap of items by dividing it by the total number of items of the two users; it therefore provides improved results for users with fewer items.

It is important to note that the actual set of metrics is not our main focus. Rather, we are interested in the adaptation process, and seek to improve recommendations by adjusting the similarity metrics of individual nodes.

4.5   Static Metric Allocations

We compare our approach to *six* static (i.e., non-adaptive) system configurations, which serve as baselines for our evaluation. In the first four, we statically allocate the same metric to all nodes from the set of metrics in Figure 6 (*Overlap*, *Big*, *OverBig*, and *Jaccard*). These baselines are static and homogeneous.

The fifth (*HeterRand*) and sixth (*HeterOpt*) baselines attempt to capture two extreme cases of heterogeneous allocation. *HeterRand* randomly associates each node with one of the four above metrics. This configuration corresponds to a system that has no a-priori knowledge regarding optimal metrics, and that does not use dynamic adaptation. *HeterOpt* associates each node with its *optimal* similarity metric. To identify this optimal metric, we first run the first four baseline configurations (static and homogeneous metrics). For each node, *HeterOpt* selects one of the metrics for which the node obtains the highest average precision. *HeterOpt* thus corresponds to a situation in which each node is able to perfectly guess which similarity metric works best for itself.

5   Experimental Results

5.1   Static Baseline

We first determine the set of optimal metrics for each node in both datasets as described in Section 4.5. To estimate variability, we repeat each experiment twice, and compare the two sets of results node by node. 43.75% of the nodes report the same optimal metrics across both runs. Of those that do not, 35.43% list optimal metrics that overlap across the two runs. In total, 79.18% of nodes' optimal metrics match either perfectly or partially across runs. Figure 7 depicts the distribution obtained in the first run for both datasets.

5.2   Basic Similitude

We first test the basic SIMILITUDE with no modifiers, and a cool-off period of two rounds. Figures 8 and 9 present precision and recall (marked SIMILITUDE (BASIC)). Figure 10 depicts the number of users selecting one of the optimal metrics, while Figure 11 shows the switching activity of users.

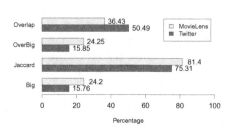

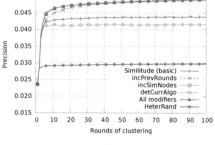

Fig. 7. Distribution of optimal metrics

Fig. 8. Precision

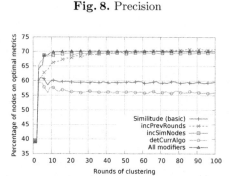

Fig. 9. Recall

Fig. 10. Nodes optimal metrics

These results show that SIMILITUDE allows nodes to both find their optimal metric and switch to it. Compared to a static random allocation of metrics (*HeterRand*), SIMILITUDE improves precision by 47.22%, and recall by 33.75%. A majority of nodes (59.55%) reach their optimal metrics, but 17.43% remain unstable and keep switching metrics throughout the experiment.

5.3   Effects of the Modifiers

detCurrAlgo has a negative effect on every aspect: precision, recall, number of nodes on optimal metrics, and stability (Figures 8 through 11). Precision and recall decrease by 5.08% and 6.93% respectively compared to basic SIMILITUDE. At the same time, the final number of nodes on their optimal metrics decreases by 6.02%, and unstable nodes increase by 35.29%.

This shows that, although reducing the current metric's score might intuitively make sense because active metrics tend to shape a node's neighbourhood to their advantage, this modifier ends up disrupting the whole adaptation process. We believe this result depends on the distribution of optimal metrics (Figure 7). Since one metric is optimal for a majority of nodes, reducing its score only causes less optimal metrics to take over. It would be interesting to see how this modifier behaves on a dataset with a more balanced distribution of optimal metrics than the two we consider here.

incPrevRounds , unlike *detCurrAlgo*, increases precision by 12.57% and recall by 24.75% with respect to basic SIMILITUDE, while improving stability by 55.92%. The number of nodes reaching an optimal metric improves by 18.81%.

As expected, *incPrevRounds* greatly improves the stability of the system; it even enhances every evaluation metric we use. The large reduction in the number of unstable nodes, and the small increase in that of nodes reaching their optimal metrics suggest that *incPrevRounds* causes nodes to settle on a metric faster, whether or not that metric is optimal. One possible explanation is that, if one metric performs especially well in a round with a particular set of neighbours, all future rounds will be affected by the score of this round.

incSimNodes, like *incPrevRounds*, improves basic SIMILITUDE on every aspect. Precision increases by 11.91%, recall by 16.88%, the number of nodes on their optimal metrics by 16.53%, and that of unstable nodes decreases by 49.26%.

With this modifier, most of the nodes switch to the same similarity metric (*Jaccard*). Since *incSimNodes* tends to boost the most used metric in each node's neighbourhood, it ends up boosting the most used metric in the system, creating a snowball effect. Given that *Jaccard* is the optimal metric for most of the nodes, it is the one that benefits the most from *incSimNodes*.

Even if completely different by design, both *incPrevRounds* and *incSimNodes* have very similar results when tested with Twitter. This observation cannot be generalised as the results are not the same with MovieLens (Figures 15 and 16).

All modifiers activates all three modifiers with the hope of combining their effects. Results show that this improves precision and recall by 29.11% and 43.99% respectively. The number of nodes on optimal metrics also increases by 32.51%. Moreover none of the nodes switch metrics after the first 25 rounds.

Activating all the modifiers causes most nodes to employ the metric that is optimal for most nodes in Figure 7, in this case *Jaccard*. This explains why no node switches metrics and why the number of nodes reaching optimal metrics (70.15%) is very close to the number of nodes with *Jaccard* as an optimal metric (75.31%). The difference gets even thinner without cool-off (Section 5.5): 73.43% of the nodes use their optimal metrics.

5.4   Weighting the Modifiers

We balance the effect of the two additive modifiers (*incPrevRounds* and *incSimNodes*) by associating each of them with a multiplicative weight. A value of 0 yields the basic SIMILITUDE, a value of 1 applies the full effect of the modifier, while a value of 0.5 halves its effect. We use a default weight of 0.5 for both of them because they perform best with this value when operating together.

Figure 12 shows the precision and recall of *incPrevRounds* and *incSimNodes* with their respective weights ranging from 0 (basic SIMILITUDE) to 1, with a 0.1 step. *incPrevRounds* peaks at a weight of 0.5 even when operating alone, while *incSimNodes* peaks at 0.7, but it still performs very well at 0.5.

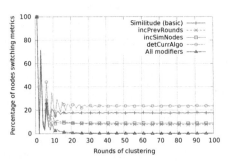

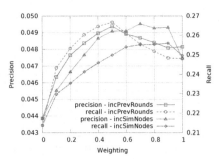

Fig. 11. Switching activity

Fig. 12. Weighting *incPrevRounds* and *incSimNodes*

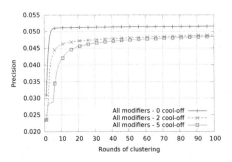

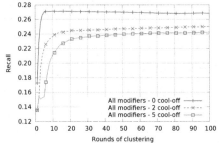

Fig. 13. Precision under different cool-off

Fig. 14. Recall under different cool-off

5.5 Varying the Cool-Off Period

As described in Section 3.1, the cool-off mechanism seeks to prevent nodes from settling too easily on a particular metric. To assess the sensitivity of this parameter, Figures 13 and 14 compare the results of SIMILITUDE with all the modifiers, when the cool-off period varies from 0 (no cool-off) to 5 rounds.

Disabling cool-off results in a slight increase in precision (5.45%) and in recall (7.23%) when compared to 2 rounds of cool-off. Optimal metrics are reached by 3.73% more nodes, and much faster, attaining up to 73.43% nodes. Removing cool-off reduces a metric's ability to optimise a neighbourhood to its advantage, as there is only a single round of clustering before the metric is tested again. While cool-off can offer additional stability in adaptive systems, the stability provided by the modifiers appears to be sufficient in our model. Cool-off, instead, leads metrics to over-settle, and produces a negative effect.

5.6 MovieLens Results

Figures 15 and 16 show the effect of SIMILITUDE on precision and recall with the different modifiers using the MovieLens dataset. The results are similar to those obtained with Twitter (Figures 8 and 9).

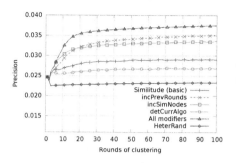

Fig. 15. Precision (MovieLens)

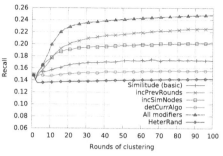

Fig. 16. Recall (MovieLens)

As with the Twitter dataset, basic SIMILITUDE outperforms *HeterRand* in precision by 24.52% and in recall by 21.02%. By the end of the simulations, 59.95% of the nodes reach an optimal metric and 15.73% still switch metrics.

The behaviour of the modifiers compared to basic SIMILITUDE is also similar. *detCurrAlgo* degrades precision by 7.58%, recall by 9.86%, the number of nodes on optimal metrics by 7.07%, and the number of nodes switching metrics by 33.40%. *incPrevRounds* improves precision by 21.02%, recall by 31.19%, the number of nodes on optimal metrics by 20.52%, and the number of nodes switching metrics by 62.08%. *incSimNodes* improves precision by 15.75%, recall by 17.38%, the number of nodes on optimal metrics by 15.12%, and the number of nodes switching metrics by 28.61%.

All modifiers improves precision by 29.11%, recall by 43.99%, the number of nodes on optimal metrics by 32.51%, and there are no nodes switching metrics after the first 25 rounds. As with the Twitter dataset, activating all the modifiers makes all the nodes use the similarity metric which is optimal for the majority of the system: *Jaccard*. The number of nodes reaching optimal metrics (79.44%) and the number of nodes with *Jaccard* as optimal metric (81.40%) are almost identical. Without cool-off, SIMILITUDE even reaches 80.57% nodes on an optimal metric, getting even closer to that last number.

5.7   Complete System

We now compare the results of the best SIMILITUDE variant (all the modifiers and 0 cool-off, noted SIMILITUDE (OPTIMISED)) with the six static configurations we introduced in Section 4.5.

For the Twitter dataset, Figure 17 shows that our adaptive system outperforms the static random allocation of metrics by 73.06% in precision, and overcomes all but one static homogeneous metrics, *Jaccard*, which is on par with SIMILITUDE (OPTIMISED). For the MovieLens dataset, Figure 18 shows very similar results where SIMILITUDE (OPTIMISED) has a higher precision than *HeterRand* by 65.85%, is on par with *Jaccard*, and has a slightly lower precision than *HeterOpt* (-2.6%). Selecting *Jaccard* statically would however require knowing

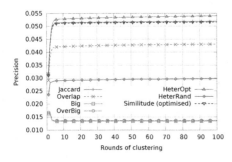
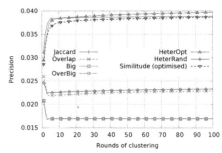

Fig. 17. SIMILITUDE against static solutions (Twitter)

Fig. 18. SIMILITUDE against static solutions (MovieLens)

that this metric performs best, which may not be possible in evolving systems (in which *Jaccard* might be replaced by another metric as users' behaviours change).

5.8   Discussion

SIMILITUDE (OPTIMISED) enables a vast majority of the nodes (73.43% for Twitter, 80.57% for MovieLens) to eventually switch to an optimal metric, which corresponds to the number of nodes having *Jaccard* as their optimal metric (Figure 7). By looking at these number, we can say that our system has the ability to discover which metric is the best suited for the system without needing prior evaluation. While this already constitutes a very good result, there remains a difference between SIMILITUDE and *HeterOpt* (the optimal allocation of metrics to nodes), which represents the upper bound that a dynamically adaptive system might be able to reach. Although achieving the performance of a perfect system might prove unrealistic, we are currently exploring potential improvements.

First, *incSimNodes* could be reworked in order to have a more balanced behaviour to avoid making the whole system use only one similarity metric, even if it is the most suited one for the majority of the nodes. Next, we observe that nodes appear to optimise their neighbourhood depending on their current metric, as opposed to basing their metric choice on their neighbourhood. This may lead to local optima because metrics perform notably better in neighbourhoods they have themselves refined. Our initial attempt at avoiding such local optima with the *detCurrAlgo* proved unsuccessful, but further investigation could result in rewarding future work. For example, we are considering decoupling the choice of the metric from the choice of the neighbourhood. Nodes may compare the performance of metrics using randomly selected neighbourhoods, and then move to the clustering process only using the best-performing metric.

Finally, it would be interesting to see how *detCurrAlgo*, *incSimNodes* and more generally SIMILITUDE behave on a dataset with a more balanced distribution of optimal metrics since their effects and results highly depend on it.

6   Related Work

Several efforts have recently concentrated on decentralised recommenders [14,24,2,6,27] to investigate their advantages in terms of scalability and privacy. Earlier approaches exploit DHTs in the context of recommendation. For example, PipeCF [14] and PocketLens [24] propose Chord-based CF systems to decentralise the recommendation process on a P2P infrastructure. Yet, more recent solutions have focused on using randomised and gossip-based protocols [5,18,4].

Recognised as a fundamental tool for information dissemination [16,23], Gossip protocols exhibit innate scalability and resilience to failures. As they copy information over many links, gossip protocols generally exhibit high failure resilience. Yet, their probabilistic nature also makes them particularly suited to applications involving uncertain data, like recommendation.

Olsson's *Yenta* [26] was one of the first systems to employ gossip protocols in the context of recommendation. This theoretical work enhances decentralised recommendation by taking trust between users into account. *Gossple* [5] uses a similar theory to enhance navigation through query expansion and was later extended to news recommendation [7]. Finally, in [15], Hegedűs et al. present a gossip-based learning algorithm that carries out 'random walks' through a network to monitor concept drift and adapt to change in P2P data-mining.

7   Conclusion

We have presented SIMILITUDE, a decentralised overlay-based recommender that is able to adapt at runtime the similarity used by individual nodes. SIMILITUDE demonstrates the viability of decentralised adaptation for very large distributed systems, and shows it can compete against static schemes.

Although promising, our results shows there is still room for improvement. In particular, we would like to see how a dataset with a more balanced distribution of optimal metrics affects SIMILITUDE and its modifiers. We also think that the *detCurrAlgo* and *incSimNodes* modifiers could benefit from further improvements, and thus bring the performance of SIMILITUDE closer to that of a static optimal-metric allocation.

Acknowledgements. This work was partially funded by the French National Research Agency (ANR) project *SocioPlug* - ANR-13-INFR-0003 (http://socioplug.univ -nantes.fr).

References

1. Movielens 1 million ratings dataset, http://grouplens.org/datasets/movielens
2. Tribler, http://www.tribler.org
3. Bai, X., Bertier, M., Guerraoui, R., Kermarrec, A.-M., Leroy, V.: Gossiping personalized queries. In: EDBT 2010 (2010)

4. Baraglia, R., Dazzi, P., Mordacchini, M., Ricci, L.: A peer-to-peer recommender system for self-emerging user communities based on gossip overlays. J. of Comp. and Sys. Sciences (2013)
5. Bertier, M., Frey, D., Guerraoui, R., Kermarrec, A.-M., Leroy, V.: The gossple anonymous social network. In: Gupta, I., Mascolo, C. (eds.) Middleware 2010. LNCS, vol. 6452, pp. 191–211. Springer, Heidelberg (2010)
6. Boutet, A., Frey, D., Guerraoui, R., Jégou, A., Kermarrec, A.-M.: Privacy-Preserving Distributed Collaborative Filtering. In: Noubir, G., Raynal, M. (eds.) NETYS 2014. LNCS, vol. 8593, pp. 169–184. Springer, Heidelberg (2014)
7. Boutet, A., Frey, D., Guerraoui, R., Jégou, A., Kermarrec, A.-M.: WhatsUp Decentralized Instant News Recommender. In: IPDPS (2013)
8. Carretero, J., Isaila, F., Kermarrec, A.-M., Taïani, F., Tirado, J.M.: Geology: Modular georecommendation in gossip-based social networks. In: ICDCS 2012 (2012)
9. Das, A.S., Datar, M., Garg, A., Rajaram, S.: Google news personalization: scalable online collaborative filtering. In: WWW (2007)
10. Demers, A., Greene, D., Hauser, C., Irish, W., Larson, J., Shenker, S., Sturgis, H., Swinehart, D., Terry, D.: Epidemic Algorithms for Replicated Database Maintenance. In: PODC 1987 (1987)
11. Facebook Inc. Facebook: Company info – statistics (March 2014), https://newsroom.fb.com/company-info/ (accessed: May 13, 2014)
12. Frey, D., Kermarrec, A.-M., Maddock, C., Mauthe, A., Taïani, F.: Adaptation for the masses: Towards decentralized adaptation in large-scale p2p recommenders. In: 13th Workshop on Adaptive & Reflective Middleware, ARM 2014 (2014)
13. Goldberg, D., Nichols, D., Oki, B.M., Terry, D.: Using collaborative filtering to weave an information tapestry. In: CACM (1992)
14. Han, P., Xie, B., Yang, F., Shen, R.: A scalable p2p recommender system based on distributed collaborative filtering. Expert Systems with Applications (2004)
15. Hegedus, I., Ormándi, R., Jelasity, M.: Gossip-based learning under drifting concepts in fully distributed networks. In: SASO 2012 (2012)
16. Jelasity, M., Montresor, A., Babaoglu, O.: T-man: Gossip-based fast overlay topology construction. Computer Networks 53(13), 2321–2339 (2009)
17. Jelasity, M., Voulgaris, S., Guerraoui, R., Kermarrec, A.-M., van Steen, M.: Gossip-based peer sampling. In: ACM TOCS, vol. 25 (2007)
18. Kermarrec, A.-M., Leroy, V., Moin, A., Thraves, C.: Application of random walks to decentralized recommender systems. In: Lu, C., Masuzawa, T., Mosbah, M. (eds.) OPODIS 2010. LNCS, vol. 6490, pp. 48–63. Springer, Heidelberg (2010)
19. Kermarrec, A.-M., Taïani, F.: Diverging towards the common good: heterogeneous self-organisation in decentralised recommenders. In: SNS 2012 (2012)
20. Konstan, J.A., Miller, B.N., Maltz, D., Herlocker, J.L., Gordon, L.R., Riedl, J.: Grouplens: Applying collaborative filtering to usenet news. In: CACM (1997)
21. Leroy, V., Cambazoglu, B.B., Bonchi, F.: Cold start link prediction. In: KDD 2010 (2010)
22. Linden, G., Smith, B., York, J.: Amazon. com recommendations: Item-to-item collaborative filtering. IEEE Internet Computing (2003)
23. Mega, G., Montresor, A., Picco, G.P.: Efficient dissemination in decentralized social networks. In: IEEE P2P 2011 (2011)
24. Miller, B.N., Konstan, J.A., Riedl, J.: Pocketlens: Toward a personal recommender system. In: TOIS (2004)
25. Moreno, A., Castro, H., Riveill, M.: Decentralized recommender systems for mobile advertisement. In: Workshop on Personalization in Mobile Applications (PEMA 2011). ACM, New York (2011)

26. Olsson, T.: Decentralised social filtering based on trust. In: AAAI 1998 Recommender Systems Workshop (1998)
27. Schiavoni, V., Rivière, E., Felber, P.: Whisper: Middleware for confidential communication in large-scale networks. In: ICDCS 2011 (June 2011)
28. Song, Y., Dixon, S., Pearce, M.: A survey of music recommendation systems and future perspectives. In: CMMR 2012 (2012)
29. Tirado, J.M., Higuero, D., Isaila, F., Carretero, J., Iamnitchi, A.: Affinity p2p: A self-organizing content-based locality-aware collaborative peer-to-peer network. Comp. Net. 54 (2010)
30. Voulgaris, S., van Steen, M.: Epidemic-style management of semantic overlays for content-based searching. In: Cunha, J.C., Medeiros, P.D. (eds.) Euro-Par 2005. LNCS, vol. 3648, pp. 1143–1152. Springer, Heidelberg (2005)
31. Yeung, C.-M.A., Liccardi, I., Lu, K., Seneviratne, O., Berners-Lee, T.: Decentralization: The future of online social networking. In: W3C Workshop on the Future of Social Networking (2009)

Concise Server-Wide Causality Management for Eventually Consistent Data Stores

Ricardo Gonçalves[(✉)], Paulo Sérgio Almeida,
Carlos Baquero, and Victor Fonte

HASLab, INESC Tec and Universidade do Minho
Portugal, Braga
{tome,psa,cbm,vff}@di.uminho.pt

Abstract. Large scale distributed data stores rely on optimistic replication to scale and remain highly available in the face of network partitions. Managing data without coordination results in eventually consistent data stores that allow for concurrent data updates. These systems often use anti-entropy mechanisms (like *Merkle Trees*) to detect and repair divergent data versions across nodes. However, in practice hash-based data structures are too expensive for large amounts of data and create too many false conflicts.

Another aspect of eventual consistency is detecting write conflicts. Logical clocks are often used to track data causality, necessary to detect causally concurrent writes on the same key. However, there is a non-negligible metadata overhead per key, which also keeps growing with time, proportional with the node churn rate. Another challenge is deleting keys while respecting causality: while the values can be deleted, per-key metadata cannot be permanently removed without coordination.

We introduce a new causality management framework for eventually consistent data stores, that leverages node logical clocks (Bitmapped Version Vectors) and a new key logical clock (Dotted Causal Container) to provides advantages on multiple fronts: 1) a new efficient and lightweight anti-entropy mechanism; 2) greatly reduced per-key causality metadata size; 3) accurate key deletes without permanent metadata.

Keywords: Distributed Systems · Key-Value Stores · Eventual Consistency · Causality · Logical Clocks · Anti-Entropy

1 Introduction

Modern distributed data stores often emphasize high availability and low latency [2,9,7] on geo-replicated settings. Since these properties are at odds with strong consistency [3], these systems allow writing concurrently on different nodes, which avoids the need for global coordination to totally order writes, but creates data divergence. To deal with conflicting versions for the same key, generated by concurrent writes, we can either use the *last-writer-wins* rule [5], which only keeps the "last" version (according to a wall-clock timestamp for example) and lose the other versions, or we can properly track each key causal

© IFIP International Federation for Information Processing 2015
A. Bessani and S. Bouchenak (Eds.): DAIS 2015, LNCS 9038, pp. 66–79, 2015.
DOI: 10.1007/978-3-319-19129-4_6

history with logical clocks [10], which track a partial order on all writes for a given key to detect concurrent writes.

Version Vectors [13] – the logical clocks used in Dynamo – are an established technique that provides a compact representation of causal histories [14]. However, Version vectors do not scale well when multiple users concurrently update the same node, as they would require one entry per user. To address this Riak, a commercial Dynamo inspired database, uses a newer mechanism – called *Dotted Version Vectors* [1] – to handle concurrent versions on the same node in addition to the concurrency across nodes. While these developments improved the scalability problem, the logical clock metadata can still be a significant load when tracking updates on lots of small data items.

In this paper, we address the general case in which, for each key, multiple concurrent versions are kept until overwritten by a future version; no updates are arbitrarily dropped. We present a solution that expressively improves the metadata size needed to track per-key causality, while showing how this also benefits anti-entropy mechanisms for node synchronization and add support for accurate distributed deletes. Brief summary of the contributions:

High Savings on Causality Metadata. Building on *Concise Version Vectors* [11], and on *Dotted Version Vectors* [1], we present a new causality management framework that uses a new logical clock per node to summarize which key versions are currently locally stored or have been so in the past. With the node clock, we can greatly reduce the storage footprint of keys' metadata by factoring out the information that the node clock already captures. The smaller footprint makes the overall metadata cost closer to last-write-wins solutions and delivers a better metadata-to-payload ratio for keys storing small values, like integers.

Distributed Key Deletion. Deleting a key in an eventually consistent system while respecting causality is non-trivial when using traditional version vector based mechanisms. If a key is fully removed while keeping no additional metadata, it will re-appear if some node replica didn't receive the delete (by lost messages or network partitions) and still has an old version (the same applies for backup replicas stored offline). Even worse, if a key is deleted and re-created, it risks being silently overwritten by an older version that had a higher version vector (since a new version vector starts again the counters with zeros). This problem will be avoided by using the node logical clock to create monotonically increasing counters for the key's logical clocks.

Anti-Entropy. Eventually consistent data stores rely on anti-entropy mechanisms to repair divergent versions across the key space between nodes. It both detects concurrent versions and allows newer versions to reach all node replicas. Dynamo [2], Riak [7] and Cassandra [9] use Merkle-trees [12] for their anti-entropy mechanism. This is an expensive mechanism, in both space and time, that requires frequent updates of an hash tree and presents a trade-off between hash tree size and risk of false positives. We will show how a highly compact and efficient node clock implementation, using bitmaps and binary logic, can be leveraged to support anti-entropy and dispense the use of Merkle-trees altogether.

2   Architecture Overview and System Model

Consider a *Dynamo-like* [2] distributed key-value store, organized as large number (e.g., millions) of virtual nodes (or simply nodes) mapped over a set of physical nodes (e.g., hundreds). Each key is replicated over a deterministic subset of nodes – called *replica nodes* for that key –, using for example consistent hashing [6]. Nodes that replicate common keys are said to be *peers*. We assume no affinity between clients and server nodes. Nodes also periodically perform an anti-entropy protocol with each other to synchronize and repair data.

2.1   Client API

At a high level, the system API exposes three operations: 1) read: key $\rightarrow \mathcal{P}(\text{value}) \times$ context; 2) write: key $\times$ context $\times$ value $\rightarrow$ (); 3) delete: key $\times$ context $\rightarrow$ ().

This API is motivated by the *read-modify-write* pattern used by clients to preserve data causality: the client first reads a key, updates the value(s) and only then writes it back. Since multiple clients can concurrently update the same key, a read operation can return multiple concurrents values for the client to resolve. By passing the read's context back to the subsequent write, every write request provides the context in which the value was updated by the client. This context is used by the system to remove versions of that key already seen by that client. A write to a non-existing key has an empty context. The delete operation behaves exactly like a normal write, but with an empty value.

2.2   Server-Side Workflow

The data store uses several protocols between nodes, both when serving client requests, and to periodically perform anti-entropy synchronization.

Serving Reads. Any node upon receiving a read request can coordinate it, by asking the respective replica nodes for their local key version. When sufficient replies arrive, the coordinator discards obsolete versions and sends to the client the most recent (concurrent) version(s), w.r.t causality. It also sends the causal context for the value(s). Optionally, the coordinator can send the results back to replica nodes, if they have outdated versions (a process known as *Read Repair*).

Serving Writes/Deletes. Only replica nodes for the key being written can coordinate a write request, while non-replica nodes forward the request to a replica node. A coordinator node: (1) generates a new identifier for this write for the logical clock; (2) discards older versions according to the write's context; (3) adds the new value to the local remaining set of concurrent versions; (4) propagates the result to the other replica nodes; (5) waits for configurable number of *acks* before replying to the client. Deletes are exactly the same, but omit step 3, since there is no new value.

Anti-Entropy. To complement the replication done at write time and to ensure consistency convergence, either because some messages were lost, or some replica node was down for some time, or writes were never sent to all replica nodes to save bandwidth, nodes perform periodically an anti-entropy protocol. The protocol aims to figure out what key versions are missing from which nodes (or must be deleted), propagating them appropriately.

2.3   System Model

All interaction is done via asynchronous message passing: there is no global clock, no bound on the time it takes for a message to arrive, nor bounds on relative processing speeds. Nodes have access to durable storage; nodes can crash but eventually will recover with the content of the durable storage as at the time of the crash. Durable state is written atomically at each state transition. Message sending from a node i to a node j, specified at a state transition of node i by $\mathsf{send}_{i,j}$, is scheduled to happen after the transition, and therefore, after the next state is durably written. Such a send may trigger a $\mathsf{receive}_{i,j}$ action at node j some time in the future. Each node has a globally unique identifier.

2.4   Notation

We use mostly standard notation for sets and maps. A map is a set of (k, v) pairs, where each k is associated with a single v. Given a map m, $m(k)$ returns the value associated with the key k, and $m\{k \mapsto v\}$ updates m, mapping k to v and maintaining everything else equal. The domain and range of a map m is denoted by $\mathsf{dom}(m)$ and $\mathsf{ran}(m)$, respectively. $\mathsf{fst}(t)$ and $\mathsf{snd}(t)$ denote the first and second component of a tuple t, respectively. We use set comprehension of the forms $\{f(x) \mid x \in S\}$ or $\{x \in S \mid Pred(x)\}$. We use $\lhd$ for domain subtraction; $S \lhd M$ is the map obtained by removing from M all pairs (k, v) with $k \in S$. We will use $\mathbb{K}$ for the set of possible keys in the store, $\mathbb{V}$ for the set of values, and $\mathbb{I}$ for the set of node identifiers.

3   Causality Management Framework

Our causality management framework involves two logical clocks: one to be used per node, and one to be used per key in each replica node.

The Node Logical Clock. Each node i has a logical clock that represents all locally known writes to keys that node i replicates, including writes to those keys coordinated by other replica nodes, that arrive at node i via replication or anti-entropy mechanisms;

The Key Logical Clock. For each key stored by a replica node, there is a
corresponding logical clock that represents all current and past versions seen
(directly or transitively) by this key at this replica node. In addition, we
attached to this key logical clock the current concurrent values and their
individual causality information.

While this dual-logical clock framework draws upon the work of Concise Version Vectors (CVV) [11], our scope is on distributed key-value stores (KVS) while
CVV targets distributed file-systems (DFS). Their differences pose some challenges
which prevent a simple reuse of CVV:

- Contrary to DFS where the only source of concurrency are nodes themselves,
  KVS have external clients making concurrent requests, implying the generation of concurrent versions for the same key, even when a single node is
  involved. Thus, the key logical clock in a KVS has to possibly manage multiple concurrent values in a way that preserves causality;
- Contrary to DFS, which considers full replication of a set keys over a set of
  replicas nodes, in a KVS two peer nodes can be replica nodes for two non-
  equal set of keys. E.g., we can have a key k_1 with the replica nodes $\{a, b\}$, a
  key k_2 with $\{b, c\}$ and a key k_3 with $\{c, a\}$; although a, b and c are peers (they
  are replica nodes for common keys), they don't replicated the exact same
  set of keys. The result is that, in addition to gaps in the causal history for
  writes not yet replicated by peers, a node logical clock will have many other
  gaps for writes to key that this node is not replica node of. This increases
  the need for a compact representation of a node logical clock.

3.1   The Node Logical Clock

A node logical clock represents a set of known writes to keys that this node
is replica node of. Since each write is only coordinated by one node and later
replicated to other replica nodes, the nth write coordinated by a node a can
be represented by the pair (a, n). Henceforth, we'll refer to this pair as a *dot*.
Essentially, a dot is a globally unique identifier for every write in the entire
distributed system.

A node logical clock could therefore be a simple set of dots. However, the set
would be unbound and grow linearly with writes. A more concise implementation
would have a version vector to represent the set of consecutive dots since the first
write for every peer node id, while keeping the rest of the dots as a separate set.
For example, the node logical clock: $\{(a, 1), (a, 2), (a, 3), (a, 5), (a, 6), (b, 1), (b, 2)\}$
could be represented by the pair $([(a, 3), (b, 2)], \{(a, 5), (a, 6)\})$, where the first
element is a version vector and the second is the set of the remaining dots.
Furthermore, we could map peer ids directly to the pair of the maximum contiguous dot and the set of disjointed dots. Taking our example, we have the map:
$\{a \mapsto (3, \{5, 6\}), b \mapsto (2, \{\})\}$.

Crucial to an efficient and compact representation of a node logical clock is the
need to have the least amount of gaps between dots as possible. For example, the

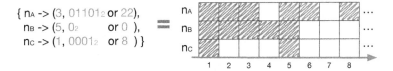

{ $n_A \rightarrow (3, 01101_2$ or $22)$,
  $n_B \rightarrow (5, 0_2$ or 0),
  $n_C \rightarrow (1, 0001_2$ or 8) }

Fig. 1. A bitmapped version vector example and its visual illustration. The bitmap least-significant bit is the first bit from the left.

dots in a node logical clock that are from the local node are always consecutive with no gaps, which means that we only need maximum dot counter mapped to the local node id, while the the the set of disjointed dots is empty.

The authors of [11] defined the notion of an *extrinsic* set, which we improve and generalize here as follows (note that an event can be seen as a write made to a particular key):

Definition 1 (Extrinsic). *A set of events E_1 is said to be **extrinsic** to another set of events E_2, if the subset of E_1 events involving keys that are also involved in events from E_2, is equal to E_2.*

This definition means that we can inflate our node logical clock to make it easier to compact, if the resulting set of dots is extrinsic to the original set. In other words, we can fill the gaps from a node logical clock, if those gaps correspond to dots pertaining to keys that the local node is not replica node of.

Taking this into consideration, our actual implementation of a node logical clock is called *Bitmapped Version Vector* (BVV), where instead of having the disjointed dots represented as a set of integers like before, we use a bitmap where the least-significant bit represents the dot immediately after the dot in the first element of the pair. A 0 means that dot is missing, while a 1 is the opposite. The actual structure of a BVV uses the integer corresponding to the bitmap to efficiently represent large and sparse sets of dots. Figure 1 gives a simple BVV example and its visual representation.

Functions over Node Logical Clocks. Lets briefly describe the functions necessary for the rest of the paper, involving node logical clocks (we omit the actual definitions due to size limitations):

- norm($base, bitmap$) normalizes the pair ($base, bitmap$). In other words, it removes dots from the disjointed set if they are contiguous to the base, while incrementing the base by the number of dots removed. Example: norm$(2, 3) = (4, 0)$;
- values($base, bitmap$) returns the counter values for the all the dots represented by the pair ($base, bitmap$). Example: values$(2, 2) = \{1, 2, 4\}$;
- add(($base, bitmap$), m) adds a dot with a counter m to the pair ($base, bitmap$). Example: add$((2, 2), 3) = (4, 0)$;

- base($clock$) returns a new node logical clock with only the contiguous dots from $clock$, i.e., with the bitmaps set to zero. Example: base($\{a \mapsto (2,2), \ldots\}$) = $\{a \mapsto (2,0), \ldots\}$;
- event(c, i) takes the node i's logical clock $clock$ and its own node id i, and returns a pair with the new counter for a new write in this node i and the original logical clock c with the new counter added as a dot. Example: event($\{a \mapsto (4,0), \ldots\}, a$) = $(5, \{a \mapsto (5,0), \ldots\})$;

3.2 The Key Logical Clock

A key logical clock using client ids is not realistic in the kind of key-value store under consideration, since the number of clients is virtually unbound. Using simple version vectors with node ids also doesn't accurately capture causality, when a node stores multiple concurrent versions for a single key [1]. One solution is to have a version vector describing the entire causal information (shared amongst concurrent versions), and also associate to each concurrent version their own dot. This way, we can independently reason about each concurrent versions causality, reducing false concurrency. An implementation of this approach can be found in *Dotted Version Vector Sets* (DVVS) [1].

Nevertheless, logical clocks like DVVS are based on per-key information; i.e., each dot generated to tag a write is only unique in the context of the key being written. But with our framework, each dot generated for a write is globally unique in the whole system. One of the main ideas of our framework is to take advantage of having a node logical clock that store these globally unique dots, and use it whenever possible to remove redundant causal information from the key logical clock.

Contrary to version vectors or DVVS, which use per-key counters and thus have contiguous ranges of dots that can have a compact representation, the use of globally unique dots poses some challenges in defining DCC and its operations: even if we only have one version per-key, we still don't necessarily have a contiguous set of dots starting with counter one. Therefore, a compact and accurate implementation of a key logical clock is problematic: using an explicit set of dots is not reasonable as it grows unbounded; neither is using a BVV- like structure, because while a single BVV per node can be afforded, doing so per key is not realistic, as it would result in many low density bitmaps, each as large as the node one. Since there may be millions of keys per node, the size of a key logical clock must be very small.

The solution is to again leverage the notion of extrinsic sets, by filling the gaps in the clock with dots pertaining to other keys, thus not introducing false causal information. The subtlety is that every key logical clock can be inflated to a *contiguous* set of dots, since every gap in the original set was from dots belonging to other keys[1].

---

[1] The gaps are always from other keys, because a node i coordinating a write to a key k that generates a dot (i, n), is guaranteed to have locally coordinated all other versions of k with dots (i, m), where $m < n$, since local writes are handle sequentially and new dots have monotonically increasing counters.

$$\mathsf{values}((d, v)) = \{x \mid (\_, x) \in d\}$$

$$\mathsf{context}((d, v)) = v$$

$$\mathsf{add}(c, (d, v)) = \mathsf{fold}(\mathsf{add}, c, \mathsf{dom}(d))$$

$$\mathsf{sync}((d_1, v_1), (d_2, v_2)) = ((d_1 \cap d_2) \cup \{((i, n), x) \in d_1 \cup d_2 \mid n > \min(v_1(i), v_2(i))\},$$
$$\mathsf{join}(v_1, v_2))$$

$$\mathsf{discard}((d, v), v') = (\{((i, n), x) \in d \mid n > v'(i)\}, \mathsf{join}(v, v'))$$

$$\mathsf{add}((d, v), (i, n), x) = (d\{(i, n) \mapsto x\}, v\{i \mapsto n\})$$

$$\mathsf{strip}((d, v), c) = (d, \{(i, n) \in v \mid n > \mathsf{fst}(c(i))\})$$

$$\mathsf{fill}((d, v), c) = (d, \{i \mapsto \max(v(i), \mathsf{fst}(c(i))) \mid i \in \mathsf{dom}(c)\})$$

Fig. 2. Functions over Dotted Causal Containers (also involving BVV)

Dotted Causal Container. Our key logical clock implementation is called Dotted Causal Container (DCC). A DCC is a container-like data structure, in the spirit of a DVVS, which stores both concurrent versions and causality information for a given key, to be used together with the node logical clock (e.g. a BVV). The extrinsic set of dots is represented as a version vector, while concurrents versions are grouped and tagged with their respective dots.

Definition 2. *A* Dotted Causal Container *(DCC for short) is a pair* $(\mathbb{I} \times \mathbb{N} \hookrightarrow \mathbb{V}) \times (\mathbb{I} \hookrightarrow \mathbb{N})$, *where the first component is a map from dots (identifier-integer pairs) to values, representing a set of versions, and the second component is a version vector (map from [replica node] identifiers to integers), representing a set extrinsic to the collective causal past of the set of versions in the first component.*

Functions over Key Logical Clocks. Figure 2 shows the definitions of functions over key logical clocks (DCC) – which also involves node logical clocks (BVV) – necessary for the rest of the paper. Function values returns the values of the concurrent versions in a DCC; $\mathsf{add}(c, (d, v))$ adds all the dots in the DCC (d, v) to the BVV c, using the standard fold higher-order function with the function add defined over BVVs. Function sync merges two DCCs: it discards versions in one DCC made obsolete by the other DCC's causal history, while the version vectors are merged by performing the pointwise maximum. The function context simply returns the version vector of a DCC, which represents the totality of causal history for that DCC (note that the dots of the concurrent versions are also included in the version vector component). Function $\mathsf{discard}((d, v), c)$ discards versions in a DCC (d, v) which are made obsolete by a VV c, and also merges c into v. Function $\mathsf{add}((d, v), (i, n), x)$ adds to versions d a mapping from the dot (i, n) to the value x, and also advances the i component of the VV v to n.

Finally, functions strip and fill are an essential part of our framework. Function $\mathsf{strip}((d, v), c)$ discards all entries from the VV v in a DCC that are covered by the corresponding base component of the BVV c; only entries with greater sequence numbers are kept. The idea is to only store DCCs after stripping the causality information that is already present in the node logical clock. Function fill adds back the dots to a stripped DCC, before performing functions over it.

Note that, the BVV base components may have increased between two consecutive strip $\mapsto$ fill manipulation of a given DCC, but those extra (consecutive) dots to be added to the DCC are necessarily from other keys (otherwise the DCC would have been filled and updated earlier). Thus, the filled DCC still represents an extrinsic set to the causal history of the current concurrent versions in the DCC. Also, when nodes exchange keys: single DCCs are filled before being sent; if sending a group of DCCs, they can be sent in the more compact stripped form together with the BVV from the sender (possibly with null bitmaps), and later filled at the destination, before being used. This causality stripping can lead to significant network traffic savings in addition to the storage savings, when transferring large sets of keys.

4 Server-Side Distributed Algorithm

We now define the distributed algorithm corresponding to the server-side workflow discussed in section 2.2; we define the node state, how to serve updates (writes and deletes); how to serve reads; and how anti-entropy is performed. It is presented in Algorithm 4, by way of clauses, each pertaining to some state transition due to an action (basically receive), defined by pattern-matching over the message structure; there is also a periodically to specify actions which happen periodically, for the anti-entropy. Due to space concerns, and because it is a side issue, read repairs are not addressed.

In addition to the operations over BVVs and DCCs already presented, we make use of: function $nodes(k)$, which returns the replica nodes for the key k; function $peers(i)$, which returns the set of nodes that are peers with node i; function $random(s)$ which returns a random element from set s.

4.1 Node State

The state of each node has five components: g_i is the node logical clock, a BVV; m_i is the proper data store, mapping keys to their respective logical clocks (DCCs); l_i is a map from dot counters to keys, serving as a log holding which key was locally written; v_i is a version vector to track what other peers have seen of the locally generated dots; we use a VV and not a BVV, because we only care for the contiguous set of dots seen by peers, to easily prune older segments from l_i corresponding to keys seen by *all* peers; r_i is an auxiliary map to track incoming responses from other nodes when serving a read request, before replying to the client. It is the only component held in volatile state, which can be lost under node failure. All other four components are held in durable state (that must behave as if atomically written at each state transition).

Algorithm 1. Distributed algorithm for node i

---

durable state:

    g_i : BVV, node logical clock; initially $g_i = \{j \mapsto (0,0) \mid j \in \mathsf{peers}(i)\}$

    m_i : $\mathbb{K} \hookrightarrow$ DCC, mapping from a key to its logical clock; initially $m_i = \{\}$

    l_i : $\mathbb{N} \hookrightarrow \mathbb{K}$, log of keys locally updated; initially $l_i = \{\}$

    v_i : VV; other peers' knowledge; initially $v_i = \{j \mapsto 0 \mid j \in \mathsf{peers}(i)\}$

volatile state:

    r_i : $(\mathbb{I} \times \mathbb{K}) \hookrightarrow (\text{DCC} \times \mathbb{N})$, requests map; initially $r_i = \{\}$

on $\mathsf{receive}_{j,i}(\mathsf{write}, k : \mathbb{K}, v : \mathbb{V}, c : \text{VV})$:

    if $i \notin \mathsf{nodes}(k)$ **then**

        $u = \mathsf{random}(\mathsf{nodes}(k))$ // pick a random replica node of k

        $\mathsf{send}_{i,u}(\mathsf{write}, k, v, c)$ // forward request to node u

    else

        $d = \mathsf{discard}(\mathsf{fill}(m_i(k), g_i), c)$ // discard obsolete versions in k's DCC

        $(n, g_i') = \mathsf{event}(g_i, i)$ // increment and get the new max dot from the local BVV

        $d' = \textbf{if } v \neq \mathsf{nil} \textbf{ then } \mathsf{add}(d, (i, n), v) \textbf{ else } d$ // if it's a write, add version

        $m_i' = m_i\{k \mapsto \mathsf{strip}(d', g_i')\}$ // update DCC entry for k

        $l_i' = l_i\{n \mapsto k\}$ // append key to log

        for $u \in \mathsf{nodes}(k) \setminus \{i\}$ **do**

            $\mathsf{send}_{i,u}(\mathsf{replicate}, k, d')$ // replicate new DCC to other replica nodes

on $\mathsf{receive}_{j,i}(\mathsf{replicate}, K : \mathbb{K}, d : \text{DCC})$:

    $g_i' = \mathsf{add}(g_i, d)$ // add version dots to node clock g_i, ignoring DCC context

    $m_i' = m_i\{k \mapsto \mathsf{strip}(\mathsf{sync}(d, \mathsf{fill}(m_i(k), g_i)), g_i')\}$ // sync with local and strip

on $\mathsf{receive}_{j,i}(\mathsf{read}, K : \mathbb{K}, n : \mathbb{N})$:

    $r_i' = r_i\{(j, k) \mapsto (\{\}, n)\}$ // initialize the read request metadata

    for $u \in \mathsf{nodes}(k)$ **do**

        $\mathsf{send}_{i,u}(\mathsf{read\_request}, j, k)$ // request k versions from replica nodes

on $\mathsf{receive}_{j,i}(\mathsf{read\_request}, u : \mathbb{I}, k : \mathbb{K})$:

    $\mathsf{send}_{i,j}(\mathsf{read\_response}, u, k, \mathsf{fill}(m_i(k), g_i))$ // return local versions for k

on $\mathsf{receive}_{j,i}(\mathsf{read\_response}, u : \mathbb{I}, k : \mathbb{K}, d : \text{DCC})$:

    if $(u, k) \in \mathsf{dom}(r_i)$ **then**

        $(d', n) = r_i((u, k))$ // d' is the current merged DCC

        $d'' = \mathsf{sync}(d, d')$ // sync received with current DCC

        if $n = 1$ **then**

            $r_i' = \{(u, k)\} \lhd r_i$ // remove (u, k) entry from requests map

            $\mathsf{send}_{i,u}(k, \mathsf{values}(d''), \mathsf{context}(d''))$ // reply to client u

        else

            $r_i' = r_i\{(u, k) \mapsto (d'', n - 1)\}$ // update requests map

periodically:

    $j = \mathsf{random}(\mathsf{peers}(i))$

    $\mathsf{send}_{i,j}(\mathsf{sync\_request}, g_i(j))$

on $\mathsf{receive}_{j,i}(\mathsf{sync\_request}, (n, b) : (\mathbb{N} \times \mathbb{N}))$:

    $e = \mathsf{values}(g_i(i)) \setminus \mathsf{values}((n, b))$ // get the dots from i missing from j

    $K = \{l_i(m) \mid m \in e \wedge j \in \mathsf{nodes}(l_i(m))\}$ // remove keys that j isn't replica node of

    $s = \{k \mapsto \mathsf{strip}(m_i(k), g_i) \mid k \in K\}$ // get and strip DCCs with local BVV

    $\mathsf{send}_{i,j}(\mathsf{sync\_response}, \mathsf{base}(g_i), s)$

    $v_i' = v_i\{j \mapsto n\}$ // update v_i with j's information on i

    $M = \{m \in \mathsf{dom}(l_i) \mid m < \min(\mathsf{ran}(v_i'))\}$ // get dots i seen by all peers

    $l_i' = M \lhd l_i$ // remove those dots from the log

    $m_i' = m_i\{k \mapsto \mathsf{strip}(m_i(k), g_i) \mid m \in M, k \in l_i(m)\}$ // strip the keys removed from the log

on $\mathsf{receive}_{j,i}(\mathsf{sync\_response}, g : \text{BVV}, s : \mathbb{K} \hookrightarrow \text{DCC})$:

    $g_i' = g_i\{j \mapsto g(j)\}$ // update the node logical clock with j's entry

    $m_i' = m_i\{k \mapsto \mathsf{strip}(\mathsf{sync}(\mathsf{fill}(m_i(k), g_i), \mathsf{fill}(d, g)), g_i') \mid (k, d) \in s\}$

4.2   Updates

We have managed to integrate both writes and deletes in a unified framework. A delete(k, c) operation is translated client-side to a write(k, nil, c) operation, passing a special nil as the value.

When a node i is serving an update, arriving from the client as a (write, k, v, c) message (first "on" clause in our algorithm), either i is a replica node for key k or it isn't. If it's not, it forwards the request to a random replica node for k. If it is: (1) it discards obsolete versions according to context c; (2) creates a new dot and adds its counter to the node logical clock; (3) if the operation is not a delete ($v \neq \text{nil}$) it creates a new version, which is added to the DCC for k; (4) it stores the new DCC after stripping unnecessary causal information; (5) appends k to the log of keys update locally; (6) sends a replicate message to other replica nodes of k with the new DCC. When receiving a replicate message, the node adds the dots of the concurrent versions in the DCC (but not the version vector) to the node logical clock and synchronizes with local key's DCC. The result is then stripped before storing.

Deletes. For notational convenience, doing $m_i(k)$ when k isn't in the map, results in the empty DCC: $(\{\}, \{\})$; also, a map update $m\{k \mapsto (\{\}, \{\})\}$ removes the entry for key k. This describes how a delete ends up removing all content from storage for a given key: (1) when there are no current versions in the DCC; (2) and when the causal context becomes older than the node logical clock, resulting in an empty DCC after stripping. If these conditions are not met at the time the delete was first requested, the key will still maintain relevant causal metadata, but when this delete is known by all peers, the anti-entropy mechanism will remove this key from the key-log l_i, and strip its remaining causal history in the DCC, resulting in a automatic and complete key and metadata removal [2].

With traditional logical clocks, nodes either maintained the context of the deleted key stored forever, or they would risk the reappearance of deleted keys or even losing new key-values created after a delete. With our algorithm using node logical clocks, we solve both cases: regarding losing new writes after deletes, updates always have new dots with increasing counters, and therefore cannot be causally in the past of previously deleted updates; in the case of reappearing deletes from anti-entropy with outdated nodes or delayed messages, a node can check if it has already seen that delete's dot in its BVV without storing specific per-key metadata.

4.3   Reads

To serve a read request (third "on" clause), a node requests the corresponding DCC from all replica nodes for that key. To allow flexibility (e.g. requiring a

---

[2] The key may not be entirely removed if in the meantime, another client has insert back this key, or made a concurrent update to this key. This is the expected behavior when dealing with concurrent writes or new insertions after deletes. Excluding these cases, eventually all keys that received a delete request will be removed.

quorum of nodes or a single reply is enough) the client provides an extra argument: the number of replies that the coordinator must wait for. All responses are synchronized, discarding obsolete versions, before replying to the client with the (concurrent) version(s) and the causal context in the DCC. Component r_i of the state maintains, for each pair client-key, a DCC maintaining the synchronization of the versions received thus far, and how many more replies are needed.

4.4   Anti-entropy

Since node logical clocks already reflect the node's knowledge about current and past versions stored locally, comparing those clocks tells us exactly what updates are missing between two peer nodes. However, only knowing the dots that are missing is not sufficient: we must also know what key a dot refers to. This is the purpose of the l_i component of the state: a log storing the keys of locally coordinated updates, which can be seen as a dynamic array indexed by a contiguous set of counters.

Periodically, a node i starts the synchronization protocol with one of its peers j. It starts by sending j's entry of i's node logical clock to j. Node j receives and compares that entry with its own local entry, to detect which local dots node i hasn't seen. Node j then sends back its own entry in its BVV (we don't care about the bitmap part) and the missing key versions (DCCs) that i is also replica node of. Since we're sending a possibly large set of DCCs, we stripped them of unnecessary causal context before sending, to save bandwidth (they were stripped when they where stored, but the node clock has probably advanced since then, so we strip the context again to possibly have further savings).

Upon reception, node i updates j's entry in its own BVV, to reflect that i has now seen all updates coordinated by j reflected in j's received logical clock. Node i also synchronizes the received DCCs with the local ones: for each key, its fills the received DCC with j's logical clock, it reads and fills the equivalent local DCCs with i's own logical clock, and then synchronizes each pair into a single DCC and finally locally stores the result after striping again with i's logical clock.

Additionally, node j also: (1) updates the i's entry in v_j with the max contiguous dot generated by j that i knows of; (2) if new keys are know known by all peers (i.e. if the minimum counter of v_j has increased), then remove the corresponding keys from the key-log l_i. This is also a good moment to revisit the locally saved DCCs for these keys, and check if we can further strip causality information, given the constant information growth in the node logical clock. As with deletes, if there were no new updates to a key after the one represented by the dot in the key-log, the DCC will be stripped of its entire causal history, which means that we only need one dot per concurrent version in the stored DCC.

5   Evaluation

We ran a small benchmark, comparing a prototype data store based on our framework, against a traditional one based on Merkle Trees and per-key logical clocks. The system was populated with 40000 keys, each key replicated in 3

Table 1. Results from a micro-benchmark run with 10000 writes

	Key/Leaf Ratio	Hit Ratio	Total Metadata	Metadata Per Repair		Average Entries Per Key L. Clock
	1	60.214 %	449.65 KB	4.30 KB		
Merkle Tree	10	9.730 %	293.39 KB	2.84 KB	VV or	3
	100	1.061 %	878.40 KB	7.98 KB	DVV	
	1000	0.126 %	6440.96 KB	63.15 KB		
BVV & DCC	–	100 %	3.04 KB	0.019 KB	DCC	0.231

nodes, and we measured some metrics over the course of 10000 writes, 10% losing a message replicating the write to one replica node. The evaluation aimed to compare metadata size of anti-entropy related messages and the data store causality-related metadata size. We compared against four Merkle Trees sizes to show how its "resolution", i.e., the ratio of keys-per-leaf impacts results.

Table 1 shows the results of our benchmark. There is always significant overhead with Merkle Trees, worse for larger keys-per-leaf ratios, where there are many false positives. Even for smaller ratios, where the "hit ratio" of relevant-hashes over exchanged-hashes is higher, the tree itself is large, resulting in substantial metadata transferred. In general, the metadata overhead to perform anti-entropy with our scheme is orders of magnitude smaller than any of the Merkle Tree configurations.

Concerning causality-related metadata size, being negligible the cost of node-wide metadata amortized over a large database, the average per-key logical clock metadata overhead is also significantly smaller in our scheme, since most of the time the causality is entirely condensed by the node-wide logical clock. With traditional per-key logical clocks, the number of entries is typically the degree of replication, and can be larger, due to entries for retired nodes that remain in the clock forever, a problem which is also solved by our scheme.

6   Related Work

The paper's mechanisms and architecture extend the specialized causality mechanisms in [11,1], apply it over a eventually consistent data store. In addition to the already mentioned differences between our mechanism and Concise Version Vectors [11], our key logical clock size is actually bounded by the number of active replica nodes, unlike PVEs (the CVV key logical clock is unbounded).

Our work also builds on concepts of weakly consistent replication present in log-based systems [15,8,4] and data/file synchronization [13]. The assignment of local unique identifiers for each update event is already present in [15], but each node totally orders its local events, while we consider concurrent clients to the same node. The detection of when an event is known in all other replicas nodes – a condition for log pruning – is common to the mentioned log-based systems; however, our log structure (the key log) is only an inverted index that tracks divergent data replicas, and thus is closer to optimistic replicated file-systems. Our design can reduce divergence both as a result of foreground user activity (both on writes, deletes, and read repair) and by periodic background anti-entropy, while using a common causality framework.

Acknowledgments. This work is financed by the FCT – Fundação para a Ciência e a Tecnologia (Portuguese Foundation for Science and Technology) within project UID/EEA/50014/2013 and scholarship SFRH/BD/86735/2012; also by the North Portugal Regional Operational Programme (ON.2, O Novo Norte), under the National Strategic Reference Framework (NSRF), through the European Regional Development Fund (ERDF), within project NORTE-07-0124-FEDER-000058; and by EU FP7 SyncFree project (609551).

References

1. Almeida, P.S., Baquero, C., Gonçalves, R., Preguiça, N., Fonte, V.: Scalable and accurate causality tracking for eventually consistent stores. In: Magoutis, K., Pietzuch, P. (eds.) DAIS 2014. LNCS, vol. 8460, pp. 67–81. Springer, Heidelberg (2014)
2. DeCandia, G., Hastorun, D., Jampani, M., Kakulapati, G., Lakshman, A., Pilchin, A., Vosshall, P., Vogels, W.: Dynamo: amazon's highly available key-value store. In: ACM SIGOPS Operating Systems Review, vol. 41, pp. 205–220 (2007)
3. Gilbert, S., Lynch, N.: Brewer's conjecture and the feasibility of consistent, available, partition-tolerant web services. ACM SIGACT News 33(2), 51–59 (2002)
4. Golding, R.A.: Weak-consistency group communication and membership. Ph.D. thesis, University of California Santa Cruz (1992)
5. Johnson, P.R., Thomas, R.H.: The maintenance of duplicate databases. Internet Request for Comments RFC 677, Information Sciences Institute (1976)
6. Karger, D., Lehman, E., Leighton, T., Panigrahy, R., Levine, M., Lewin, D.: Consistent hashing and random trees. In: Proceedings of the Twenty-Ninth Annual ACM Symposium on Theory of Computing, pp. 654–663. ACM (1997)
7. Klophaus, R.: Riak core: building distributed applications without shared state. In: ACM SIGPLAN Commercial Users of Functional Programming. ACM (2010)
8. Ladin, R., Liskov, B., Shrira, L., Ghemawat, S.: Providing high availability using lazy replication. ACM Trans. Comput. Syst. 10(4), 360–391 (1992)
9. Lakshman, A., Malik, P.: Cassandra: a decentralized structured storage system. ACM SIGOPS Operating Systems Review 44(2), 35–40 (2010)
10. Lamport, L.: Time, clocks, and the ordering of events in a distributed system. Communications of the ACM 21(7), 558–565 (1978)
11. Malkhi, D., Terry, D.: Concise version vectors in winFS. In: Fraigniaud, P. (ed.) DISC 2005. LNCS, vol. 3724, pp. 339–353. Springer, Heidelberg (2005)
12. Merkle, R.C.: A certified digital signature. In: Brassard, G. (ed.) Advances in Cryptology - CRYPTO 1989. LNCS, vol. 435, pp. 218–238. Springer, Heidelberg (1990), http://dl.acm.org/citation.cfm?id=118209.118230
13. Parker Jr., D.S., Popek, G., Rudisin, G., Stoughton, A., Walker, B., Walton, E., Chow, J., Edwards, D.: Detection of mutual inconsistency in distributed systems. IEEE Transactions on Software Engineering, 240–247 (1983)
14. Schwarz, R., Mattern, F.: Detecting causal relationships in distributed computations: In search of the holy grail. Distributed Computing 7(3), 149–174 (1994)
15. Wuu, G., Bernstein, A.: Efficient solutions to the replicated log and dictionary problems. In: Symp. on Principles of Dist. Comp. (PODC), pp. 233–242 (1984)

X-Ray: Monitoring and Analysis
of Distributed Database Queries

Pedro Guimarães and José Pereira[✉]

INESC TEC and U. Minho, Guimaraes, Portugal
pg22834@alunos.uminho.pt, jop@di.uminho.pt

Abstract. The integration of multiple database technologies, including both SQL and NoSQL, allows using the best tool for each aspect of a complex problem and is increasingly sought in practice. Unfortunately, this makes it difficult for database developers and administrators to obtain a clear view of the resulting composite data processing paths, as they combine operations chosen by different query optimisers, implemented by different software packages, and partitioned across distributed systems. This work addresses this challenge with the X-Ray framework, that allows monitoring code to be added to a Java-based distributed system by manipulating its bytecode at runtime. The resulting information is collected in a NoSQL database and then processed to visualise data processing paths as required for optimising integrated database systems. This proposal is demonstrated with a distributed query over a federation of Apache Derby database servers and its performance evaluated with the standard TPC-C benchmark workload.

Keywords: Distributed databases · Monitoring · Java instrumentation

1   Introduction

The performance of data management systems depends on how operations are mapped to different hardware and software components. This mapping is driven by the developer, by query compilation and optimisation in the system itself, and finally by database administrators. Obtaining the best performance thus depends on monitoring and analysing such mapping. Relational database management systems have traditionally included tools to expose the execution plan for a query, identifying what implementation is used for each abstract relational operation, in what order, and including a detailed accounting of I/O operations, memory pages, and CPU time used. As an example, in PostgreSQL this is provided by **EXPLAIN ANALYZE** [27] and presented graphically with pgAdmin3 [14].

Recently, driven by novel applications, there has been a growing trend towards using different data management techniques and tools for different purposes, instead of always resorting to relational database management systems [26]. For instance, the CoherentPaaS platform-as-a-service integrates various SQL and NoSQL data stores in a common framework [3,20]. Moreover, the large scale

© IFIP International Federation for Information Processing 2015
A. Bessani and S. Bouchenak (Eds.): DAIS 2015, LNCS 9038, pp. 80–93, 2015.
DOI: 10.1007/978-3-319-19129-4_7

of current applications means using distributed data stores that scale out with data size and traffic, such as HBase, trading off in the process query processing capability and transactional ACID guaranties.

This poses several challenges to monitoring and analysis. First, some of the data stores now commonly used have only minimal support for data collection on individual operations, providing only aggregate resource measurements. In fact, the additional application code needed for integration and to overcome the limitations of NoSQL data stores is likely to have no monitoring capabilities at all. Second, even when monitoring tools are available for the required data stores, they provide partial views that cannot easily be reconciled and integrated into a coherent observation, namely, by tracking its relation to a common user request. Finally, when multiple instances of a specific data store are used for scale out, such as in replication and *sharding* configurations, distributed monitoring information has to be collected and organised according to its role in a global operation, for instance, to reason about load balancing and parallelism.

This work addresses these challenges with X-Ray, a framework for monitoring and analysis of distributed and heterogeneous data processing systems. First, it provides a way to add monitoring code to applications and data stores running in the Java platform. By using bytecode instrumentation, this does not rely on the availability of the source code and can be applied conditionally to avoid overhead in production systems. Second, it provides mechanisms for tracking the interaction of multiple threads, on synchronisation primitives, and of distributed processes communicating with sockets. Finally, it provides a tool to reconcile monitoring data from multiple software components in a distributed system taking into consideration their relation to actual user requests, thus providing a cross-cutting unified view of the system's operation.

The rest of this paper is structured as follows: Section 2 introduces the X-Ray approach and how it is applied to monitor data processing systems. Section 3 describes how it is implemented using bytecode instrumentation. Section 4 evaluates the proposal with a case study and a benchmark. Section 5 contrasts the proposed approach with related work. Finally, Section 6 concludes the paper.

2   Approach

Figure 1 presents an overview of the proposed X-Ray architecture. From left to right, X-Ray targets distributed applications and data stores with software components in multiple servers, virtual hosts, and Java virtual machines. These applications generate monitoring events through the X-Ray Capture layer to the X-Ray Storage and Processing layer, to be used in the X-Ray Analysis and Visualisation layer. Label icons identify the main configuration points for the system.

The main component of X-Ray Capture uses bytecode instrumentation, a mechanism for modifying compiled programs. It uses `asm`[10], a stateless *bytecode* manipulation library modelled on the *hierarchical visitor* pattern [15]. This instrumentation inserts instructions to generate logging events and maintain context.

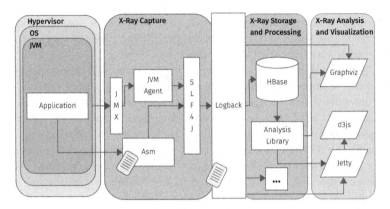

Fig. 1. Overview of the X-Ray architecture

This is the main configuration point for monitoring Java programs. Bridges or file processing can be used to obtain information about non-X-Ray-ready programs. Finally, an agent periodically monitors and collects metrics about the underlying Java runtime from Java Management Extensions(JMX) [12].

Bytecode instrumentation can be customised by choosing what methods to alter and what operations to perform. **Logback** enables processing various actions for the same message. Those actions are executed by entities called appenders, programmable in Java, and configurable with a simple XML or Groovy file.

The resulting events are routed through Simple Logging Facade for Java (slf4j), a logging facade for Java [23], and **Logback**, a logging framework implementing the (slf4j) API [22]. **Logback** works as an event spooler: it enriches events with additional information and delivers them asynchronously to the X-Ray Storage and Processing module. In the Storage and Processing module, events can be stored in HBase (the sink database), that can be configured to sustain high-throughput writes.

The Analysis Library contains analysis procedures applicable to the monitoring data, specially concerned with request tracking across software modules and components. It joins logs originating from different machines and produces a global coherent representation, interpreting remote communication events and pseudo-nodes labelled with the socket address used for the communication and connecting them in the right place on the graphs. A visual representations is then made available to the end-user, with Graphviz or D3.js, or even exported to enable further processing and interaction with external systems.

2.1   Request Tracking

The key feature of the X-Ray Capture layer is being able to chain operations performed on behalf of each end-user request, to highlight the decomposition of a data processing request in terms of software components and hardware resources. This is achieved by using tags and probes, as follows.

Instrumentation provides the ability to add tags to entities being observed. A tag is an automatically generated unique identifier that increases the data that can be collected by X-Ray, motivated by the recognition that certain computations happen in distinct contexts, even if the executed code is the same. In detail, a tag can be associated with an object or thread and through configuration instructions it is possible to generate, remove, move, or copy it to a thread or object when a method is executed. Thus, during execution tags can be associated with multiple threads and objects and flow through them.

It is also possible to associate a tag with message send and receive events in sockets thus supporting communication between different virtual machines. This takes advantage of FIFO order and the unique identifier of the socket (including both addresses and ports, as well as a timestamp) to establish a mapping between tags existing at both ends.

Probes implemented in X-Ray allow information to be collected on entry and exit(s) of selected methods. The target data – name and reference of executing class, name and signature of the method, the current thread and the parameters/return value – are accessible to all defined probes. Moreover, the probe also collects tags associated with the current object and thread.

This makes it is possible to follow a logical work unit, even if it is scattered across multiple threads and processes. The simplest usage just adds a tag to the thread on starting to execute the request and removes it on completion. This makes all work done by that thread, regardless of the software component invoked, to be associated with that request.

Consider a more complex example of an application that uses a background thread to periodically write multiple outstanding data items produced by different clients. This is harder to track as the work done by the background thread contributed to multiple requests. With X-Ray, one would copy the tag from the request thread to the object queued for the background writer. On reception, the tag would be copied from the object to the background writer thread. When the background thread uses the I/O resource, it would be tagged with the tags of all corresponding requests.

Finally, consider an example of a client/server system, where a request is partially executed at the client and at the server. In this case, one would tag the client thread upon starting the request, but also server threads whenever a remote invocation is received. Moreover, when a remote invocation is issued and received, socket tagging will map client and server side tags.

2.2 Configuration

X-Ray can be configured in two ways: using annotations or configuration files. Both have the same expressive power, but the second approach is more flexible. If these two configurations strategies are used in parallel and conflict in some parameters, the value from configuration files will override the annotations.

Annotation use implies access to source code of the program to alter, and each change in the configuration requires a program recompilation to take effect. It also results in configuration being spread over several files instead of a centralised place to read or alter everything. But this solution has certain advantages: it is simple and comes bundled with the code. Also, because it is applied directly on the entity to examine, it is not affected by refactoring.

On the other hand, configurations written in files do not require access to source code. Likewise, it is not necessary to recompile the program after each change – simply restarting the program is enough. Configurations are all grouped and separated from the code, which eases its reading or alteration and is architecturally cleaner. As for disadvantages, it is fragile in case of refactoring. Entities (class, method and package) identifiers are not exactly equal to the entities they represent so a manual search and replace may fail to modify them, and likewise IDE-assisted refactoring can also be ineffective.

2.3 Usage Methods

The first alternative to apply X-Ray is to use a custom class loader. It is configured to read configuration files and react accordingly to classes to be loaded, selectively altering them or returning the original class unchanged, as appropriate.

Because of security restrictions preventing deep and potential unsafe changes, it is not possible to alter methods in the `java.*` packages or native methods. Also if X-Ray attempted to further alter the program representation, by changing multiple times the same class, the Java Runtime Environment (JRE) would give an error (a `java.lang.LinkageError`) about an attempted duplicated class definition, which is disallowed. This makes it impossible to change instrumentation properties during the application run and seeing these changes take effect. The solution is to use the Java Agent or modify the desired configurations and restart the program through the X-Ray class loader.

Another solution is to statically modify the bytecode. Instead of modifying the program each time it is executed, it can be done just once. This is how `JarRecompiler` works: it alters all the necessary files from a JAR and saves them to a new file. This new JAR can then be normally used.

As the bytecode alteration is done just once, clients of the altered code do not need the `asm` library to run it. A disadvantage of this method is that it is less flexible - it is necessary to do a JAR recompilation every time a configuration is changed and one wants to see the effects of those changes. To mitigate it, a Maven plugin was developed for generating the altered JAR in the **package** phase. It is also not possible to alter native methods. As the recompiler acts on JAR files, it is possible to modify methods in the `java.*` packages if the input JAR corresponds to one where JRE classes are, but this is not recommended as it would permanently alter them.

The last option is a Java Agent [21, `java.lang.instrument` documentation]. Depending on the support provided by the JVM, it can be initiated along with the program by passing an argument to the command line or it can be attached to a running instance after it has started. Similar to static recompilation, it is transparent for all normal code interactions and, as the class loader solution, to test some change, a simple program re-run is enough. Depending on how agents are configured, they have the ability to alter JRE classes and native methods and redefine classes already instrumented. A disadvantage of the use of agents is that not all Java Virtual Machines (JVMs) support it. Among those that do, there is no standard way to do some things, specially initiating an agent after the virtual machine start-up [16, § 8.4.3.4].

3   Implementation

Instrumentation of Java programs to insert tags and probes starts by reading configuration files, if available, adding their commands to the framework's internal state. Classes are then loaded, either due to the program running or by statically traversing the JAR file, depending on the usage method chosen. For each of them, it scans the file and for each method decides if it should be instrumented using configuration from files and configurations acquired by reading annotations in the currently analysed class and other loaded classes.

This may require visiting the bytecode of super-classes or of the implemented interfaces if they were not already visited, as the decisions on a class may depend on information contained in other classes. If any method should be altered, the new code for the method body is generated. After going through all the class code one of these situations will happen:

1. The original code of the class was altered at some point, and so this new code is returned to the JVM to be used by the program.
2. No original code was instrumented by lack of indications; if so the original code is simply returned.

This process happens again each time a class is needed, until all are loaded and transformed. This approach is only possible because the binary representation of Java programs corresponds to a well specified, platform independent format that can be manipulated.

If any method was changed for analysis, it is altered in at least two sites: its entry and exit(s). The exits can be normal – from `return` statements – or exceptional – from `throw` statements. At method entry and exit the method and class names are collected, as well as a reference to the current object and executing thread. At method entry, parameters will be saved and at method exit, the return value is stored too.

Each time the execution flow passes through the method, indications of passage through its entry and an exit are given to X-Ray and optionally from there to other systems and all the collected information made available. Remote communication events are also listened for and reported.

3.1   Selection of Instrumentation Targets

X-Ray operates every time it is called to resolve a class, meaning, to return the bytecode associated with a class. The decision whether to instrument or not is made for each method, on a case-by-case basis. A method m in class C will be altered by X-Ray if there is configuration on: the analysed method m;

m's enclosing class C; the package of C; the original method declaration or a super implementation of m, if that indication is inheritable; a supertype that C extends or implements, if that type's configurations are to be inherited; or a package that contains a supertype C extends or implements, but only if that indication is inherited. Otherwise, the original method code is returned and the rest of the class is visited. The given conditions are tested by the order they were presented.

When a settings conflict arises the priority is given to the more specific indications, followed by the closest ones. For example if the class C of method m should log events with the TRACE level and there is an original implementation of m with log level of DEBUG, m will have the DEBUG level.

3.2   Modifications to Targets

X-Ray adds fields and other information needed for its operation. The first change is the addition of a reference to a slf4j logger object as a new static field. Tags also require the creation of a new field. These constructed fields are named in an unusual way to avoid colliding with existing code (using the "$_xray_" prefix) and with a special marker to indicate they were generated (their ACC_SYNTHETIC flag is set). This might be useful to other class manipulation or reading tools to warn them it might not be necessary to process these constructs or to enable the use of all tools simultaneously.

Before copying the original instruction to the new class representation, the necessary logging instructions are inserted. These instructions capture all the relevant execution information and pass it through calls to methods on core X-Ray classes, needed at runtime. These X-Ray methods are responsible for producing logging events following a certain structure, sending them to the defined outputs and invoking any user-defined probes.

Each event has a unique identifier associated with it. The identifier is composed of a VMID (Virtual Machine Identifier) and a sequence number. The VMID is an unique identifier for each JVM, based on some of its unique properties and it is valid as long as its IP address remains unique and constant (cfg. [21, `java.rmi.dgc.VMID` documentation][21, `java.rmi.server.UID` documentation]). The sequence number is a local identifier that is incremented once after each logged event. Each event has a type (like call logging, remote communication or performance metrics) and a time stamp.

At method entry each parameter value will be saved by X-Ray. For objects, a reference is saved and for primitive types, boxing of the original value is performed. At method exit, before the terminating statements, the return value or exception is also saved, as well as a flag indicating whether the method returned normally or not. Stored data includes also the name and reference of the current object (Java's `this`), the method name, signature and the running thread.

For the most part they are passed using slf4j parametrised messages, if not directly obtainable from logback. Other information is copied using Mapped Diagnostic Context (MDC), a per-thread key-value map, available at run-time in several code locations.

```
 1  xray("org.apache.derby.iapi.sql.execute") {
 2    instrument("NoPutResultSet") {
 3      inherit = true
 4      log "openCore()V"
 5      log "getNextRowCore()Lorg/apache/derby/iapi/sql/execute/ExecRow;"
 6    }
 7  }
 8  xray("org.apache.derby.impl")
 9
10  xray("org.apache.derby.client.am") {
11    instrument("NetResultSet") {
12      tag "next()Z"
13      send("next()Z", "?laddr", "?raddr")
14    }
15  }
16  xray("org.apache.derby.impl.drda") {
17    instrument("DRDAConnThread") {
18      tag "processCommands()V"
19      receive("processCommands()V", "?laddr", "?raddr")
20    }
21  }
```

Fig. 2. X-Ray configuration for federated Apache Derby

4   Evaluation

4.1   Case Study

The first experiment is to monitor a distributed query. The query is made to a federated SQL database management system built with Apache Derby. That database is composed of two nodes, communicating with each other. The final element of the distributed query is the client, which initiates the computation by making a request to one the servers. To satisfy the request the server must execute a sub-query on the other server, join the partial results, and return the final values of the query to the client. The goal in this case study is to apply the X-Ray framework to assess if it is possible to monitor this process, see how to do it and observe the obtained results.

Most of the configuration needed for X-Ray to do this is shown in Figure 2. In detail, lines 1 to 7 set probes on the base class of relational operators. Then, in line 8, the package implementing such operators is declared as being instrumented. This means that all classes found extending such base class, *i.e.*, all operator implementations, get instrumented.

Moreover, lines 10 to 15 target the JDBC driver, which is the entry point into Apache Derby. It sets a tag on entry of the `next()` method that is used to retrieve data. Moreover, it links this tag to a message being sent on the socket connection to the server. Some other methods in the client driver (not shown) are also instrumented in the same manner. Finally, lines 16 to 21 target the server-side protocol handler, by setting a tag on each received message and then linking it to the context of the client socket, thus relating it to the corresponding client-side context. This requires minor changes to Derby's source code, to expose the communication ports to X-Ray.

As a result we obtain Figures 3(b) and 3(a). They were obtained by saving the logs produced by client and database servers to HBase, and by invoking the analysis component to read that information from HBase, reconstruct it, and add relevant remote communication event nodes between the datastore nodes and the client.

The resulting flow graph shown in Figure 3(b), was rendered by d3.js and served by Apache Jetty. It is accessible and continuously updated at runtime. Each bar represents a logged object and its width how many times it emitted logging events to X-Ray. Figure 3(a) was produced by Graphviz from a dot file also being continuously updated. It is similar to other graphs used to represent relationships between objects. X-Ray could be used to track the relations between methods, as presented in [7,8]. All these graphics, additionally, have the added feature of also representing remote connections.

Note that node labelled as "[8]" denotes a socket connecting two processes and that the relation between parts of the computation taking place in different processes is done automatically by the X-Ray system. Furthermore, most of the nodes represent classes whose name ends in ResultSet. Except the one labelled NetResultSet, all of them were obtained from the configuration in lines 1 to 8 of Figure 2: the inheritance of configuration makes this succinct. Finally, it is clear that the structure of the computation and the amount of data handled by each software component is exposed to developers and administrators.

4.2   Performance

The performance impact of X-Ray instrumentation and probes was measured by starting a Derby server and running the TPC-C transaction processing benchmark [13]. The goal is to obtain significant statistics about the state of the database over the course of the benchmark, to see what was the overhead of using X-Ray and if it was even possible to instrument such a large code base developed by a third-party and that potentially makes use of features that conflict with the framework.

The database where the TPC-C benchmark was run is a single warehouse with approximately 200 MB of data and for the workload, 1 (one) client making requests without delay between them (i.e. with no think time). Two machines were used for these tests, both with 128 GiB of RAM, 24 cores and a disk with 7200 rpm. Their OS was Ubuntu 12.04.3 LTS (GNU/Linux 3.2.0-27-generic x86_64) and their Java environment was the Oracle JVM version 1.7.0_60. One of them was used to run the Apache Derby instance plus the benchmark client and the other was used to run HBase.

Table 1 shows results obtained with the following configurations:

Baseline. No instrumentation was used.
Instrumented. Run with the instrumentation turned on, but not using any appender.
Logging to file. Using TPC-C with instrumentation plus enabling logs to *stdout* and redirecting them to a file.

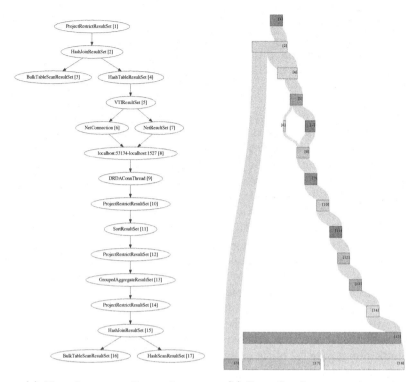

(a) Nested operator invocations.   (b) Data-flow between operators.

Fig. 3. Visualisations of a distributed SQL query

Table 1. Execution times of running TPC-C on Derby

Configuration	Latency (ms)	Throughput (tpmC)
Baseline	50.2	526
Instrumented	57.3	478
Logging to text file	64.1	414
Logging to HBase	67.4	7
Asynchronous HBase	63.3	422
Lossy asynchronous to HBase	61.4	437

Logging to HBase. Having the HBase-appender save logging information to HBase. In the HBase-appender auto-flush was turned off.

Asynchronous to HBase. Using the previous appender, but wrapped under an asynchronous appender [2,4] that performs logging in other threads, asynchronously.

Lossy synchronous to HBase. Again, the HBase-appender is employed, but this time wrapped under the asynchronous appender provided by Logback [18] that may drop messages at times of congestion.

Table 2. Space occupied and number of lines written during the benchmark

Configuration	Size (Bytes)	Size (lines)
Logging to File	317 024 499	2 040 975
Logging to HBase	436 240	260 760

For the *Logging to file* and *Logging to HBase* tests, Table 2 shows the size occupied in disk at the end of the benchmark and the number of lines written. In the case of the *Logging to file* test, the number of lines and size refer to the written file, and in the case of the *Logging HBase* run, size is the size of the data written to HBase during the benchmark, and number of lines is the number of written entries on its tables. It is possible to recognise that data written to HBase was much less than what was written in the file. But considering the total number of transactions, we have Hbase with $436240/877 \simeq 497.42$ and file with $317024499/6400 \simeq 49535.08$ bytes per transaction. This means that each set of events representing a transaction takes ≈ 99.6 times more space to represent in a file than in a table in HBase. The *Logging to file* run is portrayed to show an upper limit to logging load. In practice, better performance could be achieved by tweaking some parameters, such as changing Logback appender layout, delaying writes to disk or using several log files and removing old ones.

It is possible to see that when using instrumentation (*Instrumented*) the benchmark ran at 90.87% of the original speed; that is only a 9.13% slowdown. Although simply using logging events to HBase synchronously incurs an heavy penalty, when using an asynchronous approach, the result is far more acceptable – 88.28% of the simple instrumentation speed, or 19.77% of the original *Baseline* run. If one does not care about the possibility of dropping events, a better 16.92% can be achieved.

5   Related Work

There are already some monitoring or analysis solutions for distributed contexts. Their purposes range from assisting debugging, identifying system bottlenecks and network problems, discovering most frequent paths between nodes, to detecting potential intrusions.

NetLogger [17] has a architecture similar to X-Ray, but no support for automatic insertion of logging statements. To use it developers need to add explicit invocations to the framework to benefit from it, which forces access to source code. Pinpoint [11] does monitoring of components in a distributed system automatically, by tagging client requests with an identifier. Although useful, it only works for J2EE applications. Pip [24] allows users to configure its operation by using a domain-specific language. It with predicates about communications, times, and resource consumption can be made and at runtime those predicates can be validated or invalidated. Relations between components can be discerned by the construction of causal paths, with the help of the provided configurations and collected information. As with NetLogger, the source code is required, as annotations are used to generate events. iPath [9] is a dynamic instrumentation tool with some interesting properties for a distributed setting. It was conceived and works on distributed systems. It also allows a more focused analysis as the methods to analyse can be chosen and this selection can be altered at runtime. Yet it is a native solution and although one can choose what methods to instrument, when the call stack is walked to update the calling context information, all methods including those that were not declared for observation will be recorded in the calls information structure. Aspect-Oriented Programming (AOP) [19] has also been used for monitoring. However, on one hand it provides too much freedom when altering programs, hence, additional complexity, and on the other hand does not provide the event spooling and processing components of X-Ray. Frameworks such as AspectJ [1] could also have been used instead of asm [10], although this would add some overhead to class loading in comparison to the simple processing done now.

All these proposals, like X-Ray, require some information about the software to examine. This enables the extraction of more targeted and meaningful information. On the other hand, treating target sysems as black boxes makes the tool applicable when no internal details are known.

A system that follows the latter model is presented in [25]: considering that information about the components or middleware of a distributed service may be minimal and the source code unavailable, the proposed request tracing tool considers each component as a black box, a device that receives input, processes it in an unknown fashion and returns an output. As the processing is opaque to the rest of the system, the tracing tool follows requests, as they are passed between components until the computation associated to the request is produced (and optionally sent to the entity that made the request). A means to recognise the most frequent paths is also provided. This analysis is made on-line as the system and the logger nodes are running, without the need to stop them. Information can be collected on demand, meaning that it can enabled or disabled, or done intermittently, using sampling. The detection of communication from one component to the others is made within the kernel when a send or receive system call is used. That detection depends on SystemTap [5] hence this solution it is not OS independent and has no JVM support implemented. Another similar solution is present in [6]. It only traces network messages, without any knowledge of node internals or message semantics and infers the dominant causal paths through them. It uses timing information from RPC messages and signal-processing techniques to infer inter-call causality. But although the principle that no information exists about the components is a valid one and the results obtained are useful, for X-Ray different assumptions were made: even if the source code of a component cannot be altered and deployed, it is still available or its general API is, and so should be used.

6   Conclusions

In this paper, X-Ray, a framework for distributed systems analysis and monitoring was presented. Due to its flexible instrumentation mechanism, accepting configurations and altering bytecode accordingly, it is applicable to any system on the Java platform. The main contribution is the ability to track requests across thread and process boundaries, and to expose distributed data processing operations. Unlike existing solutions, it tries to balance the need for application-specific information, that normally require source code, with the goal of working with highly heterogeneous components.

During the qualitative analysis made when applying X-Ray to Apache Derby, its applicability and usefulness when instrumenting and analysing a large code-base was demonstrated. Derby is particularly demanding, as it makes use of dynamic code generation, which was dealt with by using the JVM agent. On the other hand, a certain amount of knowledge of the source code was still required, specially to make communication ports available to instrumentation code, but with mechanisms such as reflection and callbacks, access to the source at runtime is still not required. As for the quantitative measurements made, they confirmed that the proposed solution is lightweight and its usage does not impose an expensive overhead.

Acknowledgements. This work has received funding from the European Union's Seventh Framework Programme for research, technological development and demonstration under grant agreement no 611068, project CoherentPaaS – Coherent and Rich PaaS with a Common Programming Model (http://CoherentPaaS.eu).

References

1. The aspectj project, http://www.eclipse.org/aspectj/
2. Disruptor-based AsyncAppender for Logback, https://github.com/reactor/reactor/tree/master/reactor-logback
3. Factsheet CoherentPaaS, https://ec.europa.eu/digital-agenda/sites/digital-agenda/files/CoherentPaaS_Factsheet_v0.21_0.pdf
4. Project Reactor Homepage, http://projectreactor.io/
5. Systemtap, https://sourceware.org/systemtap/
6. Aguilera, M.K., Mogul, J.C., Wiener, J.L., Reynolds, P., Muthitacharoen, A.: Performance debugging for distributed systems of black boxes. In: Proceedings of the Nineteenth ACM Symposium on Operating Systems Principles, SOSP 2003, pp. 74–89. ACM, New York (2003), http://doi.acm.org/10.1145/945445.945454
7. Ammons, G., Ball, T., Larus, J.R.: Exploiting hardware performance counters with flow and context sensitive profiling. SIGPLAN Not 32(5), 85–96 (1997), http://doi.acm.org/10.1145/258916.258924
8. Ball, T., Larus, J.R.: Efficient path profiling. In: Proceedings of the 29th Annual ACM/IEEE International Symposium on Microarchitecture, MICRO 29, pp. 46–57. IEEE Computer Society, Washington, DC (1996), http://dl.acm.org/citation.cfm?id=243846.243857
9. Bernat, A.R., Miller, B.P.: Incremental call-path profiling: Research articles. Concurr. Comput.: Pract. Exper. 19(11), 1533–1547 (2007), http://dx.doi.org/10.1002/cpe.v19:11
10. Bruneton, E., Lenglet, R., Coupay, T.: Asm: A code manipulation tool to implement adaptable systems, http://asm.ow2.org/current/asm-eng.pdf

11. Chen, M., Kiciman, E., Fratkin, E., Fox, A., Brewer, E.: Pinpoint: Problem determination in large, dynamic internet services. In: Proceedings of the International Conference on Dependable Systems and Networks, DSN 2002, pp. 595–604 (2002)
12. Corporation, O.: Monitoring and Management of the Java Virtual Machine – Overview of the JMX Technology (The Java ™Tutorials),
    http://docs.oracle.com/javase/tutorial/jmx/overview/javavm.html
13. Council, T.P.P.: TPC-C Homepage – Version 5.11, http://www.tpc.org/tpcc/
14. pgAdmin Development Team, T.: pgAdmin III 1.20.0 documentation,
    http://pgadmin.org/docs/1.20/query.html
15. DiFalco, R.A.: Hierarchical visitor pattern. Wiki Wiki Web (2011),
    http://c2.com/cgi/wiki?HierarchicalVisitorPattern
16. Gosling, J., Joy, B., Steele, G.L., Bracha, G., Buckley, A.: The Java Language Specification, Java SE 8 Edition, 1st edn. Addison-Wesley Professional (2014)
17. Gunter, D., Tierney, B., Crowley, B., Holding, M., Lee, J.: Netlogger: A toolkit for distributed system performance analysis. In: Proceedings of the 8th International Symposium on Modeling, Analysis and Simulation of Computer and Telecommunication Systems, MASCOTS 2000, p. 267. IEEE Computer Society, Washington, DC (2000), http://dl.acm.org/citation.cfm?id=580760.823762
18. Gülcü., Pennec, S., Harris, C.: The logback manual, Chapter 4: Appenders,
    http://logback.qos.ch/manual/appenders.html#AsyncAppender
19. Kiczales, G., Lamping, J., Mendhekar, A., Maeda, C., Lopes, C., Marc Loingtier, J., Irwin, J.: Aspect-oriented programming. In: Akşit, M., Matsuoka, S. (eds.) ECOOP 1997. LNCS, vol. 1241, pp. 220–242. Springer, Heidelberg (1997)
20. Kolev, B., Valduriez, P., Jimenez-Peris, R., Martínes Bazan, N., Pereira, J.: Cloud-MdsQL: Querying heterogeneous cloud data stores with a common language. In: Gestion de Donnés – Principes Technologies et Applications (BDA) (2014)
21. Oracle Corporation: Java Platform, Standard Edition API Specification, 8th edn.
22. QOS.ch: Logback Project, http://logback.qos.ch
23. QOS.ch: Simple Logging Facade for Java (SLF4J), http://www.slf4j.org
24. Reynolds, P., Killian, C., Wiener, J.L., Mogul, J.C., Shah, M.A., Vahdat, A.: Pip: Detecting the unexpected in distributed systems. In: Proceedings of the 3rd Conference on Networked Systems Design & Implementation, NSDI 2006, vol. 3, p. 9. USENIX Association, Berkeley (2006),
    http://dl.acm.org/citation.cfm?id=1267680.1267689
25. Sang, B., Zhan, J., Lu, G., Wang, H., Xu, D., Wang, L., Zhang, Z., Jia, Z.: Precise, scalable, and online request tracing for multitier services of black boxes. IEEE Transactions on Parallel and Distributed Systems 23(6), 1159–1167 (2012)
26. Stonebraker, M.: Technical perspective: One size fits all: An idea whose time has come and gone. Commun. ACM 51(12), 76 (2008),
    http://doi.acm.org/10.1145/1409360.1409379
27. The PostgreSQL Global Development Group: PostgreSQL Documentation 9.4: EXPLAIN, http://www.postgresql.org/docs/9.4/static/sql-explain.html

Dynamic Message Processing and Transactional Memory in the Actor Model

Yaroslav Hayduk$^{(\boxtimes)}$, Anita Sobe$^{(\boxtimes)}$, and Pascal Felber$^{(\boxtimes)}$

University of Neuchatel, Switzerland
{yaroslav.hayduk,anita.sobe,pascal.felber}@unine.ch

Abstract. With the trend of ever growing data centers and scaling core counts, simple programming models for efficient distributed and concurrent programming are required. One of the successful principles for scalable computing is the actor model, which is based on message passing. Actors are objects that hold local state that can only be modified by the exchange of messages. To avoid typical concurrency hazards, each actor processes messages sequentially. However, this limits the scalability of the model. We have shown in former work that concurrent message processing can be implemented with the help of transactional memory, ensuring sequential processing, when required. This approach is advantageous in low contention phases, however, does not scale for high contention phases. In this paper we introduce a combination of dynamic resource allocation and non-transactional message processing to overcome this limitation. This allows for efficient resource utilization as these two mechanisms can be handled in parallel. We show that we can substantially reduce the execution time of high-contention workloads in a micro-benchmark as well as in a real-world application.

1 Introduction

Recent scaling trends lead to ever growing data centers and cloud computing is gaining attention. Further, the scaling trends at the CPU level let us expect increasing core counts in the following years. This causes limitations of performance gains as it is difficult to program distributed and concurrent applications efficiently. The current methods using shared memory do not keep up with the hardware scaling trends and might need to be abandoned. The actor model, initially proposed by Hewitt [1], is a successful message passing approach that has been integrated into popular local and distributed frameworks [2]. An actor is an independent, asynchronous object with an encapsulated state that can only be modified locally based on the exchange of messages. Received messages are processed sequentially avoiding the necessity of locks. With increasing numbers of actors the model is inherently parallel. To sum up, the actor model introduces desirable properties such as encapsulation, fair scheduling, location transparency, and data consistency to the programmer.

While the data consistency property of the actor model is important for preserving application safety, it is arguably too conservative in concurrent settings

A. Bessani and S. Bouchenak (Eds.): DAIS 2015, LNCS 9038, pp. 94–107, 2015.
DOI: 10.1007/978-3-319-19129-4_8

as it enforces sequential processing of messages, which limits throughput and hence scalability. With sequential processing, access to the state will be suboptimal when operations do not conflict, e.g., modifications to disjoint parts of the state and multiple read operations.

In previous work [3], we improved the message processing performance of the actor model while being faithful to its semantics. Our key idea was to use transactional memory (TM) to process messages in an actor concurrently as if they were processed sequentially. TM provides automatic conflict resolution by aborting and restarting transactions when required. However, we noticed that in cases of high contention, the performance of parallel processing dropped close to or even below the performance of sequential processing. To improve the performance of such high contention workloads, we propose to parallelize the processing of messages in a transactional context with messages that can run in a non-transactional context.

First, we determine the optimal number of threads that execute transactional operations as the performance of an application is dependent on the level of concurrency [4], [5]. To avoid high rollback counts in high contention phases fewer threads are desired. In contrast to low contention phases where the number of threads can be increased. Second, we extract messages for which we can relax the atomicity and isolation and process them as non-transactional messages.

Much of the contention in our tests was caused by read-only operations on TM objects [3]. Rollbacks could be avoided by relaxing the semantics of read operations such as proposed by Herlihy et al. [6] who introduced *early release*, which allows to delete entries from the read set. Another way is to suspend the current transaction temporarily, which is called *Escape Action* [7]. These approaches are only partly realized in current STMs such as the Scala STM (based on CCSTM [8]). Scala STM uses *Ref* objects to manage and isolate the transactional state. The Ref object does not permit accessing its internal state in a non-transactional context. Instead, Scala STM provides an *unrecorded read* facility, in which the transactional read does not create an entry in the read set but bundles all meta-data in an object. At commit time the automatic validity check is omitted, but may be done by the caller manually. However, in the presence of concurrent writes on the same value, the unrecorded read might cause conflicts and hence performance would degrade. Our proposal is to break the isolation guarantees of the Ref object in specific cases, i.e., if we limit the reads to specific isolated values, we can omit using the unrecorded read and grant direct access. By using direct access for a number of scenarios in the context of the actor model, we can process a substantial amount of read-only messages while not conflicting with messages processed in regular transactions (TM messages).

Possible candidates for such read-only operations can accept inconsistencies while not interrupting with transactional states. Examples are operations that can be used to make heuristic decisions, or operations that are known to be safe because of algorithm-specific knowledge. Furthermore, debugging and logging the current state in long-running applications are candidates for read-only operations.

The read-only and the TM messages may require different levels of concurrency. Following this observation, during high contention phases, we reduce the number of threads processing regular TM messages, which in turn allows us to increase the number of threads processing read-only messages. By handling these two message types separately (i.e., providing a separate queue for each of the message types) we can optimally use all available resources. We show the applicability of our approach by using a micro-benchmark and a real-world application.

This paper is organized as follows: In Section 2 we give an overview on related work. In Section 3 we introduce the basics of our former work and in Section 4 we discuss the proposed extensions. The benchmarks are described and evaluated in Section 5. Finally, we conclude our paper.

2   Background and Related Work

Actor models are inherently concurrent. They are widely used for implementing parallel, distributed, and mobile systems. An actor is an independent, asynchronous object with an encapsulated state that can only be modified locally based on the exchange of messages. It comprises a mailbox in which messages can be queued, as well as a set of dedicated methods for message processing [9].

The actor model provides *macro-step semantics* [10] by processing messages sequentially. As a consequence, it also guarantees the following properties:

Atomicity. The state of an actor can only be observed before or after operations took place, therefore changes on the state are perceived either all at once or not at all.

Isolation. The actor model forbids any concurrent access to the local state of an actor. This means that any operation on the state of the actor is done as if it were running alone in the system.

These characteristics make actor models particularly attractive and contribute to their popularity. Numerous implementations of actor models exist in popular languages like Java, C, C++, and Python. We decided to use Scala, which is a general-purpose language that runs on top of the JVM and combines functional and object-oriented programming patterns. The recent versions of Scala integrate the Akka Framework [11] for implementing actors. Scala also supports transactional memory (TM) [12], a programming model that provides atomicity, isolation, and rollback capabilities within transactional code regions [13]. TM provides built-in support for checkpointing and rollback, which we exploit for controlling concurrent message processing. Existing actor frameworks such as those surveyed by Karmani et al. in [2] do not include TM and differ regarding the way they handle parallelism. As an example, implementations of Habanero-Scala and Habanero-Java [14] introduce parallelism by mixing the actor model with the fork-join model (*async-finish* model). Actors can start concurrent subtasks (*async* blocks) for the handling of a single message.

When all sub-tasks complete their execution, the actor resumes its operation and can process further messages. While this approach avoids concurrent access to the actor's state, it must be used carefully as it provides no protection against synchronization hazards such as data races and deadlocks.

Parallel actor monitors (PAM) [15] support concurrent processing by scheduling multiple messages in actor queues. Using PAM, the programmer must understand the concurrency patterns within the application and define application-specific schedulers. This may prove particularly challenging for applications where concurrency patterns vary during execution. In contrast, our approach (see Section 4) removes any programmer intervention and automatically allows concurrent executions when possible.

To optimally use the resources and to improve performance, researchers proposed several mechanisms to match the level of concurrency with the current workload. Heiss and Wagner [5] discuss the problem of thrashing in concurrent transactional programs. Thrashing is a phenomenon that takes place in phases of high contention in which it is likely that the throughput suddenly drops. They propose three ways to avoid thrashing. First, they propose to set an upper bound that sets the maximum number of concurrent transactions; second, they propose to use analytical models for preventing high contention phases; and third, they propose to monitor the current load and decide dynamically on the best level of concurrency. The last approach is seen as a dynamic optimization problem that considers the relationship of concurrency level and throughput. Similarly, Didona et al. [4] propose to dynamically adjust the level of concurrency according to the number of commits and aborts. The optimal number of threads is found with the help of two phases: (1) measurement phase and (2) decision phase. In the first phase the application is profiled with a fixed number of threads, in the second phase a hill-climbing approach is applied to increase and decrease the number of threads according to the given workload, maximizing the transaction's throughput based on successful commits. While the basic idea is interesting, the variation of the thread count based on the throughput might be disadvantageous for transactions with different granularity.

3   Concurrent Message Processing

To motivate our proposed work, we relate to the enhancements of the Actor Model as presented in our former work [3]. There, we reduced the execution time without violating the main characteristics of the Actor Model. Our main idea was based on the observation that we can guarantee atomicity and isolation if we encapsulate the handling of messages inside transactions. Thanks to the rollback and restart capability of transactions, several messages can be processed concurrently, even if they access the same state. The concurrent message processing only changes the message handling provided by the Akka framework as integrated in Scala 2.10.0. Specifically, we altered the behavior of the actor's mailbox processing code. In the original Akka implementation a dispatcher is responsible for ensuring that the same mailbox is not scheduled for processing messages more than once at a given time. We adapted the dispatcher to assign each message processing to a thread of the thread pool. Further, each message

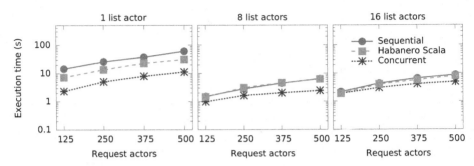

Fig. 1. Concurrent message processing in a read-dominated workload within a shared linked list

processing is handled in a transaction for which we use the default Scala STM. Our work performed well for read-dominated as well as write-dominated workloads and we outperformed the state-of-the-art Habanero Scala [14] in their distributed list benchmark shared amongst list actors with 97% of reads, 2% writes and 1% sum operations created by request actors. Figure 1 shows performance improvements over sequential processing and Habanero Scala for all numbers of list actors in a shared linked list. On the x-axis we show the effects of increasing the number of request actors (125-500), while the y-axis displays the execution time in seconds (log scale), i.e., the time needed to finish processing all requests. The lower the execution time, the better. A higher number of list actors also leads to higher contention, increased rollback counts and hence decreased performance. With 16 list actors, concurrent processing as well as Habanero Scala perform close to sequential processing.

4   Dynamic Concurrent Message Processing

For improving the performance in high contention workloads we propose the following combination of methods. First, we adapt the level of concurrency for processing actor messages according to the current contention level. Second, we extract read-only message processing from the transactional context. And third, we exploit the fact that the two types of messages do not interfere and occupy the existing threads with both types of messages according to the current contention level. As a result, we occupy all threads with work. To differentiate between these two types of messages, we adapted the concurrent mailbox implementation in Akka (as part of Scala 2.10) to handle two different queues as shown in Figure 2. One queue collects the messages to be processed in a transactional context (STM messages), and another one for the processing of read-only messages. We further adapted the actor message dispatcher such that it picks messages from both queues and forwards them for processing to the thread pool. Our new dispatcher automatically adapts the number of STM messages and read-only messages to be processed according to the current contention of the workload. The detailed principles of processing STM messages and read-only messages are described in the following sections.

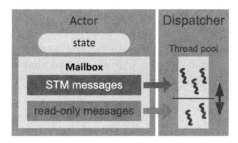

Fig. 2. The different handling of STM messages and read-only messages. Dispatcher assigns a dynamic number of threads for message processing.

4.1 STM Message Processing

At the beginning of an application we start from a random number of threads from the thread pool to process transactional messages (STM messages) and then, driven by a predefined threshold α, the level of concurrency is adapted. The dispatcher assigns the rest of the threads to process read-only messages. α is dependent on the knowledge of the current number of commits and rollbacks of transactionally processed messages and their ratio. Instead of focusing on the throughput such as Didona et al. [4], we are able to support transactions of any granularity by steering α with the commit-to-rollback ratio. If the current commit-to-rollback ratio is lower than α, we divide the number of threads processing transactional messages by two; if it is higher, we multiply them by two. We chose the commit-to-rollback ratio in combination with the fixed α threshold due to its simplicity. To find the right α value for the current workload, we consider a short profiling phase monitoring the relation of commits and rollbacks.

4.2 Read-only Message Processing

The second category of messages are read-only messages. They are handled in a separate queue from the messages that require TM context. Scala STM [16] is based on CCSTM [8] (which extends SwissTM [17]). It is a write-back TM, where writes are cached and written to the memory on commit. Further, it provides eager conflict detection for writes and lazy conflict detection for reads. Validation is done based on a global time stamp. In Scala STM transactional objects are encapsulated in so-called *Refs*. This implies that any access to a transactional object has to be within an atomic block, which ensures strong atomicity and isolation.

We argue that in some cases we can relax isolation, e.g., for performing approximate read-only operations. A ubiquitous example is a sequential data structure such as a linked list. While traversing the list in read-only mode, a concurrent write of a value, which has been already read, causes a conflict. For such cases, Scala STM provides a mechanism called *unrecorded read*. An unrecorded read is a transactional read, which returns an `UnrecordedRead` object containing the value, the version number before read, and a validity field of the read. The validity field returns true when there were no changes to the value, which helps to resolve the ABA problem [8].

In Scala STM the unrecorded read can be accessed through calling the *relaxedGet* method. By using it, we can perform a read that will not be validated during commit. The *relaxedGet* method has to be executed inside of an atomic block:

```
atomic{
    val unvalidatedValue = ref.relaxedGet({(_,_) => true})
}
```

Unrecorded reads do not yield new entries in the read set, but still need to ensure reading the latest version of a TM object. Scala STM checks for concurrent writes and forces eager conflict detection, which, in turn, causes a rollback of the writing transaction. As we see later this resolution strategy leads to similar runtime behavior as of the regular transactions.

To remove the overhead associated with unrecorded reads, we propose to provide direct access to the Ref object's data (which is safely possible due to the write-back characteristic of Scala STM). We extended Scala STM's Ref implementation with a *singleRelaxedGet* method and provide an example for generic references below.

```
class GenericRef[A](@volatile var data: A) extends BaseRef[A] {
    ...
    def singleRelaxedGet(): A = data
}
```

Its usage is then straightforward as shown in the next example:

```
val relaxedValue = ref.singleRelaxedGet()
```

As the *data* variable in *GenericRef* is marked as *volatile*, the *singleRelaxedGet* read-only operation can therefore safely interleave with other transactional write operations while guaranteeing to see the latest result. Moreover, *singleRelaxedGet* does not interfere with other transactional operations, i.e., it cannot force another transaction to roll back.

5   Evaluation

Our optimizations are expected to be most useful in applications where state is shared among many actors. Hence, to evaluate our approach, we use a benchmark application provided by Imam and Sarkar [14] that implements a stateful distributed sorted integer linked-list. It is the same benchmark as in our former work and shown in Section 3 in comparison to Habanero Scala. This benchmark is relevant as sequential data structures are typical applications for relaxed atomicity and isolation (see, e.g., *early release*). The read-only operation is a non-consistent sum that traverses each list element.

To show wider applicability we also consider a real-world scientific application that is used to simulate the hydraulic subsurface. The read-only operations in this application are used to control progress and debugging and hence should not interfere with any regular operation.

The thread pool is configured to support two scenarios. First, we specify a static ratio, in which 90% of threads are assigned to process STM messages and the rest processes read-only messages. In the second case we consider a dynamic ratio, but ensure that the number of threads assigned to process any message type never drops below the ratio of 10%. We compare the performance of our proposed *singleRelaxedGet* to the default *atomic* block and the *relaxedGet* method provided by Scala STM.

We execute the benchmarks on a 48-core machine equipped with four 12-core AMD Opteron 6172 CPUs running at 2.1GHz. Each core has private L1 and L2 caches and a shared L3 cache. The sizes of both instruction and data caches are 64KB at L1, 512KB at L2, and 5MB at L3.

5.1   List Benchmark

The list benchmark comprises two actor types: *request* and *list* actors. Request actors send requests such as *lookup*, *insert*, *remove*, and *sum*. List actors are responsible for handling a range of values (buckets) of a distributed linked list. We implemented a list element as an object containing a *value* field and a *next* field, which is wrapped in a Scala STM Ref object.

In a list with l list actors, where each actor stores at most n elements representing consecutive integer values, the ith list actor is responsible for elements in the $[(i-1) \cdot n, (i \cdot n) - 1]$ range, e.g., in a list with 4 actors and 8 entries in total, each actor is responsible for two values. A request forwarder matches the responsible list actors with the incoming requests. For the *sum* operation, we traverse each list element in every list actor. This operation is read-only and does not necessarily report a consistent value. It should not conflict with other accesses to the list.

We run the benchmark with 32 threads (to be able to divide and multiply the thread count by two) in 7 runs from which we take the median throughput and number of rollbacks for the results. Also, we create 8 list actors that are in responsible for 41,216 list elements. We create 500 request actors, where each actor sends 1,000 messages to the list. After each of the request actors finished their 1,000 requests the benchmark terminates.

To read a value from the list, we consider three different options: (1) the regular transactional read (*node.next.get()*), (2) the unrecorded read accessed via (*node.next.relaxedGet()*) and (3) our direct access (*node.next.singleRelaxedGet()*) method.

In our experiments we consider a write-dominated and a mixed workload. The write-dominated workload is configured as follows: Each request actor sends 98% of requests to modify the list (insert or remove), 1% of lookup requests and 1% of sum requests.

In the first experiments, we evaluate the impact of different access approaches to the sum operation if the threads are assigned statically. The static approach (90% STM:10% read-only) reserves 3 threads (10%) for the processing of read-only messages and 29 threads (90%) for processing STM messages. Figure 4 demonstrates the message throughput (left) and the rollback count over time (right). The shorter the line, the better the execution time. The *singleRelaxed-Get()* outperforms the other operations with respect to both, execution time (50%) and throughput (40%). However, we observe a drastic increase of rollbacks (90%). This observation is counter intuitive, as one would expect to have a lower number of rollbacks to achieve higher throughput. In fact, when we use *atomic* and *relaxedGet()* to implement the sum operation, we cause significantly more read-write conflicts. Scala STM resolves them by waiting for the write operations to finish to follow up with the execution of the read operations. On the contrary, when we use the *singleRelaxedGet()* operation, we remove transactional read operations, which increases the likelihood of concurrent write operations. As a result, we get more write-write conflicts, which are typically resolved eagerly by rolling back one of the transactions.

Since the performance of transactional operations can be further improved, we dynamically determine the optimal number of threads as described in Section 4.1. We schedule a thread, which obtains the total number of commits and rollbacks every second, and decides the optimal number of threads to schedule for the processing of STM and read-only messages. Initially, the thread counts are randomly chosen and within the first two seconds the number of threads converges to the optimal values with the help of α. For determining α we profile the application for a short time. In the case of the list benchmark this results in $\alpha = 0.21$, hence if the commit-to-rollback ratio is below α the number of threads will be reduced else increased (multiplied or divided by two).

In Figure 4 we see that the throughput and rollback values for the *atomic* and *relaxedGet()* operations are not significantly different when compared to the static approach. This behavior is expected as the operations interfere with the concurrently executing transactional write operations. This causes more contention as both the STM messages and the read-only messages are conflicting.

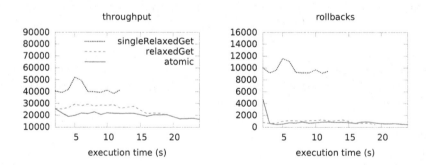

Fig. 3. Throughput (left) and rollback count (right) for the list write-dominated workload: static thread allocation

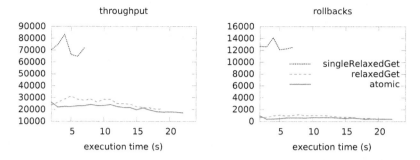

Fig. 4. Throughput (left) and rollback count (right) for the list write-dominated workload: dynamic thread allocation

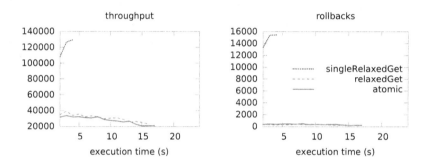

Fig. 5. Throughput (left) and rollback count (right) for the list mixed workload: static thread allocation

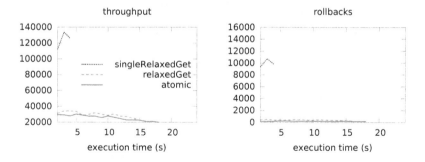

Fig. 6. Throughput (left) and rollback count (right) for the list mixed workload: dynamic thread allocation

On the contrary, the *singleRelaxedGet()* operation never conflicts with other list operations. Hence, we can efficiently use the threads not processing STM messages resulting in increased throughput (65%) and reduced runtime (70%).

In the mixed read-write workload, consisting of 50% of requests to modify the list, 49% lookup requests and 1% sum requests, we show the applicability of

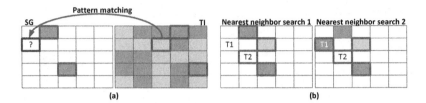

Fig. 7. (a) Matching SG point with the same pattern in the TI. (b) Two possibilities of closest neighbor pattern with probable invalidation of the closest neighbor selection if T1 finishes before T2.

singleRelaxedGet in a more read-dominant scenario. With the help of a profiling phase, we set α to 0.08. Figures 5 and 6 show similar results as the write-dominated list benchmark, amplifying the benefits of *singleRelaxedGet*. The dynamic thread assignment further reduces the rollback counts in comparison to the static assignment. In order to compare to Figure 1 the request ratio has to be increased, leading to results below 1 second for the *singleRelaxedGet*. It would hence clearly outperform the default implementation of Habanero Scala.

5.2 Simulation of the Hydraulic Subsurface

The aim of multiple-point geostatistical simulations is to simulate the hydraulic properties of the subsurface. A number of techniques has been developed for executing the simulation, the most popular of them is multiple-point geostatistics [18], which analyzes the relationship between multiple variables in several locations at a time. For its implementation, we can use the Direct Sampling simulation introduced by Mariethoz et al [19]. A simulation consists of a Training Image (TI) and a Simulation Grid (SG). The task is to fill unknown points of the simulation grid according to the known points from the training image (see Figure 7(a)). The algorithm starts with selecting a random point x to be filled in the SG. Then, it locates n closest neighbors, which are already filled. The neighbors and x are considered as a pattern, for which the algorithm searches in the TI. If found, x can be filled.

Given that in the field of hydraulic subsurface simulation the simulation grid and the training image are of a very large size, sequential processing is not efficient. Two cases of parallelization are possible: (1) the parallelization of searching within the training image, (2) the parallelization of the node filling within the simulation grid. In this paper we concentrate on the parallelization of the node filling within the SG as parallelizing the TI would only comprise independent read operations. Our implementation of the actor-based simulation considers a *main actor* that stores the SG and the TI. Consider Figure 7(b) having two points $T1$ and $T2$ to be simulated concurrently. We can see that these are close and if simulated, are likely to be part of the n closest neighbor pattern. Thus, the point that finishes first invalidates the current simulation of the other point and a synchronization mechanism is required. In our implementation, all SG points are protected by a Scala STM Ref object, which causes a rollback once a SG point is simulated that has been visited during a nearest neighbor search. Besides the main actor we implemented a number of worker actors, either simulating the SG points (*simulation actors*) or responsible for logging the current state (*log actors*). *Simulation actors* claim a number of points to be simulated and initiate the closest neighbor search and the TI matching for each of the points at the *main actor*. We run the benchmark with 32 *worker actors*, with each *simulation actor* requesting to process 30 simulation points at once, finally sending 167 messages during the benchmark.

Researchers using the multiple-point geostatistics simulation usually validate the results manually by visualizing the simulated result. Since the simulation can take several hours, intermediate results are of interest; we can use them to see whether the simulation is on the right track. This case is especially of interest, because once the points are simulated, they do not change anymore. Therefore, these intermediate results do not require full consistency and should not interfere with the main simulation. We select these messages to be handled as read-only messages sent by *log actors*. The list benchmark considered a constant number of sum messages while here, each *log actor* sends a request to the *main actor*, repeating it upon receiving a response. In the experiments we consider 8 *log actors*. The size of the SG is 750 times 750 elements and we investigate the 15 closest neighbors for each point, finally we profiled $\alpha = 1.2$. We use the sample image provided by the MPDS [19] distribution as the TI.

As shown in Figure 8 the static thread allocation results for throughput suggest that it is possible to increase the number of processed query messages with the help of *singleRelaxedGet*, while reducing the execution time in comparison to the *atomic* case by approximately 40 seconds. The total number of rollbacks, however, remains stable. Figure 9 (left) demonstrates that the dynamic thread allocation improves the execution time of the *singleRelaxedGet* by another 20 seconds. The throughput seems to decrease in comparison to the static scenario, which is not true considering the total throughput. While the amount of work performed is in both scenarios the same, we are able to successfully process more messages in the period of second 20-50 in the dynamic scenario. This can be seen

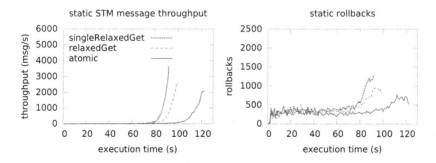

Fig. 8. Throughput (left) and rollbacks (right) of STM messages and read-only messages over time: static thread allocation

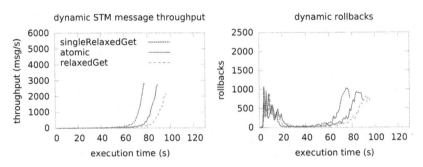

Fig. 9. Throughput (left) and rollbacks (right) of STM messages and read-only messages over time: dynamic thread allocation

by the low rollback counts shown in Figure 9 (right) for the same period. In the beginning of the execution, however, the rollback counts reflect the effects of adjusting the concurrency level. In total the dynamic scenario results in lower rollback counts than the static scenario. In all of the cases *singleRelaxedGet* in combination with the dynamic handling of STM messages is able to outperform concurrent message processing.

6   Conclusions

In this paper we introduce dynamic concurrent message processing in the actor model for high contention workloads. We propose to extract read-only messages from the transactional context if consistency is not required as well as adapt the number of threads to the workload. By handling transactional messages with a different level of concurrency we can efficiently use the remaining resources (threads in a thread pool) for processing read-only messages. We showed the applicability of our approach as well as candidates for messages processed with relaxed consistency. In a list benchmark and a real-world application we demonstrated that our approach helps reducing the execution time, while also decreasing the rollback counts. In future work we target to improve the performance by introducing a learning phase (e.g., with the help of hill-climbing) for guiding the level of concurrency.

Acknowledgement. The research leading to these results has received funding from the European Community's Seventh Framework Programme [FP7/2007-2013] under the ParaDIME Project (www.paradime-project.eu), grant agreement no 318693.

References

1. Hewitt, C., Bishop, P., Steiger, R.: A universal modular actor formalism for artificial intelligence. In: International Joint Conference on Artificial Intelligence (IJCAI), pp. 235–245 (1973)

2. Karmani, R.K., Shali, A., Agha, G.: Actor frameworks for the jvm platform: A comparative analysis. In: International Conference on Principles and Practice of Programming in Java (PPPJ), pp. 11–20 (2009)
3. Hayduk, Y., Sobe, A., Harmanci, D., Marlier, P., Felber, P.: Speculative concurrent processing with transactional memory in the actor model. In: Baldoni, R., Nisse, N., van Steen, M. (eds.) OPODIS 2013. LNCS, vol. 8304, pp. 160–175. Springer, Heidelberg (2013)
4. Didona, D., Felber, P., Harmanci, D., Romano, P., Schenker, J.: Identifying the optimal level of parallelism in transactional memory systems. In: Gramoli, V., Guerraoui, R. (eds.) NETYS 2013. LNCS, vol. 7853, pp. 233–247. Springer, Heidelberg (2013)
5. Heiss, H.U., Wagner, R.: Adaptive load control in transaction processing systems. Universität Karlsruhe (1991)
6. Herlihy, M., Luchangco, V., Moir, M., Scherer III, W.N.: Software transactional memory for dynamic-sized data structures. In: Annual Symposium on Principles of Distributed Computing (PODC), pp. 92–101. ACM (2003)
7. Moravan, M.J., Bobba, J., Moore, K.E., Yen, L., Hill, M.D., Liblit, B., Swift, M.M., Wood, D.A.: Supporting nested transactional memory in logtm. ACM SIGPLAN Notices 41(11), 359–370 (2006)
8. Bronson, N.G., Chafi, H., Olukotun, K.: CCSTM: A library-based STM for Scala. In: Annual Scala Workshop at Scala Days (2010)
9. Agha, G.A., Mason, I.A., Smith, S.F., Talcott, C.L.: A foundation for actor computation. Journal of Functional Programming, Cambridge University Press 7(1), 1–72 (1997)
10. Karmani, R.K., Agha, G.: Actors. In: Padua, D. (ed.) Encyclopedia of Parallel Computing, pp. 1–11. Springer (2011)
11. Haller, P.: On the integration of the actor model in mainstream technologies: A Scala perspective. In: Programming Systems, Languages and Applications based on Actors, Agents, and Decentralized Control Abstractions (AGERE), pp. 1–6 (2012)
12. Goodman, D., Khan, B., Khan, S., Luján, M., Watson, I.: Software transactional memories for scala. Journal of Parallel and Distributed Computing, Elsevier 73(2), 150–163 (2013)
13. Harris, T., Larus, J., Rajwar, R.: Transactional Memory. 2nd edn. Morgan and Claypool Publishers (2010)
14. Imam, S.M., Sarkar, V.: Integrating task parallelism with actors. In: International Conference on Object Oriented Programming Systems Languages and Applications (OOPSLA), pp. 753–772. ACM (2012)
15. Scholliers, C., Tanter, E., Meuter, W.D.: Parallel actor monitors. In: Brazilian Symposium on Programming Languages (SBLP) (2010)
16. ScalaSTM, http://nbronson.github.com/scala-stm/
17. Dragojević, A., Guerraoui, R., Kapalka, M.: Stretching transactional memory. ACM Sigplan Notices 44(6), 155–165 (2009)
18. Guardiano, F.B., Srivastava, R.M.: Multivariate geostatistics: Beyond bivariate moments. Geostatistics Tróia 1, 133–144 (1993)
19. Mariethoz, G., Renard, P., Straubhaar, J.: The Direct Sampling method to perform multiple-point geostatistical simulations. Water Resources Research, American Geophysical Union 46(11), 1–14 (2010)

Heterogeneous Resource Selection
for Arbitrary HPC Applications in the Cloud

Anca Iordache[✉], Eliya Buyukkaya, and Guillaume Pierre

IRISA - University of Rennes 1, 35000 Rennes, France
{ancuta.iordache,guillaume.pierre}@irisa.fr

Abstract. Cloud infrastructures offer a wide variety of resources to choose from. However, most cloud users ignore the potential benefits of dynamically choosing cloud resources among a wide variety of VM instance types with different configuration/cost tradeoffs. We propose to automate the choice of resources that should be assigned to arbitrary non-interactive applications. During the first executions of the application, the system tries various resource configurations and builds a custom performance model for this application. Thereafter, cloud users can specify their execution time or financial cost constraints, and let the system automatically select the resources which best satisfy this constraint.

1 Introduction

Cloud computing offers unprecedented levels of flexibility to efficiently deploy demanding applications. Cloud users have access to a large variety of computing resources with various combinations of configurations and prices. This allows them in principle to use the exact type and number of resources their application needs. However, this flexibility also comes as a curse as choosing the best resource configuration for an application becomes extremely difficult: cloud users often find it very hard to accurately estimate the requirements of complex applications [1].

Most cloud applications are either long-running service-oriented applications, or batch jobs which perform a computation with no user interaction during execution. Batch applications may use frameworks such as MapReduce, or simply behave as blackboxes executing arbitrary operations. Although frameworks such as Elastic MapReduce allow users to dynamically vary the number of resources assigned to a computation [2,3], other types of HPC applications require that the resource configuration must be chosen prior to execution – and kept unchanged during the entire computation.

Selecting the "right" set of resources for an arbitrary application requires a detailed understanding of the relationship between resource specifications and the performance the application will have using these resources. This is hard because the space of all possible resource configurations one may choose from can be extremely large. For example, Amazon EC2 currently offers 29 different instance types. An application requiring just five nodes must therefore choose one out of $29^5 = 20,511,149$ possible configurations.

Furthermore, users' expectations may be more complex than executing the application as fast as possible: the fastest execution may require expensive resources. Depending on the circumstances, a user may therefore want to choose

A. Bessani and S. Bouchenak (Eds.): DAIS 2015, LNCS 9038, pp. 108–123, 2015.
DOI: 10.1007/978-3-319-19129-4_9

the fastest option, the cheapest, or any option implementing a tradeoff between these two extremes.

We propose to automate the choice of resources that should be assigned to arbitrary non-interactive applications that get executed repeatedly. Upon the first few executions of the application, the system tries a different resource configuration for each execution. It then uses the resulting execution times and costs to build a custom performance model for the concerned application. After this phase, users can simply specify the execution time or the financial cost they can tolerate for each execution, and let the system automatically find the resource configuration which best satisfies this constraint.

The system indifferently supports single– and multithreaded applications built around frameworks such as MPI and OpenMP. Its only assumption is that the execution time and cost are independent from the application's input. Although slightly limiting, this assumption is met in a number of HPC applications which are optimized to perform high-volume, repetitive tasks where successive executions process inputs with the same size and runtime behavior. This is the case in particular of the two real-world applications we use in our evaluations (one in the domain of oil exploration, the other in the domain of high-performance database maintenance).

Allowing the automatic selection of computing resources for arbitrary batch cloud applications requires one to address a number of challenges. First, we need to describe arbitrary applications in such a way that a generic application manager can automate the choice of resources that the application may use. Second, we need an efficient search strategy to quickly identify the resource configurations that should be tested. Finally, we need to generate performance models that easily allow one to choose resources according to the performance/cost expectations of the users.

We propose four configuration selection strategies respectively based on uniform search of the configuration space, resource utilization optimization, simulated annealing and a resource utilization-driven simulated annealing. Evaluations show that the latter strategy identifies interesting configurations faster than the others.

Section 2 discusses related work. Section 3 shows how to abstract arbitrary applications in a single generic framework. Sections 4, 5 and 6 respectively present the system architecture, its profiling strategies, and their evaluation. Finally, Section 7 concludes.

2   Related Work

In HPC, most performance modeling techniques can be classified into analytical predictive methods, code analysis or profiling [4,5]. Analytical methods require developers to provide a model of their application. They can be very accurate, but building good models is labor-intensive and hard to automate. Moreover, user estimates of application runtimes are often highly inaccurate [1]. Code analysis automates this process, but it usually restricts itself to coarse-grained decisions such as the choice of the best acceleration device for optimizing performance [6].

In cloud environments, performance modeling was studied for specific types of applications such as Web applications. Besides the numerous techniques which dynamically vary the number of identically-configured resources to follow the request workload, one can use machine learning techniques over historical traces in order to define horizontal and vertical scaling rules to handle various types of workloads [7]. Similarly, when scaling decisions are necessary, one may dynamically choose the best resource type based on short-term traffic predictions [8]. Some other works exploit the fact that identically-configured cloud resources often exhibit heterogeneous performance [9]. For instance, one can benchmark the performance of each individual virtual machine instance before deciding how it can best be used in the application [10,11].

Performance modeling has been addressed for specific types of scientific applications. For bags-of-tasks applications, one can observe the statistical distribution of task execution times, and automatically derive task scheduling strategies to execute the bag under certain time and cost constraints [12]. Similar work has also been realized for MapReduce applications [13,14].

For arbitrary HPC applications which do not fit the MapReduce or the bags-of-tasks models, the only solution currently proposed by Amazon EC2 is to empirically try a variety of instance types and choose the one which works best [15]. CopperEgg automates this process by monitoring the resource usage of an arbitrary application over a 24-hour period before suggesting an appropriate instance type to support this workload [16]. However, as we shall see in Section 6, utilization-based methodologies do not necessarily lead to optimal results. Besides, CopperEgg does not allow the user to choose her preferred optimization criterion. Our work, in contrast, aims at finding Pareto-optimal configurations for arbitrary batch applications, and it supports the automatic selection of resources which match a given optimization criterion.

3   Handling Arbitrary Applications

Each time a user wants to launch the application, she provides a Service-Level Objective (SLO) taking one of two forms: either impose a maximum execution cost while requesting to execute as fast as possible; or impose a maximum execution time while minimizing the cost of the execution. The system is in charge of automatically selecting the resource configuration which best satisfies this SLO.

To allow a generic application manager to handle arbitrary batch applications, each SLO file contains a link to an *Application Manifest* which describes the application's structure and the type of resources it depends on to execute correctly. The manifest is typically written by the application developer.

Figure 1 shows a simple example which describes the types of resources an application needs, with their number, configuration and role. The *Configuration* attribute describes the properties that resources may have. A computing resource may thus for example specify a number of cores and memory size, while a storage resource may describe properties such as the disk size and supported IOPS. Each field may specify either a fixed value, or a set of acceptable values to choose from.

We do not specify the network capacity between provisioned machine instances in our manifests, as current clouds do not allow a user to specify such

```
ApplicationName: HelloWorld
...
Resources {
  Resource₁ (
    Type:        Virtual Machine
    Role:        Worker
    Number:      1
    Configuration: {
      Cores:   {1..16}
      Memory:  {2,4,6,8,12,
      16,24,48,64,96,124}
    }), ...
}
```

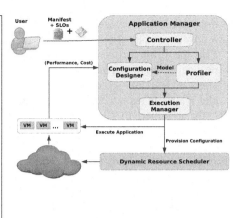

Fig. 1. Application Manifest Example   **Fig. 2.** System Overview

properties [1]. A logical extension of this work would be to also specify available bandwidth between resources, provided that the underlying cloud can take such requests into account.

Finally, one can assign a *Role* to a resource. This allows us to describe applications with multiple components potentially having specific requirements. For example, a master/slave application may separately describe *Master* and *Slave* resources.

4   System Model

This section introduces our system model supporting the automatic management of batch applications under user objectives. In the following, we explain the architecture of our system and the profiling policies we employ.

4.1   Architecture

Our system architecture is depicted in Figure 2. A user triggers an execution of the application by submitting an SLO and its associated manifest file to the application manager.

The application manager is an application-agnostic component in charge of choosing and provisioning the resource configurations, deploying and executing the application and of measuring the execution time and implied cost. Initially, it has no knowledge about the types of resources it should choose for a newly-submitted application. After loading the manifest file, in case no performance model is specified, the *Controller* forwards the application to the *Profiler* which executes the application repeatedly using a different resource configuration every time. Note that it is important for our system that execution times should be

---

[1] Amazon EC2 lets users choose a network performance level among 'Low', 'Moderate', 'High' and '10 Gigabit.' However, these qualifiers do not imply any clear guarantees on the resulting available bandwidth.

as deterministic as possible. We therefore need to rely on the cloud to minimize interferences with other co-located instances.

This profiling process continues until either a predefined number of executions has been performed or a profiling budget has been exceeded. The result of these executions (cost and execution time) is used to build a performance model which is sent to the *Configuration Designer*. If a performance model was already specified in the manifest, the *Controller* skips the *Profiler* and sends the application and its model directly to the *Configuration Designer*. Based on this model, the *Configuration Designer* then selects a configuration that satisfies the SLO and launches the execution. In both cases, the execution is handled by the *Execution Manager* which provisions the configuration through a *Dynamic Resource Scheduler* and finally executes the application on it.

Each time an application execution is performed, the system monitors its total execution time and cost, and derives a relation between them and the resource configuration. Failed executions due to a cloud failure are re-launched on identical configured resources while executions failed due to unmet application requirements are assigned a very high execution time/cost, making them unselectable in the future.

The results generated after several executions with various resource configurations can be plotted as shown in Figure 3(a). Each point represents the execution time and cost that are incurred by one particular resource configuration. The figure shows the result of an exhaustive exploration of a search space with 176 possible configurations. In a more challenging scenario the number of configurations would be much greater, and this type of exhaustive exploration would be practically unfeasible.

4.2   Pareto Frontier

It is interesting to notice that not all configurations provide interesting properties. Regardless of the application, a user is always interested in minimizing the execution time, the financial cost, or a trade-off between the two [2].

Figure 3 presents the search space of the "RTM" application used later in the evaluation. Configurations which appear at the top-right of the figure are both slow and expensive. Such configurations can be discarded as soon as we discover another configuration which is both faster and cheaper. The remaining configurations form the *Pareto frontier* of the explored search space. Figure 3(b) highlights the set of Pareto-optimal points of this application: they all implement interesting tradeoffs between performance and cost: points on the top-left represent inexpensive-but-slow configurations, while points on the bottom-right represent fast-but-expensive configurations.

The Pareto frontier (and the set of configurations leading to these points) forms the performance model that the application manager uses to choose configurations satisfying the user's SLOs. If an SLO imposes a maximum execution

---

[2] An interesting extension of this work would be to consider additional evaluation metrics such as carbon footprint. This can be easily done as long as the relevant metrics are designed such that a lower value indicates a better evaluation.

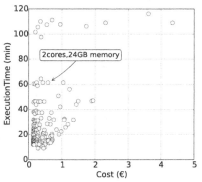 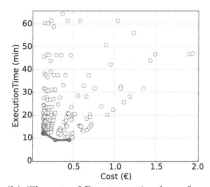

(a) Exhaustive exploration of the resource configuration space

(b) The set of Pareto-optimal configurations is shown in black

Fig. 3. Resource configuration space of the RTM application

time, the system discards the Pareto configurations which are too slow, and selects the cheapest remaining one. Conversely, if the SLO imposes a maximum cost, it discards the Pareto configurations which are too expensive, and selects the fastest remaining one.

4.3 Profiling Policies

Profiling an application requires one to execute it a number of times in order to measure is performance and cost using various resource configurations. This process may be realized in two different ways, depending on the user's preferences:

1. The *offline approach* triggers artificial executions of the application whose only purpose is to generate a performance model. In this case, the output of executions is simply discarded.
2. The *online approach* opportunistically uses the first actual executions requested by the user to try various resource configurations and lazily build a performance model.

Choosing one of these approaches requires the user to make a simple tradeoff. In offline profiling, the user will incur delays and costs of the profiling executions before a performance model has been built. On the other hand, all the subsequent executions will benefit from a complete performance model. In online profiling, although the first executions may not fulfill their SLO until a performance model has been built, the overall marginal cost and delays will be reduced.

5   Performance Profiling

The main issue when building the performance model of an application is that the space of all possible configurations is usually much too large to allow an exhaustive exploration. We therefore need to carefully choose which configurations should be tested, such that we identify the optimal configurations as quickly as possible.

5.1   Search Space

The search space of resource configurations to explore for an application is generated using the application manifest. Each resource parameter which should be chosen by the platform constitutes one dimension of the space. The number of possible configurations therefore increases exponentially as new dimensions are added, an issue often referred to as the curse of dimensionality.

In the example from Figure 1, the search space of the application has 2 dimensions (corresponding to numbers of cores and memory). This creates a total of $16 \times 11 = 176$ possible configurations (due to 16 possible numbers of cores, and 11 possible memory sizes). Within these 176 configurations, only a subset of them may offer interesting tradeoffs between performance and cost.

5.2   Search Strategies

The goal of the profiling process is to search through the space of possible configurations and to quickly identify configurations that implement interesting performance/cost tradeoffs. It aims not only to find the fastest or the cheapest configuration but also configurations which offer interesting tradeoffs between these two extremes.

We define four strategies that can be used to explore a configuration space:

Uniform Search strategy explores stepwise points in the resource search space to select a configuration for the profiling process. As shown in Algorithm 1, the application is executed for all combinations of stepwise resource values (lines 2-5). Although uniform search is extremely simple, it may waste time exploring large areas which are unlikely to deliver interesting performance/cost tradeoffs. In addition, low exploration step values result in high complexity, while using high step values (to decrease the complexity) may skip relevant configurations.

Utilization-Driven strategy is a simplified version of the CopperEgg strategy [16]. It iteratively refines an initial resource configuration by monitoring the resource utilization generated by the application. As shown in Algorithm 2, the algorithm starts with a random resource configuration (lines 1-2), and monitors the utilization of each resource type in configurations (lines 8-9). If a resource is highly used by the application, the algorithm then allocates a higher amount

---

Algorithm 1. Uniform Search

Input: Application A, Resources $R = \{R_1, R_2, ..., R_n\}$
Output: Set of configurations, their execution time and cost $S_{r,t,c}$
1: $S_{r,t,c} \leftarrow \emptyset$
2: **for** $r_1 = min_1$ to max_1 by $step_1$ **do**
3:      **for** $r_2 = min_2$ to max_2 by $step_2$ **do**
4:          ...
5:          **for** $r_n = min_n$ to max_n by $step_n$ **do**
6:              $r \leftarrow \{r_1, r_2, ..., r_n\}$
7:              $(t, c) \leftarrow$ execution time and cost of running A on r
8:              $S_{r,t,c} \leftarrow S_{r,t,c} \cup \{(r, t, c)\}$
9:          ...

Algorithm 2. Utilization-Driven

Input: Application A, Resources $R = \{R_1, R_2, ..., R_n\}$
Output: Set of configurations, their execution time and cost $S_{r,t,c}$
1: $r \leftarrow \{r_1, r_2, ..., r_n\}$ where r_i is a uniform random sample of $R_i \in R$
2: $Q \leftarrow \{r\}$
3: $S_{r,t,c} \leftarrow \emptyset$
4: **while** $Q \neq \emptyset$ **do**
5:     $r \leftarrow$ dequeue(Q)
6:     $(t, c) \leftarrow$ execution time and cost of running A with resource configuration r
7:     $S_{r,t,c} \leftarrow S_{r,t,c} \cup \{(r, t, c)\}$
8:     **for** $i = 1$ to $|R|$ **do**
9:         **if** R_i is over- **or** underutilized **then**
10:            **if** R_i is overutilized **then**
11:                $r_i' \leftarrow$ next value of R_i (value after r_i)
12:            **else if** R_i is underutilized **then**
13:                $r_i' \leftarrow$ previous value of R_i (value before r_i)
14:            $enqueue(Q, \{r_1, r_2, ..., r_i', ..., r_n\})$

---

of this resource in the hope of delivering better performance (lines 10-11). On the other hand, if a resource utilization is low, the algorithm then reduces this resource amount in the hope of reducing resource costs (lines 12-13). Otherwise, it stops its exploration once there is no configuration that neither overuses nor underuses its resources. This strategy is simple and intuitive but, as we shall see later, it may stop prematurely whenever it reaches a local minimum in the search space.

Standard Simulated Annealing (SA) is a well known generic algorithm for global optimization problems [17]. It initially tries a wide variety of configurations, then gradually focuses its search around configurations that were already found to be interesting. To control how many bad configurations are accepted as interesting, it relies on a global time-varying parameter called the temperature.

Algorithm 3 shows the SA routine applied to the resource configurations. The algorithm starts with a random resource configuration (line 1), and explores new configurations in the neighborhood of the current configuration (line 5). The *neighbor()* function determines a new configuration by drawing random values around the current configuration using a normal distribution determined by the temperature. $rate_{learn}$ is a scale constant for adjusting updates and *upper* and *lower* are the parameter r's interval bounds. The temperature decreases gradually (line 10), which means that the algorithm accepts new configurations to explore with slowly decreasing probability (lines 8-10). Due to its convergence to optimal solution in a fixed amount of time, simulated annealing quickly explores the search space, focusing most of its efforts in the "interesting" parts of the search space.

In order for the algorithm to explore configurations that are both cost-efficient and performance-efficient, we evaluate each configuration based on the product between the cost and the execution time it generates. The minimization of the product is guaranteeing the minimization of at least one of them. Using this utility function the algorithm explores the entire Pareto frontier, instead of focusing on optimizing only the execution time or the cost.

Algorithm 3. Standard SA

Input: Application A, Resources R, Temperatures $T_{cooling}$ and $T_{current}$
Output: Set of configurations, their execution time and cost $S_{r,t,c}$
1: $r \leftarrow \{r_1, r_2, ..., r_n\}$, r_i is random value of resource $R_i \in R$
2: $(t, c) \leftarrow$ execution time and cost of running A with resource configuration r
3: $S_{r,t,c} \leftarrow \{(r, t, c)\}$
4: **while** $T_{current} > T_{cooling}$ **do**
5:     $r_{new} \leftarrow neighbor(r, T_{current})$
6:     $(t_{new}, c_{new}) \leftarrow$ execution time and cost of running A with resource configuration r_{new}
7:     $S_{r,t,c} \leftarrow S_{r,t,c} \cup \{(r_{new}, t_{new}, c_{new})\}$
8:     **if** $Probability_{Acceptance}((t, c), (t_{new}, c_{new}), T_{current}) > random()$ **then**
9:         $r, t, c \leftarrow r_{new}, t_{new}, c_{new}$
10:     decrease $T_{current}$

$neighbor(r, T_{current})$

1: $\sigma \leftarrow min(sqrt(T_{current}), (upper - lower)/(3 * rate_{learn}))$
2: $updates \leftarrow random.Normal(0, \sigma, size(r))$
3: $r_{new} \leftarrow r + updates * rate_{learn}$
4: **return** r_{new}

Algorithm 4 $NeighborDirectedSA(r, T_{current})$

1: **if** $Probability_{directed} < random()$ **then**
2:     **for** $i = 1$ to $|R|$ **do**
3:         **if** r_i is over- **or** underutilized **then**
4:             **if** r_i is overutilized **then**
5:                 $\sigma \leftarrow 1 - r_i$
6:                 $r_{new_i} \leftarrow r_i + random.Normal(0, \sigma, 1)$
7:             **else if** r_i is underutilized **then**
8:                 $\sigma \leftarrow r_i$
9:                 $r_{new_i} \leftarrow r_i + random.Normal(0, \sigma, 1)$
10:         **else**
11:             $r_{new_i} \leftarrow r_i$
12:     **if** no update has been done **then**
13:         $r_{new} \leftarrow neighbor(r, T_{current})$
14: **else**
15:     $r_{new} \leftarrow neighbor(r, T_{current})$
16: **return** r_{new}

Directed Simulated Annealing is a variant of the previous algorithm. As shown in Algorithm 4, the difference lies in the implementation of the *neighbor()* function: instead of choosing configurations randomly around the current best one, Directed Simulated Annealing uses resource utilization information to drive the search towards better configurations. If a resource is under-utilized (resp. over-utilized), Directed SA increases (resp. decreases) this resource value by a random amount. Otherwise, if the monitoring data cannot offer any direction to drive the search, Directed SA updates the resource value in any direction. This strategy can therefore be seen as a combination of the Utilization-Driven and the Standard Simulated Annealing strategies.

6 Evaluation

This section evaluates the search strategies presented in the previous section. We focus on three evaluation criteria: (i) the convergence speed of different search strategies towards identifying the full set of Pareto-optimal configurations; (ii) the quality of configurations we can derive from these results when facing various SLO requirements; and (iii) the costs and delays imposed by offline vs. online profiling.

We base our evaluations on two real HPC applications:

- *Reverse Time Migration* (RTM) is a computationally-intensive algorithm used in the domain of computational seismography for creating 3D models of underground geological structures [18]. It is typically used by oil exploration companies to repeatedly analyze the geology of fixed-sized areas. We use a multithreaded, single-node implementation of this application.
- *Delta Merge* (DM) is a re-implementation of an important maintenance process in the SAP HANA in-memory database [19]. This operation is used to merge a table snapshot with subsequent update operations (which are kept separately) in order to generate a new snapshot. For consistency reasons the database table must remain locked during the entire operation. It is therefore important to minimize the execution time of Delta-Merge as much as possible.

Both application manifests define resource configurations between 1 and 16 CPU cores and 11 discrete values between 2 and 124 GB of memory. We simplify the RTM case by imposing a CPU frequency of 2.2 GHz for the physical machine hosting the VMs, while for DM we authorize 4 possible values. This creates a relatively small search space with 172 configurations for RTM and a significantly larger one for DM. Figure 3 shows the result of this exhaustive evaluation for RTM.

We run experiments in the Grid'5000 testbed [20]. For RTM, we use machines equipped with two 10-core CPUs running at 2.2 GHz, 128 GB of RAM and 10 Gb Ethernet connectivity. Additional machines with different CPU frequency, number of cores and amount of memory are used for executing the DM application.

All machines run a 64-bit Debian Squeeze 6.0 operating system with the Linux-2.6.32-5-amd64 kernel. We use QEMU/KVM version 0.12.5 as the hypervisor. We deploy the OpenNebula cloud infrastructure in these machines so our application manager can request dynamic VM configurations via the OCCI interface. We repeated all experiments three times, and kept the average values for execution time.

As our applications typically run within tens of minutes, we define execution costs for resources on a per-minute basis according to a simple cost model derived from a linear regression over the price of cloud resources at Amazon EC2:

$$Cost_{VM} = 0.0396 * N_{Cores} + 0.0186 * N_{Memory(GB)} + 0.0417$$

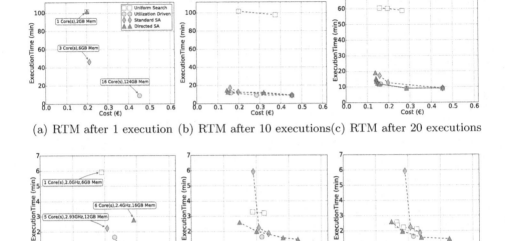

(a) RTM after 1 execution (b) RTM after 10 executions(c) RTM after 20 executions

(d) DM after 1 execution   (e) DM after 10 executions   (f) DM after 20 executions

Fig. 4. Pareto frontiers for RTM (a,b,c) and DM (d,e,f)

When using cores of different frequency, the cost is scaled accordingly. Note that our system does not rely on this simplistic cost model. It is general enough to accept *any* other function capable of giving a cost for any VM configuration.

6.1   Convergence Speed

To understand which search strategy identifies efficient configurations faster, we compute the Pareto frontiers generated by each strategy after 10 and 20 executions. The results are presented in Figure 4.

In the case of Uniform Search, we use a step equal to the unit for each dimension of the search space. It therefore actually completes an exhaustive search of the configuration space. We can observe that this strategy converges very slowly. It eventually finds the full Pareto frontier, but only after it completes its exhaustive space exploration.

The Utilization-Driven strategy starts from a randomly generated configuration in the search space. This randomly-chosen starting point creates a different search path for each run of this strategy. In the worst case, this strategy starts with a configuration which neither over- nor underutilizes its resources, so the search stops after a single run. In the best case, the algorithm starts from a configuration already very close to the Pareto frontier, in which case it actually identifies a number of good configurations. We show here an average case (neither the best nor the worst we have observed): it quickly identifies a few interesting configurations but then stops prematurely so it does not identify the entire frontier.

Table 1. Performance after 10 executions of RTM under cost (C) constraints. The values correspond to the average and standard deviation of 100 runs of the search techniques.

SLO ⟍ Strategy	Cost < 0.15 €		Cost < 0.25 €		Cost < 0.35 €	
	Time	Failed	Time	Failed	Time	Failed
Uniform Search	-	100%	60.21 min ± 0.00	0%	58.91 min ± 0.00	0%
Utilization-driven	16.82 min ± 4.50	83%	18.56 min ± 7.44	1%	18.62 min ± 7.77	0%
Standard SA	13.01 min ± 2.17	15%	13.12 min ± 5.74	2%	11.46 min ± 3.78	1%
Directed SA	12.67 min ± 1.58	0%	12.00 min ± 0.24	0%	11.34 min ± 1.21	0%
Exhaustive search	*12.07 min*	-	*11.84 min*	-	*9.12 min*	-

Finally, Standard SA and Directed SA also start from randomly generated configurations. We can however observe that they converge faster than the others towards the actual Pareto frontier. For both applications, after just 10 iterations they already identified many interesting configurations. We can note that Directed SA converges faster than Standard SA.

6.2 SLO Satisfaction Ratio

Another important aspect of the search result is the range of SLO requirements it can fulfill, and the quality of the configurations that will be chosen by the platform under these SLOs. We now compare the quality of solutions proposed by the different search strategies after having had the opportunity to issue just 10 profiling executions.

Table 1 presents the execution times that would be observed with the RTM application if the SLO imposed various values of maximum cost. Several search techniques rely on random behavior so we compute the average and standard deviations of 100 runs of each profiling technique. We also show the number of runs where the strategy failed to propose a configuration for a given SLO. Conversely, Table 2 shows the costs that would be obtained with the RTM application after defining a maximum execution time. For both tables we also show the performance that would result from an exhaustive search of the entire space. Tables 3 and 4 show similar results for the DM application.

It is clear from all the tables that Directed SA provides better configurations. With its good approximation of the entire Pareto frontier, it can handle all SLOs from the table. The other strategies have only a partial or sub-optimal frontier and cannot find configurations for demanding SLOs. At the same time, when several strategies can propose solutions that match the SLO constraint, the solutions found by Directed Simulated Annealing are almost always better, with a lower standard deviation.

6.3 Profiling Costs

Another important aspect is the time and cost incurred by the profiling process which can be minimized based on user's choice on profiling approach: offline or online.

Table 5 presents the cost and duration overhead of offline profiling for the RTM application using 20 experiments. The utilization-driven strategy appears

Table 2. Performance after 10 executions of RTM under time (T) constraints. The values correspond to the average and standard deviation of 100 runs of the search techniques.

SLO Strategy	Time < 10.00 min		Time < 20.00 min		Time< 30.00 min	
	Cost	Failed	Cost	Failed	Cost	Failed
Uniform Search	-	100%	-	100%	-	100%
Utilization-driven	0.28 € ± 0.00	98%	0.16 € ± 0.01	33%	0.17 € ± 0.05	6%
Standard SA	0.35 € ± 0.08	36%	0.16 € ± 0.05	0%	0.15 € ± 0.05	0%
Directed SA	0.40 € ± 0.08	30%	0.14 € ± 0.00	0%	0.14 € ± 0.00	0%
Exhaustive search	*0.28 €*	-	*0.13 €*	-	*0.13 €*	-

Table 3. Performance after 10 executions of DM under cost (C) constraints. The values correspond to the average and standard deviation of 100 runs of the search techniques.

SLO Strategy	Cost < 0.02 €		Cost < 0.04 €		Cost < 0.06 €	
	Time	Failed	Time	Failed	Time	Failed
Uniform Search	2.23 min ± 0.00	0%	2.10 min ± 0.00	0%	2.10 min ± 0.00	0%
Utilization-driven	2.11 min ± 0.25	74%	2.14 min ± 0.64	22%	2.20 min ± 0.91	12%
Standard SA	3.47 min ± 1.42	26%	2.14 min ± 0.92	5%	1.97 min ± 0.63	3%
Directed SA	2.62 min ± 1.10	7%	1.66 min ± 0.18	0%	1.60 min ± 0.16	0%
Exhaustive search	*1.81 min*	-	*1.46 min*	-	*1.46 min*	-

Table 4. Performance after 10 executions of DM under time (T) constraints. The values correspond to the average and standard deviation of 100 runs of the search techniques.

SLO Strategy	Time < 2.00 min		Time < 3.00 min		Time< 4.00 min	
	Cost	Failed	Cost	Failed	Cost	Failed
Uniform Search	-	100%	0.02 € ± 0.00	0%	0.02 € ± 0.00	0%
Utilization-driven	0.03 € ± 0.02	49%	0.03 € ± 0.02	10%	0.03 € ± 0.02	4%
Standard SA	0.04 € ± 0.02	28%	0.02 € ± 0.01	6%	0.02 € ± 0.01	1%
Directed SA	0.02 € ± 0.01	1%	0.02 € ± 0.00	0%	0.02 € ± 0.00	0%
Exhaustive search	*0.01 €*	-	*0.01 €*	-	*0.01 €*	-

to be cheap and fast, but this is only due to the fact that it stops after a small number of iterations.

Uniform Search starts its exploration from the cheapest available resource types which incur long execution times, thus, the execution becomes expensive.

Standard SA is slightly cheaper and faster than Directed SA mostly due to a an initial temperature chosen too low which means that the algorithm converges quickly before issuing 20 executions (we use the SciPy [21] implementation of SA).

Directed SA does not have this limitation as it does not rely all the time on the temperature to choose a next configuration. This strategy therefore explores more configurations, thus having a higher total cost and execution time than Standard SA. On the other hand, it identifies more optimal configurations.

Figure 5 shows the execution times and costs incurred by the user using the Directed Simulated Annealing strategy in conjunction with online profiling. In this case, no artificial execution is generated. On the other hand, as we can see

Table 5. Total cost and duration overhead for an offline profiling of RTM limited to 20 executions. The values represent the average of 100 profiling processes with each search technique.

Strategy	Total cost	Duration
Uniform Search	19.92 €	1727.93 min
Utilization-driven	2.63 €	234.51 min
Standard SA	7.09 €	426.41 min
Directed SA	9.38 €	635.39 min

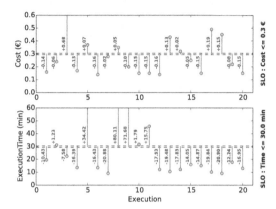

Fig. 5. Cost and Execution Time fluctuation in an online profiling of RTM limited to 20 executions

in the figure, many executions violate an arbitrary SLO of 0.30 €. However, it is interesting to notice that the overall group of execution remains within its aggregated budget (with a negative cost overhead of -0.21 €). Similarly, when applying an arbitrary SLO of 30 minutes of execution time, numerous individual executions violate the SLO but overall the execution time overhead is again negative (-20.82 minutes).

We conclude that the search based on Directed Simulated Annealing shows the fastest convergence to optimal configurations and provides a better satisfaction for the SLOs. It generates good configurations to be used when creating an application profile in a smaller number of executions.

For users willing to tolerate SLO violations on individual executions, the online profiling strategy provides obvious benefits: it remains within the aggregate time or budget of the overall profiling phase, and therefore offers fast and cost-effective generation of a full performance model. On the other hand users unwilling or unable to tolerate individual SLO violations can revert to the offline strategy, at the expense of artificial executions which consume both time and money.

7   Conclusion

Assigning the appropriate computational resources for efficient execution of arbitrary cloud applications is a difficult problem. We presented an automatic profiling methodology that allows a application-agnostic platform to select resources according to an SLO.

Our work so far relies on the assumption that execution time and cost are independent from the input. The next step in our agenda consists in modeling applications with input-dependent performance.

Acknowledgments. This work was partially funded by the FP7 Programme of the European Commission in the context of the Harness project under Grant Agreement 318521. Experiments were carried out using the Grid'5000 experimental testbed, developed under the INRIA ALADDIN development action with support from CNRS, RENATER and several Universities as well as other funding bodies.

References

1. Tang, W., Desai, N., Buettner, D., Lan, Z.: Job scheduling with adjusted run-time estimates on production supercomputers. Elsevier Journal of Parallel and Distributed Computing (2013)
2. Amazon Elastic MapReduce, http://aws.amazon.com/elasticmapreduce/
3. Azure Batch, http://azure.microsoft.com/en-us/services/batch/
4. Allan, R.: Survey of HPC performance modelling and prediction tools. Technical Report DL-TR-2010-006, Science and Technology Facilities Council (July 2009)
5. Pllana, S., Brandic, I., Benkner, S.: A survey of the state of the art in performance modeling and prediction of parallel and distributed computing systems. IJCIR 4(1) (2008)
6. Beach, T.H., Rana, O.F., Avis, N.J.: Integrating acceleration devices using Comet-Cloud. In: Proc. ORMaCloud Workshop (June 2013)
7. Vasic, N., Novakovic, D., Miucin, S., Kostic, D., Bianchini, R.: DejaVu: Accelerating resource allocation in virtualized environments. In: Proc. ACM ASPLOS (March 2012)
8. Fernandez, H., Pierre, G., Kielmann, T.: Autoscaling Web applications in heterogeneous cloud infrastructures. In: Proc. IEEE IC2E (March 2014)
9. Dejun, J., Pierre, G., Chi, C.H.: EC2 performance analysis for resource provisioning of service-oriented applications. In: NFPSLAM-SOC (November 2009)
10. Dejun, J., Pierre, G., Chi, C.H.: Resource provisioning of Web applications in heterogeneous clouds. In: Proc. USENIX WebApps (June 2011)
11. Farley, B., Juels, A., Varadarajan, V., Ristenpart, T., Bowers, K.D., Swift, M.M.: More for your money: exploiting performance heterogeneity in public clouds. In: SOCC (2012)
12. Oprescu, A.M., Kielmann, T., Leahu, H.: Budget estimation and control for bag-of-tasks scheduling in clouds. Parallel Processing Letters 21(2) (June 2011)
13. Verma, A., Cherkasova, L., Campbell, R.H.: ARIA: automatic resource inference and allocation for mapreduce environments. In: Proc. ICAC (2011)
14. Tian, F., Chen, K.: Towards optimal resource provisioning for running MapReduce programs in public clouds. In: Proc. IEEE CLOUD (2011)
15. Amazon Web Services, http://aws.amazon.com/blogs/aws/choosing-the-right-ec2-instance-type-for-your-application/
16. CopperEgg: AWS sizing tool, http://copperegg.com/aws-sizing-tool/
17. Wikipedia.org: Simulated annealing
18. CGC: Reverse time migration, http://www.cgg.com/default.aspx?cid=2358

19. Sikka, V., Färber, F., Lehner, W., Cha, S.K., Peh, T., Bornhövd, C.: Efficient transaction processing in SAP HANA database – the end of a column store myth. In: SIGMOD (2012)
20. Grid'5000, http://www.grid5000.fr/
21. SciPy, http://docs.scipy.org/doc/scipy/reference/generated/scipy.optimize.anneal. html#scipy.optimize.anneal

Practical Evaluation of Large Scale Applications

Tiago Jorge[✉], Francisco Maia, Miguel Matos, José Pereira, and Rui Oliveira

INESC TEC and U. Minho
{tiago.jorge,francisco.maia,miguelmatos,jop,rco}@di.uminho.pt
http://www.haslab.pt

Abstract. Designing and implementing distributed systems is a hard endeavor, both at an abstract level when designing the system, and at a concrete level when implementing, debugging and evaluating it. This stems not only from the inherent complexity of writing and reasoning about distributed software, but also from the lack of tools for testing and evaluating it under realistic conditions. Moreover, the gap between the protocols' specifications found on research papers and their implementations on real code is huge, leading to inconsistencies that often result in the implementation no longer following the specification. As an example, the specification of the popular Chord DHT comprises a few dozens of lines, while its Java implementation, OpenChord, is close to twenty thousand lines, excluding libraries. This makes it hard and error prone to change the implementation to reflect changes in the specification, regardless of programmers' skill. Besides, critical behavior due to the unpredictable interleaving of operations and network uncertainty, can only be observed on a realistic setting, limiting the usefulness of simulation tools. We believe that being able to write an algorithm implementation very close to its specification, and evaluating it in a real environment is a big step in the direction of building better distributed systems. Our approach leverages the MINHA platform to offer a set of built in primitives that allows one to program very close to pseudo-code. This high level implementation can interact with off-the-shelf existing middleware and can be gradually replaced by a production-ready Java implementation. In this paper, we present the system design and showcase it using a well-known algorithm from the literature.

Keywords: Testing and evaluation · Distributed systems · Simulation and emulation

1 Introduction

Real distributed systems are often built around several collaborating middleware components such as a membership or coordination service. The correctness and performance of these systems depends not only on the particular algorithm used to solve the problem, but also on the interactions among the supporting middleware components. Despite its importance and criticality, experimentally assessing such distributed systems in a large scale setting is a daunting task. Unfortunately, interesting behavior - and bugs - often arise exclusively in large

© IFIP International Federation for Information Processing 2015
A. Bessani and S. Bouchenak (Eds.): DAIS 2015, LNCS 9038, pp. 124–137, 2015.
DOI: 10.1007/978-3-319-19129-4_10

scale settings where intra-component concurrency, the interleaving among components' operations and network uncertainty, expose the system to previously overlooked issues. This is aggravated by the fact that the very conditions that cause the problems to appear in the first place are often hard to determine, and harder to reproduce. Simulators such as ns-2 [12] or PeerSim [11] partially address this problem, but their usefulness is limited to validating the design and specification, not production code. This requires maintaining the simulation and real implementations in tandem, which due to the huge gap in complexity between them, becomes error-prone and time consuming as we have witnessed first-hand several times [10]. Test beds such as PlanetLab [3] or a cloud infrastructure allow to perform very large scale deployments, but system observability and reproducibility of testing conditions on normal and faulty conditions poses several challenges. As a matter of fact, not only a coherently global observation is physically impossible, but also the system's behavior remains largely unpredictable and unreproducible. Other tools allow to run real code but are limited to a particular framework and language [8], or are limited in scope [2,14,5], thus precluding the integration with required off-the-shelf middleware components and providing only rough estimates of system behavior and performance.

In this paper, we take a different approach to the problem. Instead of building yet another simulator, we rely on the MINHA [1] platform [4] and extend it with capabilities to write distributed algorithms at a high abstraction level. Briefly, MINHA virtualizes multiple Java Virtual Machines (JVM) instances in a single JVM while simulating key environment components, reproducing the concurrency, distribution, and performance characteristics of a much larger distributed system. By virtualizing time, it is possible to get a global observation of all operation and system variables, while simulation models make it possible to reproduce specific testing conditions. This allows to run and evaluate unmodified Java code in real, yet reproducible conditions.

In this work we extend MINHA to provide a simplified API that features common distributed systems functionality allowing to write algorithms very concisely. Despite this, such code still runs as real code and can interact with off-the-shelf middleware components. This allows one to not only develop and test algorithms faster but also to incrementally replace the concise implementations, close to pseudo-code, with fully fledged Java implementations for critical parts of the system. Since MINHA accurately reflects the cost of executing real code, succedaneum components can be used with the guarantee that its behavior can be analyzed, controlled and evaluated under precise reproducible conditions, thus minimizing measurements fluctuations. Arguably, working closer to the specification allows better reasoning about the problem at hand and therefore easier detection and correction of problems. This is achieved through the JSR-223 Java Scripting API [7] which allows to run scripting languages inside the JVM. We consider the Python programming language in particular, but our approach lends itself to be used in any language supported by JSR-223.

---

[1] www.minha.pt

The rest of this paper is organized as follows. We begin by providing background on important characteristics of MINHA and JSR-223 in Section 2. Then we describe our system in Section 3 and present a concrete use case by providing the implementation of the Chord DHT in Section 4. Related work is debated in Section 5 and, finally, Section 6 concludes the paper and discusses future work.

2 Background

In this section we provide some background and context for our framework. We describe two frameworks on which our own work relies, MINHA and JSR-223.

The MINHA [4] framework is capable of virtualizing multiple JVM instances in a single JVM. It is able to do so simulating a real distributed environment by virtualizing the network, CPU scheduling and by virtualizing most of the standard Java APIs. As a consequence, it is possible to run multiple instances of any Java application in a single machine. Each instance believes it is running in its own machine and runs without the need to adapt any of its code. By running multiple instances of an application in a single JVM, MINHA reduces significantly the resources typically required for evaluating it in a large scale scenario. This makes large scale evaluation practical.

One critical advantage of MINHA is the fact it virtualizes time. Once time is virtualized, it is possible to perform a global system observation at any moment of the simulation. Moreover, contrary to execution in a real environment, there is no overhead introduced by observation and control or even by debugging, so execution time can be considered for analysis. Global observation of system state and each application instance variables greatly eases the process of detecting and solving problems the application may exhibit.

Another important aspect of the MINHA platform is that environments and software models can be replaced by simulation models, and incorporated in a standard test harness to be run automatically as code evolves. By resorting to simulated components and running the system with varying parameters, the impact of extreme environments can be assessed and reproducing testing conditions becomes automatic. Thanks to this holistic approach, when a component does not yield the expected results, the developer can quickly identify and fix any problem that may exist, and reevaluate the new component version for the same exact conditions. The ability to easily replace software components or mock them allows for iterative development and allows for component-targeted evaluation and validation, which greatly eases the development of reliable software.

Additionally, MINHA not only allows to run real applications, but it also virtualizes a significant part of a modern Java platform, thus providing unprecedented support for running existing code. In particular, the virtualization of threading and concurrency control primitives provides additional detail when simulating concurrent code, as is usually the case of middleware components. Code is run unmodified and time is accounted using the CPU time-stamp counter to closely obtain true performance characteristics.

MINHA's API allows the invocation of arbitrary methods, several scheduling options, asynchronous invocations, and callbacks. As presented in Listing 1.1,

```
World  world  =  new  World ( ) ;
Entry<Main >[]  e  =  world . createEntries (10);
for ( int  i =0;  i<e . length ;  i++)
     e . queue ( ) . main (" test . Main" ,  "arg0" ,  "arg1" );
world . runAll (e );
world . close ( );
```

Listing 1.1. Asynchronous invocation of 10 identical MINHA entries

creating and invoking a number of identical application instances is quite straight forward. Basically, each **entry** object will represent an application instance running in its own host to which it is passed the application to run as a parameter. In this case the application is **test.Main** and ten instances of this application are run. These and other utilities that allow to create and control entries for user defined interfaces, make it very simple to simulate large scale applications without having to modify its code.

The JSR-223 Java Scripting API [7] is a framework that allows developers to run scripting language code in the JVM. Any JSR-223 compliant scripting language can be used. This way, it becomes possible to write Java applications that can be easily customizable and extendable in a scripting language of choice. Possible languages include Python (via Jython), JavaScript (via Rhino) or Lua (via LuaJ). This flexibility is also very useful for reusing code from existing protocols implemented in a scripting language. Scripting languages are convenient because they are easy to learn and use, allow complex tasks to be performed in relatively few steps, thus requiring less lines of code, and code testing can be made on the fly with handy interpreters. Mainly, their conciseness allow one to prototype ideas quickly, focusing on early proof of concept implementations close to pseudo-code.

Importantly, access between the scripting language and regular Java classes is bidirectional, meaning that the scripting language has access to regular Java and vice-versa. Therefore, algorithms programmed in our simplified API can still access other middleware components such as a group communication toolkit. As shown in Listing 1.2, one can expose an object (**File f**) as a variable to the script, that, as such, can access it and call methods on it. On the other hand, it is also possible to define a script object (**var o = new Object()**), expose it to the Java class, and invoke methods on it through the **Invocable** interface.

The flexibility in choosing any JSR-223 compliant scripting language, together with its bidirectional exposure, are determining factors for the integration of components written in different languages.

```
public  class  Bidirect  {
 public  static  void  main ( String [] args ) throws  Exception  {
   ScriptEngineManager  manager  =  new  ScriptEngineManager ();
   ScriptEngine  engine  =  manager . getEngineByName (" JavaScript ");
   // Script to Java
   File  f  =  new  File (" test . txt ");
   engine . put (" file " ,  f );
   engine . eval (" print ( file . getAbsolutePath ())");
```

```
// Java to Script
String s = "var o=new Object(); o.hi=function(n){print('Hi
    '+n);}";
engine.eval(s);
Invocable inv = (Invocable) engine;
Object o = engine.get("o");
inv.invokeMethod(o, "hi", "Script Method" );
 }
}
```

Listing 1.2. Example of Bidirectional access between scripts and Java

3   Framework Design

As described previously, the MINHA framework allows to run unchanged Java applications in a simulated environment. It allows us to instantiate an arbitrary large number of *peers*, each with its own IP address, as if they were running in their own machines. To each peer it is possible to assign a Java application or service to run. In the same simulation, different peers may run different applications and may interact with each other through the (simulated) network.

Naturally, it is the responsibility of the developer to implement all the communication code for the application. Moreover, as it is real Java code, the developer must deal with all the implementation details of socket management, data marshalling / unmarshalling and message dispatching. This can be a serious drawback when the application is still in early design and prototyping phase. In fact, having developers focusing on these tasks prevents them from dedicating time to the core components of the protocol.

Our framework provides a way of concisely prototyping real code distributed algorithms. These prototypes can be tested and validated in large-scale simulations leveraging MINHA. Integrating the JSR-223 scripting framework, we allow each MINHA peer to run any JSR-223 compliant scripting language code. Additionally, by providing a high level API to the developer, our framework hides lower level intricacies from the developer, such as all the boilerplate code relating to thread and socket management, data marshalling / unmarshalling, and event dispatching.

In Figure 1 we depict the framework architecture and the exposed high level API. The API consists in three system primitives and four types of methods each application must implement. The three primitives are *send*, *call* and *periodic*. Two of the primitives abstract message dispatch - *send* - and remote procedure call - *call* - without the developer needing to write any communication code. The *periodic* primitive allows the user to register, at boot time, service methods to be invoked periodically. In order to make a runnable application, besides implementing these periodic methods themselves, the developer needs to provide a *boot* method, a *get_state* method and all those events remotely invoked with *send* or *call*, locally triggered through *receive*. Method *boot* is invoked by the platform before actually running the application and should be used to bootstrap

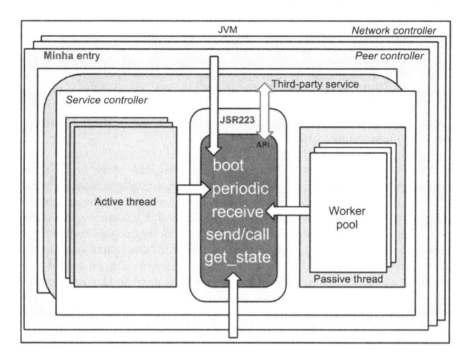

Fig. 1. Framework architecture

the application data structures and any required initializing procedures. The *get_state* method should return a representative state of the peer for system observation purposes. Finally, *receive* is invoked each time a message is delivered to the application and triggers the target event having the necessary logic to process such message. Besides the API, the framework is organized in three main components built on top of MINHA: network controller, peer controller and service controller.

Network Controller: In MINHA multiple virtual JVMs can be run in each JVM, significantly reducing the resources required by typical alternatives. This component is responsible for interfacing our framework with MINHA. The system parameters are specified in a YAML configuration file. The number of peers to run and the number of simulation rounds to perform are two of the required configuration parameters. The network controller creates a MINHA host, which runs in a virtualized JVM, for every peer to run. Alongside this step, each one of this hosts is assigned a unique IP address by the MINHA platform. The component is also responsible for loading both the script engine for each peer and all the user-defined scripts, which implement the framework's API. After instantiating all peers and scheduling their start-up, it initiates the MINHA simulation. Because this component interfaces with the MINHA platform it can perform operations outside the simulation environment. In particular, the network controller is able to globally observe the system. In the current implementation, this is achieved by having all applications implement the *get_state* method. The *get_state* method implementation is application dependent and should return a representative state of the peer. The goal is to be able to globally observe the state of the system by being able to inspect, for the same virtual time, the inner state of every peer in the system. This observation can be done periodically according to user configuration.

Peer Controller: This controller corresponds to a MINHA entry, or peer. This component will run the user application, which can actually consist of a stack of what we call services. These services can be smaller applications or protocols that are used as building blocks for a larger application. For instance, in a typical epidemic application [9], different protocols are used as they rely on each other. In our platform, each service is implemented in a JSR-223 compliant language and implementing the exposed API. Alternatively, a service can also be a third-party off-the-shelf application whose specific interface is exposed to the other services leveraging the bidirectional characteristic of the JSR-223 framework. With all the services ready, the user then declares, in the configuration file, which services to run on each peer and, for each service, specific configuration parameters it may require. At runtime, the peer controller loads the list of services to run and their respective configurations, such as protocol specific parameters, port, and times for periodic behavior. It then instantiates each service by invoking the correspondent *boot* method, exposing in the scripting side all the necessary Java objects such as loggers and communication end-points. Only then it starts the service controller for each service. Third-party services are also instantiated and started through their specific interfaces. All services have access to the list of other services available, which enables integration.

Service Controller: The service controller is responsible for the mechanisms necessary to offer the API abstraction of the framework. It schedules the necessary threads to allow periodic invocation of protocol methods, according to configuration. It handles message passing by managing the necessary sockets for inter-peer communication as well as data marshalling and unmarshalling mechanisms. Since distributed protocols can have multiple periodic procedures executing concurrently, one active thread is started for each cyclic method registered through the *periodic* primitive. Each thread will then periodically invoke, through JSR-223, its respective procedure. A passive thread listens for messages continuously and assigns a worker for processing each incoming message through *receive*, which in turn inspects the message type and invokes the corresponding event, whose implementation the user must provide.

4 Use Case

In this section we present a concise implementation of the well-known Chord distributed hash table [13], as a use case that shows the benefits of using our framework. Chord maps keys to nodes in a peer-to-peer structured infrastructure. When joining the network, a node receives a unique identifier that determines its position in a ring. Every node is responsible for the keys that fall between itself and its predecessor, keeping track of the latter and maintaining a **finger** table whose entries point to nodes at an exponentially increasing distance, the first one corresponding to its successor. For completeness, we provide the specification found in the Chord paper in Listing 1.3.

The corresponding implementation in our system using Python is presented on Listing 1.4. The **boot** initializes the protocol. Specifically note the registration of all the cyclic procedures using the **periodic** primitive. These are stabilization tasks which have to be performed at regular intervals. Namely, function **stabilize** verifies that a node is its own successor's predecessor and notifies the successor, function **fix_fingers** iteratively refreshes fingers, and **check_pred** checks if a node's predecessor has failed. At the end of initialization, function **join** is invoked, allowing the node to join the Chord ring. Here, only its successor is set, since its predecessor will be updated as part of the stabilization mechanism.

```
1   n.find_successor(id)
2       if(id ∈ (n,successor))
3           return successor;
4       else
5           n' = closest_preceding_node(id);
6           return n'.find_successor(id);

7   n.closest_preceding_node(id)
8       for i = m downto 1
9           if(finger[i] ∈ (n,id))
10              return finger[i];
11      return n;

12  n.join(n')
13      predecessor = nil;
14      successor = n'.find_successor(n);

15  n.stabilize()
16      x = successor.predecessor;
17      if(x ∈ (n,successor))
18          successor = x;
19      successor.notify(n);

20  n.notify(n') :
21      if(predecessor is nil or n' ∈ (predecessor,n))
22          predecessor = n'
```

```
23   n.fix_fingers ()
24      next = next + 1;
25      if (next > m)
26         next = 1;
27      finger [next] = find_successor (n + 2^{next-1});

28   n.check_predecessor ()
29      if (predecessor has failed)
30         predecessor = nil;
```

Listing 1.3. Chord specification as found in the original researh paper [13]

Primitives **call** and **send** respectively perform a non-blocking and blocking (waits for a returned result) communication with another node in the overlay. Their arguments include the destination IP, the name of the event to trigger, and its necessary parameters. The receiver node then invokes **receive** (from the super-class), which in turn applies the correspondent event. Such events include function **find_successor**, that looks for the successor of a given identifier, **get_pred** for returning the predecessor, **poke** working as a *ping*, and **notify** for telling a node that its predecessor might be incorrect. Notice that an extra parameter, **src**, is provided to each event, corresponding to the sender's IP. This is necessary because some protocols require pairwise interactions. Finally, function **closest_preceding_node** returns the highest predecessor of a given identifier found in the finger table, and **between** (from utilities) determines the inclusion of a value in a given range.

All these procedures correspond to executable code that can be readily deployed. As most of the complexity is hidden inside our infrastructure, we end up with an extremely concise specification. In fact, excluding **boot** and the single comment line, and without compromising code legibility, we have 35 LOC, an increase of only 17% over the pseudo-code from the original paper (compare with Listing 1.3), which does not contain initialization code, and a decrease of 15% over SPLAY's implementation [8] (also excluding initialization).

```
1    class ChordService(P2Pservices.Service):
2       def boot(self, **kwargs):
3          self.m = kwargs['m']
4          self.iD = random.randint(1, 2**self.m)
5          self.pred = None
6          self.finger = [None] * self.m
7          self.refresh = 0
8          self.periodic(stabilize, fix_fingers, check_pred)
9          self.join(kwargs['start_node'])

10      def join(self, n):
11         self.pred = None
12         self.finger[0] = self.call(n.ip, find_successor, self.iD)

13      def closest_preceding_node(self, iD):
14         for n in reversed(self.finger):
15            if n != None and between(n.iD, self.iD, iD):
16               return n
17         return self
```

```
18    def stabilize(self):
19        x = self.call(self.finger[0].ip, get_pred)
20        if x != None and between(x.iD,self.iD,self.finger[0].iD):
21            self.finger[0] = x
22        self.send(self.finger[0].ip, notify, self)

23    def fix_fingers(self):
24        self.refresh = (self.refresh % self.m) + 1
25        self.finger[self.refresh-1] = self.find_successor((self.iD
              + 2**(self.refresh-1)) % 2**self.m)

26    def check_pred(self):
27        if self.pred != None:
28          try:
29              self.call(self.pred.ip, poke)
30          except Timeout:
31              self.pred = None


32    # invoked by receive
33    def find_successor(self, src, iD):
34        if between(iD, self.iD, self.finger[0].iD):
35            return self.finger[0]
36        n = self.closest_preceding_node(iD)
37        return self.call(n.ip, find_successor, iD)

38    def get_pred(self, src):
39        return self.pred

40    def poke(self, src):
41        pass

42    def notify(self, src, n):
43        if self.pred==None or between(n.iD,self.pred.iD,self.iD):
44            self.pred = n
```

Listing 1.4. Concise implementation of Chord.

As for the configuration, consider for instance the YAML file shown in Listing 1.5. A simulation of twenty rounds (**simulation_rounds**) is defined for a network of one thousand peers (**number_of_peers**), each round running for sixty seconds (**round_time**) of simulated time (time units are in milliseconds). After each round a global observation is performed over the entire network, therefore **simulation_rounds** specifies the number of snapshots to be taken. Each peer runs a single protocol, **ChordService**, whose parameters have to be provided also. General protocol parameters include, for instance, the **port** where the service will run (here 32143), as well as the **periodic_interval** for cyclic procedures (five seconds in this case). Configurations specific to the protocol are also defined, in this case **m** is set to ten, resulting in a ring space of 1024 positions.

```
# simulation config
number_of_peers: 1000
simulation_rounds: 20
round_time: 60000
services: [ChordService]

# service config
ChordService:
  port: 32143
  periodic_interval: 5000
  m: 10 # 2^m nodes and keys, with identifiers of length m
...
```

Listing 1.5. YAML file with simulation and service parameters.

5 Related Work

Considering the current approaches to large scale evaluation of distributed systems, PlanetLab [3] is a very valuable global research network for assessing large-scale distributed systems, by allowing experimentation in live networks of geographically dispersed hosts. In a more lightweight approach, network emulators such as ModelNet [15] can reproduce some of the characteristics of a networked environment, such as delays and bandwidth, allowing users to evaluate unmodified applications across various network models, each machine in the cluster hosting several end-nodes from the emulated topology. However, in these test beds, system observability and reproducibility of testing conditions on normal and faulty environments poses several challenges. Despite that existing technologies allow to partially observe the state of the system, a coherently global observation is physically impossible. The lack of knowledge about the system seriously hinders the ability to find and address problems, which is further aggravated by failures and non predictable interactions due to concurrency.

A common approach to this problem is to build a simulation model, that frees testing from the availability of the target platform for deployment and provides perfect observability. Simulators such as ns-2 [12] or PeerSim [11] have been shown to scale to very large systems. However, they can only validate the design and simulation model not the real implementation. This requires maintaining the simulation and real implementations in tandem which is error-prone and time consuming.

An interesting trade-off is achieved by JiST (Java in Simulation Time) [2], an event-driven simulation kernel that allows code to be written as Java threaded code, but avoids the overhead of a native thread by using continuations. JiST does not however virtualize Java APIs and thus cannot be used to run most existing Java code, neither does it accurately reflect the actual overhead of Java code in simulation time. Neko [14] provides the ability to use simulation models as actual code, provided its event-driven API is used instead of the standard

Java classes. It also does not accurately reflect the actual cost of executing code, as it uses a simple model that allows the relative cost of the communication and computation to be adjusted. Protopeer [5] allows switching between event-driven simulation and a real deployment without modifying the application. This is achieved by abstracting time and the networking API which offers a limited set of operations. The simulated network can be subject to message delay and loss following models already available or others customized by the developer. The major drawback of Protopeer is the requirement of using a specific API thus precluding the use of off-the-shelf middleware components.

The approach of MINHA [4] is closer to CESIUM [1], which also accurately reflects the cost of executing real code in simulated resource usage. MINHA does however virtualize a significant part of a modern Java platform, thus providing unprecedented support for running off-the-shelf code. In particular, the virtualization of threading and concurrency control primitives provides additional detail when simulating concurrent code, as is usually the case of middleware components.

SPLAY [8] is an integrated system that facilitates the design, deployment and testing of large-scale distributed applications. It also allows developers to express algorithms in a concise, simple language that highly resembles pseudocode found in research papers. However, SPLAY limits the developer to the Lua language [6] and does not offer facilities for an incremental integration with off-the-shelf existing middleware.

6 Discussion and Future Work

In this paper, we present a unified solution for practical testing and validation of large-scale applications. We achieve this by extending the MINHA simulation platform with a framework for flexibly and concisely prototyping distributed algorithms. The framework allows to effortlessly integrate prototypes with existing middleware components and test them in the large.

We believe this framework can effectively ease the development of large scale distributed systems. Not only ideas can be quickly prototyped and tested but, when developing a complex system, each component can be mocked and progressively improved while the entire system keeps working as a whole. This progressive and iterative development process definitely contributes for higher quality applications.

We plan to assess the platform by implementing a broad number of protocols. With this effort we intend not only to show the usefulness of the framework but also to build a library of useful services that can be used in subsequent applications. Implementing different kinds of protocols will enable us to ensure a considerable expressiveness level for the framework, rather than taking the risk of making it biased towards a particular type of distributed applications. An automated and simplified mechanism for deploying these applications on real environments is also in the scope of our short-term work, this in order to take full advantage of supporting real code. Last but not least, we plan to evaluate the performance of the framework itself. Rather than evaluating the distributed applications themselves, we will assess the simulation overhead and scalability, taking our library of protocols as an increasingly rich benchmark.

Acknowledgment. The research leading to these results has received funding from the European Union Seventh Framework Programme (FP7/2007-2013) under grant LeanBigData, agreement no. 619606.

References

1. Alvarez, G.A., Cristian, F.: Applying simulation to the design and performance evaluation of fault-tolerant systems. In: Proceedings of the Sixteenth Symposium on Reliable Distributed Systems, pp. 35–42. IEEE (1997)
2. Barr, R., Haas, Z.J., van Renesse, R.: Jist: An efficient approach to simulation using virtual machines. Software: Practice and Experience 35(6), 539–576 (2005)
3. Bavier, A.C., Bowman, M., Chun, B.N., Culler, D.E., Karlin, S., Muir, S., Peterson, L.L., Roscoe, T., Spalink, T., Wawrzoniak, M.: Operating systems support for planetary-scale network services. In: NSDI, vol. 4, p. 19 (2004)
4. Carvalho, N.A., Bordalo, J., Campos, F., Pereira, J.: Experimental evaluation of distributed middleware with a virtualized java environment. In: Proceedings of the 6th Workshop on Middleware for Service Oriented Computing, p. 3. ACM (2011)
5. Galuba, W., Aberer, K., Despotovic, Z., Kellerer, W.: Protopeer: From simulation to live deployment in one step. In: Eighth International Conference on Peer-to-Peer Computing, P2P 2008, pp. 191–192. IEEE (2008)
6. Ierusalimschy, R., De Figueiredo, L.H., Celes Filho, W.: The implementation of lua 5.0. J. UCS 11(7), 1159–1176 (2005)
7. JCP - Java Community Process: JSR-223 Java Scripting API (2006), https://www.jcp.org/en/jsr/detail?id=223
8. Leonini, L., Rivière, É., Felber, P.: Splay: Distributed systems evaluation made simple (or how to turn ideas into live systems in a breeze). In: NSDI, vol. 9, pp. 185–198 (2009)
9. Maia, F., Matos, M., Vilaça, R., Pereira, J., Oliveira, R., Riviere, E.: Dataflasks: epidemic store for massive scale systems. In: 2014 IEEE 33rd International Symposium on Reliable Distributed Systems (SRDS), pp. 79–88. IEEE (2014)
10. Matos, M., Felber, P., Oliveira, R., Pereira, J.O., Riviere, E.: Scaling up publish/subscribe overlays using interest correlation for link sharing. IEEE Transactions on Parallel & Distributed Systems 24(12), 2462–2471 (2013)
11. Montresor, A., Jelasity, M.: PeerSim: A scalable P2P simulator. In: Proc. of the 9th Int. Conference on Peer-to-Peer (P2P 2009), Seattle, WA, pp. 99–100 (September 2009)
12. The Network Simulator NS-2, http://www.isi.edu/nsnam/ns/
13. Stoica, I., Morris, R., Liben-Nowell, D., Karger, D.R., Kaashoek, M.F., Dabek, F., Balakrishnan, H.: Chord: a scalable peer-to-peer lookup protocol for internet applications. IEEE/ACM Transactions on Networking 11(1), 17–32 (2003)

14. Urban, P., Défago, X., Schiper, A.: Neko: A single environment to simulate and prototype distributed algorithms. In: Proceedings of 15th International Conference on Information Networking 2001, pp. 503–511. IEEE (2001)
15. Vahdat, A., Yocum, K., Walsh, K., Mahadevan, P., Kostić, D., Chase, J., Becker, D.: Scalability and accuracy in a large-scale network emulator. ACM SIGOPS Operating Systems Review 36(SI), 271–284 (2002)

Cheap and Cheerful: Trading Speed and Quality for Scalable Social-Recommenders

Anne-Marie Kermarrec[1], François Taïani[2], and Juan M. Tirado[1(✉)]

[1] INRIA Rennes, 35042 Rennes, France
{anne-marie.kermarrec,juan-manuel.tirado}@inria.fr
[2] University of Rennes 1 - IRISA - ESIR, Rennes Cedex, France
francois.taiani@irisa.fr

Abstract. Recommending appropriate content and users is a critical feature of on-line social networks. Computing accurate recommendations on very large datasets can however be particularly costly in terms of resources, even on modern parallel and distributed infrastructures. As a result, modern recommenders must generally trade-off quality and cost to reach a practical solution. This trade-off has however so far been largely left unexplored by the research community, making it difficult for practitioners to reach informed design decisions. In this paper, we investigate to which extent the additional computing costs of advanced recommendation techniques based on supervised classifiers can be balanced by the gains they bring in terms of quality. In particular, we compare these recommenders against their unsupervised counterparts, which offer lightweight and highly scalable alternatives. We propose a thorough evaluation comparing 11 classifiers against 7 lightweight recommenders on a real Twitter dataset. Additionally, we explore data grouping as a method to reduce computational costs in a distributed setting while improving recommendation quality. We demonstrate how classifiers trained using data grouping can reduce their computing time by 6 while improving recommendations up to 22% when compared with lightweight solutions.

1 Introduction

As web and on-line services continuously grow to encompass more facets of our lives, personalization and recommendation are emerging as key technologies to help users exploit the deluge of data they are submitted to. This is particularly true in social-networking applications (Facebook, Google+, Linkedin, Twitter), which receive, store, and, process a continuously growing mass of information produced for tens to hundreds of millions of users daily.

Implementing a recommendation mechanism that works for such a large user base over terabytes of data is a highly challenging task: an ideal solution should be accurate, lightweight, and easily scale to the distributed and cloud environments in which modern recommenders are being deployed [1]. Traditional approaches to user recommendation in social networks have so far heavily relied on topological metrics to identify new users or items that might be of interest to

A. Bessani and S. Bouchenak (Eds.): DAIS 2015, LNCS 9038, pp. 138–151, 2015.
DOI: 10.1007/978-3-319-19129-4_11

a user. These approaches, pioneered by Liben and Nowell [16], can be *unsupervised*, in which a topological metric (e.g. number of common neighbors, length of shortest path) is used directly to predict links in the underlying social graph and thus derive recommendations. These approaches are typically lightweight, and scale well, but can provide sub-optimal recommendations, and tend to depend on the suitability of the chosen metrics for a particular dataset.

In recent years, a second strand has therefore emerged that exploit classifiers developed for machine learning to improve on these earlier approaches [18,17,24,19]. These classifiers often use as inputs the same topological metrics developed for unsupervised learning, and are trained on a part of the social-graph to construct an appropriate prediction model. Due to this training phase, these methods can better adapt to the specifics of individual datasets. They are also able to combine several metrics into one predictor [14], and thus offer a natural path to merge different types of information into a recommender, including topological data, semantic information based on the content consumed and produced by users [18,24], or geographic information in geolocated social networks (Foursquare, Gowalla) [19].

Unfortunately, training such supervised models can require very large training sets (up to twice as large as the prediction set [17]), and be particularly costly in terms of computation time, even on today's highly distributed, highly parallel infrastructures found in datacenters and cloud providers. Computation costs are in turn a fundamental decision factor [13] used to select practical on-line recommenders, and has led companies as prominent as Netflix [1] to discard improved, but particularly costly solutions that were difficult to deploy in their target environment (in Netflix's case, Amazon's public cloud).

Almost no information exists nowadays about this fundamental trade-off, balancing training's computation cost on modern infrastructures and the quality of the returned recommendation. This lack of analysis is highly problematic, as it leads to researchers to focus almost exclusively on quality metrics that ignore a decision factor that is key to practitioners. In this paper, we analyze this very trade-off, and present an extensive study that contrast the benefits brought by supervised classifiers against their computational costs on parallel architectures under a wide range of operational assumptions. First, we describe a method that combines topology-based and content-based information to improve the quality of recommendations. Second, we explore the utilization of data grouping methods to reduce the computation time required to train classifiers while improving recommendations. We carry out a thoroughly evaluation using a real dataset extracted from Twitter that demonstrates the benefits our approach can bring to scalable user-recommenders.

This work is structured at follows. In Section 2 we state the problems of user recommendation. Section 3 briefly introduces the related work. Section 4 describes our approach. Section 5 describes the evaluation of this approach and finally we conclude in Section 6.

2   Problem Statement

The tremendous growth of users data in modern on-line services has made recommendation a key enabling technology in the last few years [4]. This is particularly true in on-line social networks such as Facebook, Twitter, or Weibo, which allow users to maintain an on-line web of social connections, where they produce and consume content. These networks serve up to hundreds of millions of users (for instance Facebook reported 1.15 billion monthly active users in June 2013 [8]), and must select recommendation techniques able to scale to their user-base, while being amenable to the highly distributed infrastructures in which these services are typically deployed. The ability to scale and distribute recommendation algorithms has been shown in the past to play a key role in their acceptability: Netflix for instance revealed in 2012 that it had not adopted the winning algorithms of its own one million dollar Netflix prize, in part because of the engineering challenges raised to port the algorithm to their distributed infrastructure (hosted by Amazon) [1].

In this work, we focus on the problem of recommending users to other users. This problem can be compared to the link prediction problem [16] where we try to predict when the user u will create a link with another user v. In order to do this, we have to compute a recommendation score ($score(u, v)$) or score function indicating the interest of u to create a link with v. How to compute this score, depends on the taken approach. One common approach is to use *unsupervised* models consisting of a generic solution that is oblivious to the distinguishing features of the dataset. A second approach uses supervised models, consisting of classifiers trained with an excerpt of data extracted from the target dataset. Generally, this score is given by a pre-computed model that has been previously trained using the information available in the system. The general approach is to provide the system with a representative number of observations in order to compute an accurate model. Once a score function is chosen, we can compute a matrix of scores among the users in the system and chose the largest scored users as recommendations. Computing the score among all the users is not practical, therefore only a small subset is scored. Normally only a subset of close neighbors are score for each user during the recommendation. Apart from the time cost of computing the score of the neighbors, we have to consider the cost of training the supervised models. This aspect is generally ignored, although it is a major constraint in the design of distributed user-recommenders.

3   Related Work

The problem of link prediction has been addressed in two separated strands. A first approach follows the seminal work of Liben-Nowell and Kleinberg [16] using metrics based on the network topology [23,2]. As observed by Yien et al. [25] these metrics only reflect changes in the network topology being oblivious to the creation of links regarding other aspects contained into the users metadata. In this sense, Schifanella et. al [21] find tags to be a good link predictor. However, in [7] authors find that tags are not very effective for link-prediction in their explored datasets.

A second approach employs methods to combine different features in order to exploit all the available information in the systems. Rowe et al. [18] exploit Twitter semantics using logistic regression. Authors claim the need for topical affinity between users to create links. Although their work has some resemblance with the one we present, their work differs from our approach in the utilization of topics instead of natural language and the analysis of just one classifier. Scellato et al. [19] use supervised learning to predict links in a location-based social network. The authors train a set of classifiers with different location and social-based metrics finding that the combination of these metrics results into an improvement of recommendations. They find that a combination of location and social-based metrics does not significantly improve recommendations compared with only location-based recommenders. Wang et al. [24] present a framework for link-prediction based on an ensemble of classifiers trained with graph features and similarity metrics. They claim a 30% improvement of recommendations when compared with other approaches. However, they ignore the elapsed time in the training process using an exhaustive amount of information during training.

Although the aforementioned works emphasize the combination of different data sources in order to improve recommendations, none of the mentioned works present any conclusion about computational costs. In practice, many of these systems are not scalable and only practical for centralized designs [13]. However, the utilization of methods exploiting different features in user-recommenders has not been analyzed from a computational perspective that may facilitate the design of distributed solutions.

4   Proposed Approach

User-recommendation is essentially a classification problem where we determine whether a candidate is relevant for a user or not. A $score(u, v)$ function determines the probability of u to establish a link with the candidate v after comparing both users. In socially oriented systems for any user u we find his outgoing edges (social links) $\Gamma(v)$ and part of the content u has consumed or generated. The content can have different formats such as tagged content (e.g. YouTube videos) or natural language text (e.g. posts, tweets). Both of them can be managed in bags of words [18] consisting of a vector containing all the words (or tags) employed by the user. Each user has an associated corpus C_u containing all the employed words, where $P_u(i)$ is the probability of finding the word i into the corpus.

Both $\Gamma(v)$ and C_v can be employed to compute similarity metrics that can be used as score functions ($score(u, v)$). These metrics have been widely used in distributed systems where the user has a partial vision of the network [22,5] and also in graph-based solutions [16,3]. The main reason for their utilization is that they are computationally light and summarize relevant features users may

Table 1. $score(u,v)$ functions based on content and graph information

Content-based score functions		
Jensen-Shannon	js	$\frac{1}{2}\sum_i P_u(i)\log\frac{P_u(i)}{P_v(i)} + \frac{1}{2}\sum_i P_v(i)\log\frac{P_v(i)}{P_u(i)}$ with $i \in C_u \cap C_v$
Jaccard	$jacc$	$\|C_u \cap C_v\|/\|C_u \cup C_v\|$
Cosine	cos	$1 - \dfrac{\sum_i w_u(i)w_v(i)}{\sqrt{\sum_i w_u(i)^2}\sqrt{\sum_i w_v(i)^2}}, i \in C_u \cap C_v$
Adamic-Adar	aa	$\sum_{i \in C_u \cap C_v} 1/\log P_u(i)$
Graph-based score functions		
Jaccard	$jaccf$	$\|\Gamma(u) \cap \Gamma(v)\|/\|\Gamma(u) \cup \Gamma(v)\|$
Adamic-Adar	aaf	$\sum_{i \in \Gamma(u) \cap \Gamma(v)} 1/\log\|\Gamma(i)\|$
Preferential attachment	pa	$\|\Gamma(u)\|\|\Gamma(v)\|$

have in common. Table 1 shows the score functions used in this work and their notation.

The Jensen-Shannon divergence measures the distance between two corpuses using the probability distribution of the words used by each user. The Jaccard coefficient is a common metric that measures the probability of sharing items between users. Cosine distance considers the elements and their occurrences as the dimensions of two vectors. Adamic-Adar weights rare common features [16]. Finally, preferential attachment considers the probability of connecting two users proportionally to their connectivity degree. For the Jaccard and Adamic-Adar metrics we present a content-based and a social graph based version.

The aforementioned score functions can be directly used as unsupervised score-based classifiers to compute the probability of u and v to become connected or not. However, in some scenarios computing recommendations remains a challenge. For example, cold-start recommendations [20] will probably fail as there is no available data. In other scenarios the score can be biased. For example, if u and v have similar content and a low number of common links, probably v is not relevant to u. They share similar topics but are distant neighbors. And similarly, a low content score wit a great social similarity indicates close users although they consume different contents. Combining both approaches (content-based and social-based) at the same time can improve recommendations in scenarios where only one approach may be insufficient.

4.1 Supervised Multi-score Recommenders

There is an extensive literature in supervised classification algorithms [15] that take advantage of different statistic features. Supervised classifiers have to be trained with a given set of observations (training dataset) each one containing a set of features and the class belonging to. Depending on the classifier and the training dataset, the classifier will come up with a different classification model.

In our approach, we propose to use a training dataset with entries containing $\{s_1, s_2, ..., s_n, c\}$ where s_i is a score function (Table 1) and c indicates whether users u and v are connected (1 if connected, 0 otherwise). Ideally, for every user u in the social graph, we can create a training dataset and then train the corresponding classifier. However, this is not a scalable solution as we would need to compute as many classifiers as users in the system. Additionally, computing a single model for the whole dataset requires to identify a sample representative enough which is a difficult task. In order to cope with this problem, we split the graph into manageable groups and compute classifiers for these groups. Intuitively, groups composed of users with similar features should have similar classification models. This permits to train personalized recommendation models for samples of users. Additionally, by splitting the problem we can consider the parallelization through distribution using paradigms such as Map-reduce.

Algorithm 1. Supervised score-based model training

1: **for** each group g **do**
2:     $T \leftarrow \{\}$ training set
3:     U random sample of users belonging to g
4:     //Fill the training dataset
5:     **for** $u \in U$ **do**
6:         $N \leftarrow neighborsSelection(u, d)$
7:         **for** $n \in N$ **do**
8:             Compute each similarity metric i
9:             $s_i \leftarrow score_i(u, n)$
10:            $c \leftarrow connected(u, n)$
11:            Add $[s_1, s_2...s_n, c]$ to T
12:        **end for**
13:    **end for**
14:    //Find the best classification model
15:    $B_i \leftarrow \{\}$
16:    **for** each classifier i **do**
17:        $B_i^c \leftarrow \{\}$
18:        **for** each configuration c **do**
19:            Train M_c using configuration c and cross-fold validarion over T
20:            Add AUC_{M_c} to B_i^c
21:        **end for**
22:        $M_i \leftarrow$ model with largest value from B_i^c
23:        Save M_i, discard the other models
24:    **end for**
25:    $M_g \leftarrow$ model with largest AUC from B_i
26: **end for**

Algorithm 1 describes the steps carried out to train and find the most suitable model for each group of users g. First, we define the training set T for each group g. For each g, we select a sample of users U large enough to be representative but small enough to be computationally feasible. The users are chosen using the $neighborsSelection(u, d)$ function as explained in Section 4.2. For each of the users in U we compute the score functions and add them to the training set T. Once we have all the training sets, we can compute the best classification model. Considering the most adequate classifier for a given social graph a priori is a difficult task. Different classifiers show different performance depending on the incoming training set. We propose to simultaneously train several classifiers using cross-fold validation over T. For each classifier we train models M_c for a set of pre-determined configurations (if the classifier accepts additional configuration), compute the obtained AUC (Area Under the ROC Curve) for M_c. The AUC measures the predictive power of the model between 0 and 1. Values larger than 0.5 indicate better performance than a random classifier. The model with the largest AUC will finally be selected as the classifier for the group (M_g).

4.2   Training Set Users Selection

The training set T described in Algorithm 1 must contain a proportional ratio of observations belonging to both classes (connected and non-connected) in order to get an accurate classifier. We select a random sample of users U from group g. Then for each user u in U we compute the features corresponding to a connected and a non-connected user. Selecting a connected user we just have to select one v belonging to $\Gamma(u)$ and compute the different $score(u, v)$ functions. However, the remaining users in the graph could be considered as non-connected examples. We propose a social distance approach to determine which users to consider as non-connected.

We define the social distance d as the minimal number of links u has to traverse in order to find user v. Previous works observe that most of the new links in social networks are established for small values of d [25]. We use the social distance to determine when a user shall be considered as an example of connected or non-connected class in the training set. For $d = 1$ we consider the users to be connected as they are currently neighbors. Then for $d > 1$ we consider non-connected samples. According to this assumption, for large values of d a classifier must find easier to distinguish between connected and non-connected users during training. Figure 1 describes how the $neighborsSelection(u, d)$ function works. In Figure 1a we have the original directed social graph. In Figure 1b we use $d = 2$ selecting users 3, 7 and 8 (green) as connected examples with 5 and 6 as non-connected taking 4 as the origin. Similarly, in Figure 1c we use $d = 3$ being 9 the only non-connected candidate.

5   Evaluation

We evaluate our approach using a Twitter dataset extracted using the public Twitter API [1]. We have crawled Twitter's social graph for users in the London area extracting their tweets and list of followings (users they follow) before July 28th 2013. Our dataset accounts for 106,385 users with 11,111,386 following links and a total of 21 million tweets. The median of the distribution is 94 followings with 80% of the users having less than 265 followings.

---

[1] http://dev.twitter.com/docs/api/1.1

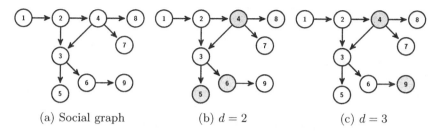

Fig. 1. Example of training set users selection using $d = 2$ and $d = 3$. Vertex 4 indicates the starting user. Vertices 3, 7 and 8 indicate examples of connected users. With $d = 2$ vertices 5 and 6 are non-connected vertices. With $d = 3$ the non-connected vertex is 9.

We aim to understand how a combination of graph and user content information can improve user recommendations and how we can reduce the computational overhead in order to facilitate the scalability of this process. We use the score functions defined in Table 1 in order to compare two users in terms of social and content similarities. We use the tweets to compute the content-based score functions. Tweets use natural language that may reduce the amount of information we can extract from them. For that reason, we first remove stop words and punctuation symbols (except hashtags).

We use a set of representative classifiers available in the R Caret package [11]. This package offers a unified interface for a large number of classifiers, simplifying the implementation. Table 2 enumerates the classifiers we have used for our experiments. We choose these classifiers in order to have a representative set with various classifiers that may get some benefit from our approach. For each training we use cross-fold validation with 10 folds. Then we select a sample of random users with a variable social distance d and compute the AUC to measure the quality of recommendations. In order to compare the computational cost of training we show the average elapsed time for 5 executions. All the experiments are carried out in a non-fully dedicated 8 Intel Xeon cores machine with 32 GBytes of memory.

Table 2. Summary of employed classifiers used in the evaluation and their abbreviated names

Method	Abbreviated name
Bagging	*bagFDA*
Gradient boosted models [9]	*gbm,blackboost*
Decission tree	*C5.0Tree*
Random forests [6]	*parRF*
K-nearest neighbors	*knn*
Multivariate adaptive regression splines [10]	*earth*
Logistic regression	*glm,glmnet*
General additive models	*gam*
Support Vector Machine	*svmLinear*

5.1 Single-Score Recommenders

In this section, we show the quality of recommendations simply using score functions as recommenders. For clarity, we analyze the recommendation power depending on the nature of the score (graph-based or content-based), the number of user followings and the social distance d of the users in the evaluation set. The results showed in Figure 2 indicate that increasing the social distance d improves the performance of recommenders. However, graph-based recommenders are more accurate than content-based. In particular, we observe that the AUC increases for users with a larger number of followings. This could be due to the cold-start effect that limits the amount of available information. However, in the case of content-based recommenders we observe that the number of followings do not substantially modify the recommendations.

5.2 Supervised Multi-score Recommenders

After analyzing the recommendations obtained using score functions, we explore the recommendations obtained with multi-score recommenders. We use the same evaluation set employed in the previous section with $d \leq 2$. First we only combine score functions from graph-based (Figure 3a) and content-based (Figure 3b) score functions. Then we combine both in order to check how by combining data sources we can improve recommendations (Figure 3c).

For graph-based multi-score recommenders (Figure 3a) we observe a significant improvement for the users with less than 100 followings. This improvement is particularly relevant for users with less than 10 followings achieving a 22% improvement (0.71 AUC compared with graph-based single-score that only achieved 0.58). However, we do not observe relevant improvements for content-based multi-score recommenders (Figure 3b) compared with the single-score version. Finally, the combination of all the scores (Figure 3c) significantly improves the recommendations of some classifiers such as *glm* or *svmLinear*. In the other cases there is an improvement of the recommendations, although it is not very significant.

5.3 Train Set Grouping

In the previous section we show how using multi-score classifiers improves recommendations. However, in order to facilitate the deployment of a distributed solution we have to consider the computation cost of training classifiers. The elapsed time training a classifier depends on the amount of data and the classifier itself. Additionally, as described in Algorithm 1 our approach considers the training of several models in order to find the most accurate model. This operation may require a significant amount of time. In order to reduce this time while keeping the quality of recommendations, we split users into groups.

In our experiments we split the dataset into five equally-sized groups depending on the number of outgoing edges. The reason behind this partition is to reduce the diversity of features found in each training set. Intuitively, users

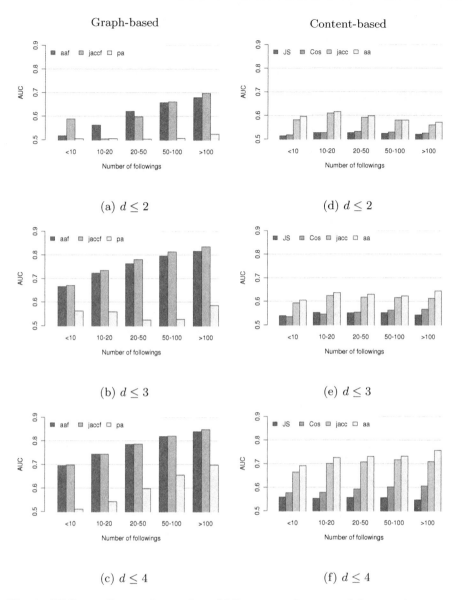

Fig. 2. AUC according to the number of followings and the social distance for content-based similarity metrics

with the same number of outgoing links may have similar profiles, and therefore it would be easier to find a model to classify them. We assume that the information regarding each user (followings and content) is fully available when computing the scores. In Figure 4 we plot the elapsed average time for training and the AUC per classifier using a multi-score recommender combining graph and content-based scores. We classify the same set of users employed in the

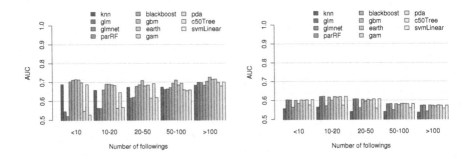

(a) Graph-based multi-score recom- (b) Content-based multi-score recommenders   menders

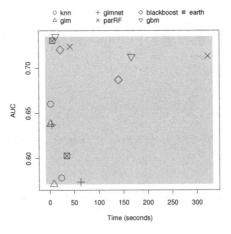

(c) Graph and content-based multi-score
recommenders

Fig. 3. AUC for multi-score recommenders using graph-based scores, content-based scores and both kind of scores

Fig. 4. Comparison of AUC and time used in model training. The right and left areas indicate the results not using and using groups respectively.

previous section with and without grouping (left and right highlighted areas respectively).

We observe an increment of the AUC for all the classifiers with a significant time reduction after grouping. In some cases like *parRF* the AUC slightly improves while the training is 6 times faster. In other cases like the *earth* classifier, the AUC increment is more significant than the saved time. This experiment shows how partition permits to reduce the training time while not affecting the quality of recommendations.

5.4   Discussion

There are many aspects to be evaluated in a recommendation system. We know the evaluation presented in this paper is not complete. However, we think that many of the results presented in this work are promising and open the door for new ideas in the development of scalable recommendation systems that can combine multiple sources of information. Our experiments demonstrate how training classifiers using classic user comparison metrics can improve recommendations. We observe that there is a significant improvement when dealing with users offering small amounts of data. Furthermore, we demonstrate how classifiers trained with metrics based on different sources of information we can get 22% better recommendations than the best value obtained simply using these metrics. The combination of graph and content-based slightly improves recommendations. However, this result may vary in other datasets.

Group partitioning demonstrates to be a good approach to reduce the average elapsed time in classifiers training. Additionally, we observe how recommendation improves for all the evaluated classifiers after grouping. This result is particularly promising in order to develop distributed recommender systems using supervised classifiers. Grouping data with common features improves recommendations. This makes possible to reduce the amount of training data, and therefore the elapsed training time. In this work, we only provide one group partitioning strategy based on the number of outgoing links of the user. A large number of partition techniques based on topology features can be explored [12]. However, our main goal is to demonstrate the importance of group partitioning in terms of recommendations and time. Exploring other grouping techniques remains for future work. Finally, the reduction in the time needed to train the models makes possible to compute a larger number of models. And facilitates the parallelization of the recommendation process. Our experiments indicate that the *gbm* (Gradient Boosted Modelling) classifier gets the best results in almost every scenario. However, this result can differ depending on the dataset.

6   Conclusions

In this work we explore the design of scalable solutions for social recommenders. First, we propose the utilization of supervised classification methods for user recommendation in social networks. We describe a method that combines topology-based and content-based similarity metrics to improve the quality of recommendations. Second, we explore the utilization of data grouping methods to reduce the computation time required to train classifiers and make easier the deployment of distributed solutions. We carry out a thoroughly evaluation using a real dataset extracted from Twitter that demonstrates the benefits of our approach. In particular, we find that our solution improves the quality of recommendations by 22% compared with unsupervised solutions. Additionally, we observe that data grouping permits to speedup the training of classifiers by 6.

Our work shows promising results and opens several directions in the development of scalable social recommenders. We plan to extend our study about the effects of data grouping in the quality of recommendations and how it facilitates the deployment of scalable solutions. Additionally, we will extend our evaluation to other datasets.

Acknowledgments. This work was partially funded by the French ANR project SocioPlug (ANR- 13-INFR-0003), and by the DeSceNt project granted by the Labex CominLabs excellence laboratory (ANR- 10-LABX-07-01).

References

1. Amatriain, X., Basilico, J.: Netflix recommendations: Beyond the 5 stars (April 6, 2012), http://techblog.netflix.com/2012/04/netflix-recommendations-beyond-5-stars.html (accessed September 20, 2013)
2. Backstrom, L., Leskovec, J.: Supervised random walks: predicting and recommending links in social networks. In: Proceedings of the Fourth ACM International Conference on Web Search and Data Mining, WSDM 2011, pp. 635–644 (2011)
3. Barabasi, A.L., De, J., Lettres, P., Al, L., Cimento, N., Jeong, H., Jeong, H., Neda, Z., Neda, Z., Barabasi, A.L.: Measuring preferential attachment in evolving networks. Europhysics Letters 61(61), 567–572 (2003)
4. Bobadilla, J., Ortega, F., Hernando, A., Gutiérrez, A.: Recommender systems survey. Knowledge-Based Systems 46(0), 109–132 (2013)
5. Boutet, A., Frey, D., Guerraoui, R., Jégou, A., Kermarrec, A.-M.: WhatsUp Decentralized Instant News Recommender. In: IPDPS 2013 (May 2013)
6. Breiman, L.: Random forests. Machine Learning 45(1), 5–32 (2001)
7. Brzozowski, M.J., Romero, D.M.: Who should i follow? recommending people in directed social networks. In: ICWSM (2011)
8. Facebook Inc. Key facts (2013), https://newsroom.fb.com/Key-Facts (accessed October 2, 2013)
9. Freund, Y., Schapire, R.E.: A decision-theoretic generalization of on-line learning and an application to boosting. Journal of Computer and System Sciences 55(1), 119–139 (1997)
10. Friedman, J.H.: Multivariate Adaptive Regression Splines. The Annals of Statistics 19(1), 1–67 (1991)
11. Kuhn, M., Contributions from Jed Wing, Weston, S., Williams, A., Keefer, C., Engelhardt, A., Cooper, T.: caret: Classification and Regression Training. R package version 5.16-24 (2013)

12. Gonzalez, J.E., Low, Y., Gu, H., Bickson, D., Guestrin, C.: Powergraph: Distributed graph-parallel computation on natural graphs. In: Proceedings of the 10th USENIX Conference on Operating Systems Design and Implementation, OSDI 2012, pp. 17–30. USENIX Association, Berkeley (2012)

13. Gupta, P., Goel, A., Lin, J., Sharma, A., Wang, D., Zadeh, R.: Wtf: the who to follow service at twitter. In: WWW, pp. 505–514 (2013)

14. Hasan, M., Zaki, M.: A survey of link prediction in social networks. In: Aggarwal, C.C. (ed.) Social Network Data Analytics, pp. 243–275. Springer, US (2011)

15. Kotsiantis, S.B.: Supervised machine learning: A review of classification techniques. In: Proceedings of the 2007 Conference on Emerging Artificial Intelligence Applications in Computer Engineering: Real Word AI Systems with Applications in eHealth, HCI, Information Retrieval and Pervasive Technologies, pp. 3–24. IOS Press, Amsterdam (2007)

16. Liben-Nowell, D., Kleinberg, J.: The link prediction problem for social networks. In: Proceedings of the Twelfth International Conference on Information and Knowledge Management, CIKM 2003, pp. 556–559. ACM (2003)

17. Lichtenwalter, R.N., Lussier, J.T., Chawla, N.V.: New perspectives and methods in link prediction. In: Proceedings of the 16th ACM SIGKDD International Conference on Knowledge Discovery and Data Mining, KDD 2010, pp. 243–252. ACM, New York (2010)

18. Rowe, M., Stankovic, M., Alani, H.: Who will follow whom? exploiting semantics for link prediction in attention-information networks. In: Cudré-Mauroux, P., et al. (eds.) ISWC 2012, Part I. LNCS, vol. 7649, pp. 476–491. Springer, Heidelberg (2012)

19. Scellato, S., Noulas, A., Mascolo, C.: Exploiting place features in link prediction on location-based social networks. In: Proceedings of the 17th ACM SIGKDD International Conference on Knowledge Discovery and Data Mining, KDD 2011, pp. 1046–1054. ACM, New York (2011)

20. Schein, A.I., Popescul, A., Ungar, L.H., Pennock, D.M.: Methods and metrics for cold-start recommendations. In: Proceedings of the 25th Annual International ACM SIGIR Conference on Research and Development in Information Retrieval, SIGIR 2002, pp. 253–260. ACM, New York (2002)

21. Schifanella, R., Barrat, A., Cattuto, C., Markines, B., Menczer, F.: Folks in folksonomies: social link prediction from shared metadata. In: Proceedings of the Third ACM International Conference on Web Search and Data Mining, WSDM 2010, pp. 271–280 (2010)

22. Tirado, J.M., Higuero, D., Isaila, F., Carretero, J., Iamnitchi, A.: Affinity p2p: A self-organizing content-based locality-aware collaborative peer-to-peer network. Comput. Netw. 54(12), 2056–2070 (2010)

23. Valverde-Rebaza, J., de Andrade Lopes, A.: Structural link prediction using community information on twitter. In: 2012 Fourth International Conference on Computational Aspects of Social Networks (CASoN), pp. 132–137 (2012)

24. Wang, C., Satuluri, V., Parthasarathy, S.: Local probabilistic models for link prediction. In: Seventh IEEE International Conference on Data Mining, ICDM 2007, pp. 322–331. IEEE (2007)

25. Yin, D., Hong, L., Davison, B.D.: Structural link analysis and prediction in microblogs. In: Proceedings of the 20th ACM International Conference on Information and Knowledge Management, CIKM 2011, pp. 1163–1168. ACM, New York (2011)

Replication of Recovery Log — An Approach to Enhance SOA Reliability

Anna Kobusińska[⊠] and Dariusz Wawrzyniak

Institute of Computing Science
Poznań University of Technology, Poznań, Poland
{akobusinska,dwawrzyniak}@cs.put.poznan.pl

Abstract. Along with development of SOA systems, their requirements in terms of fault-tolerance increase and become more stringent. To improve reliability of SOA-based systems and applications, a RESERVE service, providing an external support of web services recovery, has been designed. In this paper we propose to enhance the resilience of RESERVE by replication of log with recovery information, and address problems related to deployment of this solution.

Keywords: SOA · Rollback-recovery · Message-logging · Replication

1 Introduction

Service-oriented systems (SOA) are increasingly adopted by industry in various areas of computing. Many web services, especially those found in critical or vital domains (e.g. healthcare, finance, defense, etc.), have stringent requirements in terms of availability and reliability. Since in most cases failures of such services are unacceptable, their dependability has to be ensured [1]. However, building a dependable SOA systems is a difficult task, due to their specific properties. SOA systems are highly dependent on the remote web service components of various characteristics, which are autonomous and loosely-coupled. Web services usually run on heterogeneous platforms, and are hosted by different organizations. Such services may be unavailable for an unknown reason, and for an undetermined amount of time. Moreover, their providers may refuse or be unwilling to cooperate with other providers to overcome failures of their services. They also may not be able to take part in fault-tolerance processing because of applied fault-tolerance policies. Therefore, services should not be relied upon, when the fault-tolerant mechanisms are to be provided.

As a consequence, we have proposed RESERVE service, which aims in increasing SOA fault-tolerance [2]. RESERVE provides an external support of web services rollback-recovery with the use of a well-known mechanism of message-logging [5,9], and ensures that in the case of failure of one or more system components (i.e. web services or their clients) a consistent state of distributed

---

This work was supported by the Polish National Science Center under Grant No. DEC-2011/03/D/ST6/01331 and the Grant No. 09/91/DSPB/0571.

A. Bessani and S. Bouchenak (Eds.): DAIS 2015, LNCS 9038, pp. 152–157, 2015.
DOI: 10.1007/978-3-319-19129-4_12

processing is recovered. The interactions exchanged between clients and services are saved by RESERVE in the form of message log, stored in the persistent storage, which is assumed to survive all failures. Such an assumption is difficult to be guaranteed in real-life [8]. Additionally, although a persistent storage supports reliability, due to significant MTTR (mean time to recovery), its crash results in log unavailability for a substantial period of time. This way, another point vulnerable to crash is introduced, which can reduce system availability. Therefore, in this paper we propose to implement the persistent storage used in RESERVE service as a replicated log containing the recovery information. Along with the replication of a message log, also the logic of the module of RESERVE, called Recovery Management Unit (RMU), which is responsible for the implementation of a recovery process has to be replicated. Although a general idea of log and RMU replication is straightforward [7], and relies on storing messages necessary for recovery of system participants in replicas, its implementation raises several problems, which have to be solved. Among them are: synchronization of logs kept by different replicas, handling replicas failures, combining the replication of recovery information with the recovery processing. In this paper we discuss how the above problems may be resolved in the context of RESERVE.

The paper is organized as follows. Sections 2 and 3 present system model and general idea of RESERVE, respectively. Section 4 discusses the possible approach to replication of RESERVE recovery log. Finally, Section 5 concludes the paper and presents the future directions of our work.

2   System Model

Throughout this paper, a distributed SOA system is considered [6]. It consists of service providers that keep resources, and deliver — in the form of provided web services — a specified functionality to clients. Web services are autonomous and loosely-coupled. They have a well-defined and standardized interface that defines how to use them. Clients invoke services by sending requests, so service invocation results in a computation, subsequent reply to the requesting client, and possible resource state changes. Service execution may also encompass the collaboration of other services (without compromising the autonomy of each individual service). It is assumed that both clients and services are piece-wise deterministic. Services can concurrently process only such requests that do not require access to the same or interacting resources. Otherwise, the existence of a mechanism serializing access to resources, which uniquely determines the order of operations, is assumed. Communication in the considered system is stateless — each request contains all the information necessary to understand the request, independently of any requests that may have preceded it. The considered communication channels are reliable (the reliability is ensured by the retransmission of messages), but they do not guarantee FIFO property. Additionally, the crash-recovery model of failures is assumed, i.e., system components may fail and recover after crashing a finite number of times [1]. Failures may happen at arbitrary moments, and we require any such failure to be eventually detected, for example by a Failure Detection Service [3]. We assume that each service provider may have its own reliability policy and may use different local mechanisms that provide fault tolerance.

3   ReServE Architecture

In this Section, the design choices and concepts behind ReServE service are presented. The detailed description of ReServE has already been presented in [2,4], and is summarized here in order to make a paper self-contained. Due to the fact that interactions between clients and services result in a computation and possible resource state changes, they entail the client-service inter-dependencies. Upon a failure of one of interacting processes, such dependencies may force other processes that did not fail to rollback. Otherwise, states of processes could reflect situations impossible in any correct failure-free execution. Due to SOA assumption on autonomy of services, the failure of one process should not influence the processing of the others. Since service providers do not provide information on the internal implementation of services, it is not known which events introduce inter-process dependencies and result in state changes. Therefore, in general, the recovery of a failed service should be isolated to avoid the cascading rollbacks of other processes. Above observation had an impact on the concept of ReServE functionality. ReServE intercepts the communication between processes and logs all performed interactions (requests of service invocations and the appropriate replies) in a persistent storage of *Recovery Management Unit* (*RMU*). The intercepted messages reflect the complete history of communication, which is used to recover the consistent system state in the case of failure. However, since in SOA participants of processing may have their private mechanisms providing reliability, their state after the failure may be partially reconstructed with the use of local mechanisms. Therefore, only those messages, the processing of which was not reflected in services' (clients') recovered state, should be processed again. The task of *RMU* is to find such messages, and reissue them to the service in the same order as before the failure. After re-execution of recovered requests *RMU* intercepts replies from the service, because they have already been sent to clients and other services during the failure-free execution. *RMU* module ensures also the idem potency of obtained requests. If it obtains the client's request, to which the response has already been saved in its persistent storage, then such a saved response is sent to the client immediately, without the need of sending the request to the service once again. Thus, the same message (i.e., the message with the same identification number) may be send by a client multiple times, with no danger of multiple service invocations. Another two modules of ReServE service are *Service Intermediary Modules* (*SIM*) and *Client Intermediary Module* (*CIM*). *CIM* and *SIM* serve as proxies for clients and servers and hide the details of rollback-recovery. For this purpose, both modules intercept messages issued by clients and servers, so they allow to fully control the flow of messages in the system. Additionally, *SIM* monitors the services' status and react in the case of its eventual failure by initiating and managing the service rollback-recovery.

4   Replication of Recovery Information

In this Section we propose to replicate the RMU module of RESERVE service, instead of using the persistent storage. From the perspective of clients and services, introducing RMU replication is transparent. Each service has a dedicated replica of RMU module, in which it is registered, called a *Leader*. Analogically, each client has a default RMU replica, called *Interceptor*. We assume that each request issued by a client is first replicated, before it is sent to the service. Analogically, the service reply is replicated, before it is sent back to the client.

The crucial issue arising from replication is consistency. Since the replication in the context of this paper concerns log, i.e. a set of requests and replies, and adding elements to a set is commutative, i.e. it does not pose a risk of conflicts, thus consistency maintenance boils down to preserving replica completeness. The completeness is important for message safety in the sense of the ability to survive RMU replica crash. We assume that a message is safe if it can be obtained by a given number N of replicas, despite the crash of some log servers. A number N ranges from 1 to $\mid RMU \mid$. When $N = \mid RMU \mid$, all correct replicas hold the message, and the highest level of message safety is achieved. At the same time the system availability (response time), is decreased because before the message is sent to its recipient, first all N replicas have to acknowledge the fact that they obtained the message. In turn, in the worst case, only one complete replica is required to survive the crash, and to hold the message. In such situation, the level of system reliability is the smallest, but its availability is uttermost, as the message obtained by the RMU replica is immediately passed to its recipient. In the proposed solution it is a role of a *Leader* to check safety of messages.

The idea of replicating the request among RMU replicas is the following: each time the *Interceptor* obtains the new request, it adds it to the log $\mathcal{M}$ (being a set of requests and replies exchanged between clients and services, and stored by each RMU replica), and broadcasts it to other replicas. The fact of delivering request to a replica is acknowledged by the communication channel, and results in adding such a RMU replica to the set $\mathcal{A}$ (a set of RMU replicas that acknowledged obtaining the request). The *Leader*, after obtaining request from *Interceptor*, can immediately send a reply to the client and to *Interceptor*, provided it possess the matching reply in its log $\mathcal{M}$. Otherwise, *Leader* is responsible for forwarding the request to SIM of the requested service. Since in the considered replication scheme the request is forwarded only after N requests replicas exist, the knowledge on the number of replicas maintained in the system is essential. For this purpose, each RMU replica, after obtaining a request and storing it in its log, sends acknowledgment to *Leader* that updates its set $\mathcal{A}$. But, since the receipt of request can be acknowledged by some RMU replicas either to *Interceptor* or to *Leader* (for example in the case of communication channels with a low bandwidth between the RMU replica and *Leader*), *Interceptor* informs *Leader* , by sending its $\mathcal{A}$ to the *Leader*, which RMU replicas possess a request. In turn, *Leader* expands its set $\mathcal{A}$ on the basis of information obtained from *Interceptor*. Additionally, *Leader* broadcasts request to all RMU replicas that did not confirm obtaining this message neither to *Interceptor*, nor to *Leader*.

The purpose of the re-broadcast of request is to allow *RMU* replica that have just recovered from the failure to take part in the replication. In case one *RMU* replica acts as both the *Interceptor*, and the *Leader*, the procedure of updating the set $\mathcal{A}$ is simplified. There may be *RMU* replicas which do not belong to the set, although they possess the request message replica. However, this does not affect the correctness of the proposed solution. After performing the request, service provider returns the reply through its *SIM* to the *Leader*. When *Leader* obtains reply for the first time, it stores it in the log $\mathcal{M}$, and broadcast it to all *RMU* replicas to replicate reply along with its corresponding request. Finally, the *Leader* sends reply to the client. The architecture of replicated RESERVE is shown in Fig.1.

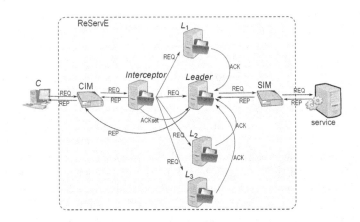

Fig. 1: ReServE — replication of recovery log

Despite reliable communication channels, an *Interceptor, Leader,* and other *RMU* replicas can fail, which effectively disturbs the communication between clients and service providers. In order to mask transient communication failures, the client reissues its request when no reply has been received within a given time. Thus, the role of the *RMU* replica is twofold: keep requests for the purpose of service recovery, and replies for the purpose of client recovery or for filtering duplicated request. In the case of the *Leader* crash another *RMU* replica must be elected to take the responsibility for further communication with the service. The *Interceptor* suspects the *Leader* crash in two cases. First, when the acknowledgment of obtaining a request broadcasted by the *Interceptor* is not delivered to *Leader*, and when the acknowledgment of obtaining by the *Leader* a request reissued by the client is not delivered. In both cases the *Interceptor* starts the *Leader* election procedure.

5   Conclusions and Future Work

In RESERVE service considered until now, we have assumed that each service component can be the subject of failure, except of persistent storage of *RMU*, where the message log is stored. Since this approach understates the robustness of message log, in this paper we proposed the preliminary concept of the alternative solution, based on the replication of RMU and its log.

Applying the replication mechanism will always introduce an overhead. But, the preliminary performance tests show that in the case of the specic message size, the overall costs of the proposed approach based on the replication are not inferior to the cost associated with the costs of saving messages in the stable storage. Thus, the proposed solution is competitive with the one based on persistent storage, because at similar costs, it increases recovery log availability.

Our future work encompasses the introduction of detailed protocol of recovery log replication, formal proof of its corectness, and detailed empirical evaluation.

References

1. Avizienis, A., Laprie, J.-C., Randell, B., Landwehr, C.: Basic concepts and taxonomy of dependable and secure computing. IEEE Transactions on Dependable and Secure Computing 1(1), 11–33 (2004)
2. Brzeziński, J., Danilecki, A., Hołenko, M., Kobusińska, A., Kobusiński, J., Zierhoffer, P.: D-reserve: Distributed reliable service environment. In: Morzy, T., Härder, T., Wrembel, R. (eds.) ADBIS 2012. LNCS, vol. 7503, pp. 71–84. Springer, Heidelberg (2012)
3. Brzeziński, J.: Dependability infrastructure for SOA applications. In: Ambroszkiewicz, S., Brzeziński, J., Cellary, W., Grzech, A., Zieliński, K. (eds.) Advanced SOA Tools and Applications. SCI, vol. 499, pp. 203–260. Springer, Heidelberg (1991)
4. Danilecki, A., Hołenko, M., Kobusińska, A., Szychowiak, M., Zierhoffer, P.: ReServE service: An approach to increase reliability in service oriented systems. In: Malyshkin, V. (ed.) PaCT 2011. LNCS, vol. 6873, pp. 244–256. Springer, Heidelberg (2011)
5. Elmootazbellah, N., Elnozahy, A.L.: A survey of rollback-recovery protocols in message-passing systems. ACM Computing Surveys 34(3), 375–408 (2002)
6. OASIS. Reference Architecture Foundation for Service Oriented Architecture - Version 1.0 (October 2009)
7. Pedone, F., Wiesmann, M., Schiper, A., Kemme, B., Alonso, G.: Understanding replication in databases and distributed systems. In: Proceedings of the 20th International Conference on Distributed Computing Systems, Taipei, Taiwan, April 10-13, pp. 464–474 (2000)
8. Rao, S., Alvisi, L., Vin, H.M.: The cost of recovery in message logging protocols. In: SRDS, pp. 10–18 (1998)
9. Shahzad, F., Wittmann, M., Kreutzer, M., Zeiser, T., Hager, G., Wellein, G.: A survey of checkpoint/restart techniques on distributed memory systems. Parallel Processing Letters 23(4) (2013)

Leader Election Using NewSQL Database Systems

Salman Niazi[1]([✉]), Mahmoud Ismail[1], Gautier Berthou[2], and Jim Dowling[1,2]

[1] KTH - Royal Institute of Technology, Stockholm, Sweden
{smkniazi,maism,jdowling}@kth.se
[2] SICS - Swedish ICT, Stockholm, Sweden
{gautier,jdowling}@sics.se

Abstract. Leader election protocols are a fundamental building block for replicated distributed services. They ease the design of leader-based coordination protocols that tolerate failures. In partially synchronous systems, designing a leader election algorithm, that does not permit multiple leaders while the system is unstable, is a complex task. As a result many production systems use third-party distributed coordination services, such as ZooKeeper and Chubby, to provide a reliable leader election service. However, adding a third-party service such as ZooKeeper to a distributed system incurs additional operational costs and complexity. ZooKeeper instances must be kept running on at least three machines to ensure its high availability. In this paper, we present a novel leader election protocol using NewSQL databases for partially synchronous systems, that ensures at most one leader at any given time. The leader election protocol uses the database as distributed shared memory. Our work enables distributed systems that already use NewSQL databases to save the operational overhead of managing an additional third-party service for leader election. Our main contribution is the design, implementation and validation of a practical leader election algorithm, based on NewSQL databases, that has performance comparable to a leader election implementation using a state-of-the-art distributed coordination service, ZooKeeper.

1 Introduction

One of the main difficulties when designing a replicated distributed system is to ensure that the nodes will reach agreement on the actions to take. Agreement protocols are complex to design and inefficient in terms of throughput and latency, for example, classical Paxos [1] in a failure-recovery model. As a result, most distributed systems rely on a unique leader node to coordinate the tasks running in the system. For this *leader* pattern to work correctly the nodes need to be able to solve the general agreement problem [2] in order to agree on which one of them is the leader. Solving this problem is the purpose of the leader election protocol.

Leader election protocols are a fundamental building block that play a central role in many scalable distributed systems such as stateful middleware [3],

© IFIP International Federation for Information Processing 2015
A. Bessani and S. Bouchenak (Eds.): DAIS 2015, LNCS 9038, pp. 158–172, 2015.
DOI: 10.1007/978-3-319-19129-4_13

distributed filesystems [4], and distributed databases [5]. The typical role of a leader is to propose global state updates and to disseminate them atomically among the nodes. Having a unique leader is imperative to avoid multiple leaders proposing conflicting updates that would compromise the integrity of the system. Additionally, the failure of the leader should not affect the system availability. Moreover, the detection of the leader failure and the election of a new leader should be low latency events (at most, in the order of seconds).

Implementing an algorithm that provides both uniqueness of the leader and low latency is very challenging. In order to avoid errors and to curtail development time, developers often rely on third-party, standalone coordination services such as Chubby [6] and ZooKeeper [7]. These services have the advantages of being widely used and well tested but they introduce additional operational costs and complexity as they must be kept running on at least three machines if the leader-election service itself is to be highly available.

Many existing distributed systems use highly available relational databases or key-value stores to manage their persistent data. Why not build the leader election service using the database as a shared memory? This would allow developers to exploit the leader pattern without paying the extra operational cost of a dedicated coordination service. Implementing the leader election using shared memory is not a new problem; Guerraoui [8] and Fernandez [9, 10] have shown that a leader election service can be implemented using shared memory. However, in partially synchronous systems, these solutions do not guarantee that there will be a unique leader while the system is unstable. They only guarantee that nodes will eventually agree on a leader once the system has stabilized. As a result, these solutions are not widely used in production systems.

In contrast, we propose an algorithm based on locking and transaction primitives provided by the database to guarantee that there is at most one leader in the system at any given time. Traditional highly available relational database management systems are not suitable for building our leader election service, since it can take long time for transactions to complete if a database node failure occurs, which would slow down the leader election process. However, NewSQL systems have emerged as a new class of distributed, in-memory databases that are optimized for on-line transaction processing (OLTP) and have low timeouts for transactions, thus, making them a viable platform for building our leader election service.

In this paper, we present a practical leader election service based on shared memory in a NewSQL database. Our implementation uses the Network Database (NDB) storage engine for MySQL Cluster [5], but our approach is generalizable to all NewSQL databases. Our main contribution is to prove that two-phase commit can be used to implement practical leader election algorithm. We validate our algorithm and show that its performance is comparable to a leader election algorithm implemented using ZooKeeper [7] for cluster sizes of up to 800 processes.

2   NewSQL Database Systems

Although a database can be used as shared memory to implement leader election, some databases do not provide sufficient primitives to implement a reliable leader election service. Our leader election service requires a highly available database with support for transactions and locking primitives. Additionally, the database must ensure that database node failures and slow clients do not cause transactions to take too long to complete (commit or abort). We will now discuss different types of database systems and their suitability for leader election service.

Highly Available Relational Databases typically provide high-availability using either an active-standby replication protocol that provides eventually consistent guarantees for data (as used in SQLServer [11] and MySQL [12]) or a shared-state replication protocol, as used in Oracle RAC [13]. For the active-standby model, a crash of the active node will result in the leader election service being unavailable until the standby node takes over. There are no guarantees on how long this failover will take, and, in practice, it can take from seconds up to minutes to complete depending on the degree of lag at the standby node. Moreover, until the failover completes, the system remains vulnerable to failures as the standby node now becomes a single point of failure. For shared-state databases, it can take up to a minute for transactions to complete if a database node failure occurs (the default distributed lock timeout in Oracle RAC is 60 seconds [13]). For these reasons, traditional highly available relational databases are not suitable for building leader election services.

NoSQL Systems are highly available, but they only provide eventually consistent guarantees for data [14, 15]. This make them unsuitable as the basis for a leader election service, as eventually consistent data may lead to multiple leaders in the system.

NewSQL Systems are a new class of highly available databases that can scale in performance to levels reached by NoSQL systems, but still provide ACID guarantees and a SQL-based declarative query interface [16, 17]. NewSQL systems achieve high performance and scalability by redesigning the internal architecture of traditional databases, often to a shared-nothing architecture, that take better advantage of modern multi-core hardware along with increasingly cheap in-memory storage. NewSQL systems can be scaled-out by adding additional nodes. What makes NewSQL systems a viable platform for building a leader election service is that they typically have low timeouts for locks and transactions. Some notable NewSQL systems are the NDB storage engine for MySQL Cluster [5], FoundationDB [18], and VoltDB [19].

3   System Model and Eventual Leader Election

Processes. The system consists of a time varying finite set of processes p_1, p_2, p_3 ... p_n. Each process has a unique id assigned by a function that returns monotonically increasing ids. All the processes are assumed to behave according to their protocol specification, that is, the processes are not Byzantine. A process can fail by crashing, but until a process crashes it will execute the protocol and it will not halt for an indefinite amount of time. When a process fails it stops executing all operations. A failed process can recover after the failure, but it is assigned a new id by the monotonically increasing function. There is no restriction on the number of processes that can fail or join during the execution of leader election protocol.

The underlying system is partially asynchronous, as it is impossible to develop a leader election service for purely asynchronous systems [20]. In partially synchronous systems there are positive upper and lower bounds on the communication and processing latency. These synchrony primitives of the system are eventually determined by the application. Before these time bounds are determined, a distributed application may not function as expected. The time after which the lower and upper time bounds hold is called global stabilization time (GST). The protocol proceeds in rounds. The duration of these rounds expand until the GST is reached. Moreover, each process' local clock drift is significantly smaller than the round time of protocol.

Shared Memory. All processes communicate through reliable atomic registers (shared memory) implemented using rows in a table in the database. A reliable atomic register is always available, moreover, if two read operations r_1 and r_2 return w_1 and w_2 respectively and r_1 precedes r_2 then w_1 precedes w_2. Atomic registers can easily be implemented in a relational database using a strong enough transaction isolation level. To be considered correct, a process must successfully read and write the register values within a heartbeat period, that can expand during the execution of the protocol.

Leader Election Service. Eventually a correct process with the lowest id in the system will be elected as the leader. The service ensures that a correct leader is elected again in the subsequent rounds. Our service provides stronger guarantees than Ω [2]. With Ω there could be multiple leaders if the GST has not been reached. With the help of transactions, our leader election guarantees at most one leader at any given time and guarantees following properties:

- **Integrity**: there should never be more than one leader in the system.
- **Termination**: a correct process eventually becomes a leader.
- **Termination**: all invocations of the primitive *getLeader()* invoked by a correct process should return the leader's id.

4   Leader Election in a NewSQL Database

Logically, all processes communicate through shared registers (implemented as rows in a table). Each process has its own counter that it updates periodically (in a transaction) to indicate that it is still alive. Each process maintains a local history of the all processes descriptors. Process descriptor contains id, counter, ip and port information. Using the local history a process is declared dead if it fails to update its counter in multiple consecutive rounds. A process declares itself to be the leader when it detects that it has the smallest id among all the alive processes in the system. The leader evicts failed processes, and it is also responsible for increasing the heartbeat *round time* to accommodate slow processes.

All processes run in parallel, concurrency control could be handled with a transaction isolation level set to *serializable*, ensuring that conflicting transactions will execute one after another. For example, if two processes, P_a and P_b, want to become leader simultaneously then the transactions will automatically be ordered such that if P_a manages to execute first then P_b is put on hold. The transaction P_b waits until transaction P_a has finished.

However, due to poor performance [21], NewSQL systems typically do not provide serializable as the default transaction isolation level, if they even support it at all. The strongest isolation level supported by NDB is the *read committed* isolation level, guaranteeing that any data read is committed at the moment it is read. However, it is not sufficient for implementing a reliable leader election service. We use row-level locking to implement stronger isolation levels for transactions. Row-level locking complicates the design, but allows for more fine-grained concurrency control and thus, higher throughput.

Algorithm 1. Leader Election

Require: VARS   ▷ Atomic Register. Holds max id,T_p and evict flag
Require: DESCRIPTORS   ▷ Set of atomic registers that stores all descriptors

1: id = ⊥, role = non_leader, leader = ⊥

2: **procedure** PERIODICHEARTBEATTASK
3:    **while** true **do**
4:        **begin transaction**   ▷ Begin new round
5:            **if** role = leader | id = ⊥ | forceExclusiveLock **then**
6:                acquire ***exclusive lock*** on VARS *register*
7:                forceExclusiveLock = false
8:            **else**
9:                acquire ***shared lock*** on VARS *register*
10:            read all DESCRIPTORS   ▷ No locks needed
11:
12:            updateCounter()
13:            leaderCheck()
14:            DESCRIPTORS ≫ history   ▷ Add to history
15:
16:            T_p = VARS.getTimePeriod()

```
17:            if  role = leader & VARS.evictFlag = true  then
18:                T_p = VARS.updateTimePeriod(T_p + Δ)
19:                VARS.evictFlag = false
20:            L_hbt = currentTime()                    ▷ Leader's lease start time
21:        commit transaction
22:        sleep(forceExclusiveLock ? 0 : T_p)  ▷ Immediately retry with higher locks
```

```
23: procedure UPDATECOUNTER
24:     if  id ∈ DESCRIPTORS then
25:         updateDescriptor(id, getCurrentCounter()+1)
26:     else
27:         if  id != ⊥ then                          ▷ Case: evicted
28:             if  transaction lock mode is not exclusive  then
29:                 forceExclusiveLock = true
30:                 VARS.setEvictFlag()
31:                 return
32:             id = VARS.incrementMaxID()
33:             insertDescriptor(id)
```

```
34: procedure LEADERCHECK
35:     P_s = history.getSmallestAliveProcess()
36:     if  P_s.id = id then
37:         if  transaction lock mode is not exclusive then
38:             forceExclusiveLock = true
39:             return
40:         role = leader
41:         removeDeadNodes()                          ▷ Evict processes
42:     else
43:         role = non_leader
44:         leader = P_s                                ▷ Possible leader
```

```
45: procedure ISLEADER
46:     if  role = leader  then
47:         elapsed_time = currentTime() - L_hbt         ▷ Lease check
48:         if  elapsed_time < (T_p * Max_mhb - μ) then
49:             return true
50:     return false
```

```
51: procedure GETLEADER
52:     if  role = leader & isLeader()  then
53:         return this
54:     else if  role = non_leader  then
55:         return leader
```

4.1 Shared Memory Registers

We implement shared memory registers using rows in tables. Transactions ensure atomicity of the registers. The atomic register VARS stores global parameters such as the maximum allocated process id, and the duration of heartbeat rounds. The maximum allocated process id is used in monotonic id generation. It also stores a boolean flag that is used to change the heart beat round time to cater for slow processes. VARS is backed by single row in a table that contains all the global variables. DESCRIPTORS represents a set of registers that store information about all the alive process. It is backed by a table where each row contains a process descriptor.

Our database, NDB, supports two main locking modes: *shared* (read) and *exclusive* (write) locks. Multiple transactions can concurrently obtain shared locks on an object. However, only one transaction can obtain an exclusive lock on an object.

Every processes is an element of one of two disjoint sets. The first set contains the majority of processes. These are non-leader processes that only update their counter in each round. The second set of processes contains the leader process, processes contending to become the leader, and processes that have not yet obtained a unique id. Usually this group is very small, and it depends upon the amount of churn in the system.

All the processes in the first set can run concurrently as they only update their own counters. However, the processes in the second set may take decisions or change the state of the global variables which can effect other processes. Therefore, all the transactions of the processes in the second set are serialized. For example, assume the leader wants to evict a slow process. By taking exclusive locks, the leader process prevents the slow process from committing any updates to shared state. When the slow process' transaction is scheduled, it will notice its id is missing and it will have to rejoin the system. Similarly, if two processes are contending to become the leader then their operations should be serialized to prevent a system state where there are multiple leaders. Moreover, the first round of new processes are also serialized to generate monotonically increasing ids.

4.2   Leader Election Rounds

Each round encapsulates its operations in a transaction that starts by taking a lock on the VARS register which acts as a *synchronization point*. Processes belonging to the first group acquire shared locks while the processes in the second group acquire exclusive locks on the VARS register, lines 5 – 9.

After acquiring locks on the VARS register all the processes descriptors are read without any locks (read committed). The processes update their counters and check if they can become the new leader. Each process maintains a history of process descriptors to identify dead processes, lines 12 – 14. Now, we explain these operations in more detail from the perspective of both groups of processes.

A new process starts by taking exclusive locks in the first round. It obtains a new monotonically increasing id and stores its descriptor, lines 32 –33. An exclusive lock is required to update the maximum process id in the VARS register. An evicted process will not find its descriptor, as it has been deleted. The evicted process cannot obtain a new process id if it does not hold an exclusive lock on the VARS register. In such a case, the transaction is immediately retried using exclusive locks, see lines 5, and 27 – 31. Additionally, the evicted process sets a flag to inform the leader that it was evicted prematurely, see line 30.

The service then checks for changes in the group membership. A process is declared dead if it fails to update its counter in multiple consecutive rounds. The threshold, Max_{mhb}, determines the number of rounds a process can miss before it is declared dead. The Max_{mhb} is usually set to ≥ 2. The process elects itself to be the leader if it has the smallest id among the alive processes. The leader process cleans the DESCRIPTORS register by removing the dead processes. If a non-leader process, that holds a shared lock, finds out that it can become the leader then it immediately retries the transaction with exclusive locks. It becomes the leader and removes the dead descriptors. If the process does not have the smallest id then it sets its role to *non_leader* and stores the descriptor of the process that has smallest id in a local variable, lines 34 – 44.

4.3   Global Stabilization Time (GST)

The time bounds for communication and processing latencies are not known in advance. For large systems the initial round time for periodically updating the counter may not be sufficiently long enough so that all processes mange to update their counters in a single round. Moreover, the round time must be automatically adjusted to cater for slow processes; otherwise, the system may not stabilize. In our implementation, only the leader process increases the round time by updating the VARS register (which is read by all processes).

Slow processes are evicted by the leader. When a process finds out that it was evicted, it obtains a new id and set a flag in the VARS register to notify the leader that it was wrongfully suspected. When the leader process finds that the evicted flag is set it increases the round time by a constant value Δ, see lines 16 – 18.

4.4   Leader Lease

Our solution ensures that there is never more than one leader in the system. However, this *invariant* is difficult to enforce before the GST has reached. Additionally, in order to reduce contention on the registers, methods like *isLeader*() and *getLeader*() return information stored in the local variables. On a slow process these variables may contain stale values. For instance, assume a slow process, L_a, becomes the leader. After becoming the leader L_a fails to update its counter in multiple consecutive rounds. Later, a new process becomes a leader and L_a is evicted. However, L_a will remain oblivious of the fact that it has been evicted, and its function *isLeader()* will keep on returning true until L_a manages to read new values from the registers.

In order to ensure *integrity* of the leader election service each leader process stores a local lease. Whenever the leader process updates its counter, it acquires a lease for the duration of $(T_p * Max_{mhb} - \mu)$. The constant, μ, is to accommodate for clock drifts. Before committing the transaction, a timestamp is stored in L_{hbt}, which indicates the start of the leader lease time, line 20. The lease is the the maximum time during which the leader cannot be evicted by other processes. If the leader is slow and it fails to update its counter then the lease will eventually expire and the process will voluntarily yield its leader role, line 45 – 50. The election of a new leader will happen after the lease of previous leader has expired, see theorem 1 for more details.

4.5   Dealing with Failures

Note that the transactions only guarantee the atomicity of the registers. Read committed isolation ensures that, during transaction execution, partial results (changes in the registers) are not be visible to other transactions until the transaction has committed. When a transaction fails the database rollbacks only the partial changes in the registers. However, it is the responsibility of the application to rollback all the local variables, such as *role*, L_{hbt}, T_p, and *id*. For clarity reasons we do not show code listing to rollback local variables.

5   Proof

In this section we prove the safety (at most one leader invariant) and the liveness (termination) properties of our leader election algorithm.

Theorem 1. *There is never more than one leader in the system.*

Proof. In order to prove that there cannot be two leaders, L_s and L_n, in the system at the same time we will prove that (I) two processes cannot declare themselves as leader simultaneously (II) a process cannot become leader while another process still sees itself as leader.

Case I: In order to become a leader both the processes, L_s and L_n, need to acquire exclusive locks at the beginning of the transaction. As a result the transactions for L_s and L_n will be serialized. If L_s manages to acquire the exclusive lock first, it will update the counter and elect itself as a leader (assuming the transaction commits). L_n will wait until L_s releases the lock. L_n will acquire the locks after L_s commits the transaction, and it will find out that L_s has already became the leader. As a result L_n will not declare itself the leader.

In a case where L_s halts after acquiring the exclusive lock, the database will timeout L_s's transaction and release the lock. The database will rollback the transaction and L_s will have to re-acquire the exclusive lock in order to become a leader. L_s has to reset its local role variable to *non_leader*.

Case II: When a process becomes the leader it acquires a lease that is valid for $(T_p * Max_{mhb} - \mu)$. The process voluntarily gives up the leader role if it fails to renew the lease before it expires. In order to ensure that a process L_n cannot become the leader while a slow leader L_s still has a valid lease, the protocol needs to ensure that the time needed by L_n to suspect L_s is higher than the time duration of L_s's lease.

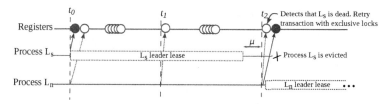

Fig. 1. Black and white circles represent exclusive and shared locks, respectively. Process L_s is a slow leader that does not update the counter after t_0. Process L_n becomes leader after the lease for L_s expires.

Assume the processing and network latencies of the process L_n are *zero*. Furthermore, the process L_n performs a heartbeat (read and update the registers) soon after L_s commits an update. The process L_n will find out that L_s is alive. After that, it will have to read the registers Max_{mhb} times before it can suspect L_s. Max_{mhb} heartbeat rounds will take $(T_p * Max_{mhb})$ seconds, assuming that L_n's clock drift is negligible. Thus, the minimum time that L_n needs to suspect L_s and elect itself as leader is $(T_p * Max_{mhb})$, which is strictly more than the lease time of L_s. The assumption that L_n does not have any processing and network latencies represents a worst case scenario. In a real system the latencies will always have some positive value which will increase the time needed by L_n to declare L_s as dead. The constant, μ, should be configured to be higher than the upper bound on clock drift for any process in the system. In practical systems, NTP, GPS, atomic clocks are used to ensure low bounds on clock drift.

An illustration of this worst case scenario is presented in Figure 1 where $Max_{mhb} = 2$. The leader L_s is faulty and it does not update the counter after t_0. At time t_2 the process L_n detects that L_s is faulty and it can become the new leader. As L_n does not hold the exclusive lock, it immediately retries the transaction, acquires the exclusive lock and becomes the leader. The lease of L_s expires after $T_p * 2 - \mu$, which is less than the time L_n must wait to detect the failure of the process L_s.

Theorem 2. *A correct process eventually becomes the leader.*

Proof. Assume a system configuration of $p_1, p_2, p_3...p_k...p_n$ processes. Additionally, assume p_k is the only correct process that repeatedly manages to update its counter every Max_{mhb} rounds. All the other processes are incorrect such that these processes do not always manage to update the counter within Max_{mhb} rounds. A correct process is never suspected by any process in the system. We show that the process p_k eventually becomes a leader and retains the leader role in the subsequent rounds.

Assume all the processes have just started and the history of each process is empty. The process p_1 will declare itself to be the leader and it will retain the role for $T_p * Max_{mhb} - \mu$ seconds. During the first Max_{mhb} rounds no process will be evicted. If p_1 is an incorrect process which fails to update the counter, its lease for the leadership will expire. In the round $(Max_{mhb} + 1)$ a process with least id that managed to update the counter, while p_1 was the leader, will become the new leader. The new leader will evict p_1 along with other suspected processes, if any. An evicted process might rejoin the system, but it is will be assigned with a new id by the monotonically increasing function. The eviction of incorrect processes will continue until p_k becomes the process with the least id in the system. The process p_k will elect itself as the new leader. As the process p_k is correct it will not miss any heartbeats and it will retain the leader role in subsequent rounds.

6   Evaluation

We have implemented the leader election using in-memory, highly-available, distributed database called NDB (Version 7.4.3), the storage engine for MySQL Cluster [5]. NDB is a real-time, ACID-compliant, relational database with no single point of failure and support for row-level locking. We use the native Java API for NDB, ClusterJ, as it provides lower latency and higher throughput than the SQL API that uses the MySQL Server.

All the experiments were performed on nodes behind a single 1 Gbit switch, where the network round trip time between any two nodes is in single digit millisecond range. The NDB setup consisted of six data nodes (6-core AMD Opteron 2.6 GHz, 32GB RAM) with replication factor of 2. We compare our solution with a leader election solution implemented using ZooKeeper. The ZooKeeper setup consisted of three quorum nodes (6-core AMD Opteron, 32GB RAM). We used the leader election library for ZooKeeper (Version 3.4.6) from the Apache Curator project (Version 2.7.1). Each ZooKeeper client creates a sequential ephemeral node in predetermined directory. Each node registers a *watch* (callback request) for its predecessor. Upon a node failure its successor is notified. The successor checks if there are any nodes with smaller sequential number. If there are no smaller nodes available then it elects itself as the new leader; otherwise, it registers a new watch for its new predecessor.

In the experiments the initial heartbeat round time was set to 2 seconds and Max_{mhb} was set to 2. To accurately determine the failover time all the clients were run on a single machine (12-core Intel Xeon 2.8 GHz, 40 GB RAM). All experiments were performed fifteen times and the graphs show the average results, with the error bars showing the standard deviation of the results. In each experiment N processes are started. When all processes have joined the system, the round time is continuously monitored for changes. If it does not change for a certain time (three minutes) then the system is considered stable. After the system has stabilized the leader process is repeatedly killed 50 times to measure failover time.

Figure 2a shows the relation between network size and the time to elect a new leader. Up to 200 processes the service consistently elects a new leader in around five seconds. However, when the network sizes increases beyond 200 nodes the time to elect new leader also increases. This can also be observed in figure 2b which shows the relationship between round time and the network

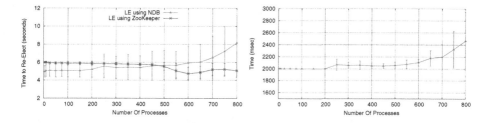

(a) Average time to elect a new leader.   (b) Heartbeat round time after GST.

Fig. 2. Performance of leader election service with the default configuration settings for NDB (MySQL Cluster). Figure 2a shows the average time to elect a new leader when the current leader process fails. Figure 2b shows the increase in the heartbeat round time when the leader detects contention on the registers.

size. For network sizes up to 200 processes, all the processes manage to update the counter before they are suspected by the leader process. However, when the network size increases beyond 200, contention on the registers prevents some processes from writing to the shared register for consecutive heartbeats. The leader processes detects contention on the registers when an evicted process raises the evict flag. The leader process increases the heartbeat delay to release the contention on the registers, which has the side-effect of also increasing the leader failover time. In the experiments, the heartbeat delay increment (Δ) was set to 50 milliseconds.

In the implementation of leader election using ZooKeeper, the time to elect a new leader is determined by two configuration parameters: *tick time* and *session timeout*. We set these values as low as possible to quickly elect a new leader in case of a leader failure. The lowest allowable values for *tick time* is 2 seconds, and *session timeout* is 4 seconds. In order to accurately determine the fail over time all leader election processes were run on one (12-core Intel Xeon 2.8 GHz, 40 GB RAM) machine. Up to 400 processes ZooKeeper constantly elects a new leader in six seconds. However the time to elect new leader starts to drop if we increase the number of clients on the same machine. This is because of the contention on the CPU and main memory because of which the processes slowed down. When a leader is killed it may have already skipped a heartbeat. This results in quicker reelection of a new leader. Due to memory limitations we could not add more than 800 processes in the experiment.

7   Related Work

Leader election is a well studied problem. All the related research can be classified into two broad categories: shared memory and message passing based leader election protocols.

Guerraoui et al. presented the first failure detector, Ω, that was implemented using shared memory for an eventually synchronous system [8]. The protocol is write optimal, only the leader process writes to the shared memory, and all other non-leader processes only read shared memory. Fernandez et al. further investigated the problem in systems where all processes are not eventually synchronous [9, 10]. In [9], they propose solutions for systems which require only one process to eventually behave synchronously. All other process can behave fully asynchronously provided that their timers are well behaved. In [10], two t-resilient protocols are presented that require a single, eventually synchronous, process and $t - f$ processes with well behaved timers, where t is the maximum number of processes that may fail, and f is maximum number of processes that can fail in a single run. For synchronous systems, a leader election algorithm using shared memory is presented in [22], where a semaphore is used to prevent multiple writers from concurrently updating the counter.

The first leader election protocols using message passing are timer-based. Processes send messages to each other to indicate they are alive. A process is suspected if it fails to send a heartbeat message within a time bound. If a heartbeat is received from a suspected process the timer is increased to accommodate for slow processes. Eventually time bounds for processing and communication latencies are determined for the given system by successively increasing the timer upon receiving a message from a suspected process. Some notable leader election protocols in the message passing paradigm using timers are [23–25].

Mostefaoui et al. presented a time-free implementation of failure detectors [26]. It allows the communication and processing times to always increase. The protocol assumes that the query-response messages obey a certain pattern. The protocol requires a correct process p and $f + 1$ processes from a set Q such that if processes repeatedly wait to receive messages from $n - f$ processes, then eventually the messages from p are always among the first $n - f$ messages received by each process in Q. Here n is the system size and f is the maximum number of processes that can fail. The protocol works for any value of f (i.e., $1 \leq f < n$).

8   Conclusions

We have shown that a reliable leader election service can be implemented using two phase commit transactions in the NDB storage engine, a NewSQL database. Our solution ensures that there is never more than one leader, and the time taken for leader election is comparable to ZooKeeper for clusters of up to 800 processes. Our algorithm enables distributed systems that already use NewSQL databases to save the operational overhead of deploying a third-party service, such as ZooKeeper, for leader election, as our algorithm can easily be re-implemented for other NewSQL databases.

Acknowledgement. This work funded by the EU FP7 project "Scalable, Secure Storage and Analysis of Biobank Data" under Grant Agreement no. 317871, and by Swedish e-Science Research Center (SeRC) as a part of the e-Science for Cancer Prevention and Control (eCPC) project.

References

1. Lamport, L.: Paxos made simple. ACM Sigact News 32(4), 18–25 (2001)
2. Chandra, T.D., Hadzilacos, V., Toueg, S.: The weakest failure detector for solving consensus. J. ACM 43(4), 685–722 (1996)
3. Junqueira, F.P., Reed, B.C.: The life and times of a zookeeper. In: Proceedings of the 28th ACM Symposium on Principles of Distributed Computing, p. 4. ACM (2009)
4. Shvachko, K., Kuang, H., Radia, S., Chansler, R.: The hadoop distributed file system. In: Mass Storage Systems and Technologies, pp. 1–10 (May 2010)
5. Ronström, M., Oreland, J.: Recovery Principles of MySQL Cluster 5.1. In: Proc. of VLDB 2005, pp. 1108–1115. VLDB Endowment (2005)
6. Burrows, M.: The chubby lock service for loosely-coupled distributed systems. In: Proceedings of the 7th Symposium on Operating Systems Design and Implementation, OSDI 2006, pp. 335–350. USENIX Association, Berkeley (2006)
7. Hunt, P., Konar, M., Junqueira, F.P., Reed, B.: Zookeeper: Wait-free coordination for internet-scale systems. In: Proceedings of the 2010 USENIX Conference on USENIX Annual Technical Conference, USENIXATC 2010, p. 11 (2010)
8. Guerraoui, R., Raynal, M.: A Leader Election Protocol for Eventually Synchronous Shared Memory Systems, pp. 75–80. IEEE Computer Society, Alamitos (2006)
9. Fernandez, A., Jimenez, E., Raynal, M.: Electing an eventual leader in an asynchronous shared memory system. In: Dependable Systems and Networks, DSN 2007, pp. 399–408 (June 2007)
10. Fernandez, A., Jimenez, E., Raynal, M., Tredan, G.: A timing assumption and a t-resilient protocol for implementing an eventual leader service in asynchronous shared memory systems. In: ISORC 2007, pp. 71–78 (May 2007)
11. Sqlserver @ONLINE (January 2015), http://www.microsoft.com/en-us/server-cloud/products/sql-server/
12. Mysql :: The world's most popular open source database @ONLINE (January 2015), http://www.mysql.com/
13. White paper: Xa and oracle controlled distributed transactions @ONLINE (June 2010), http://www.oracle.com/technetwork/products/clustering/overview/distributed-transactions-and-xa-163941.pdf
14. Lakshman, A., Malik, P.: Cassandra: A decentralized structured storage system. SIGOPS Oper. Syst. Rev. 44, 35–40 (2010)
15. Riak, basho technologies @ONLINE (January 2015), http://basho.com/riak/
16. Stonebraker, M., Madden, S., Abadi, D.J., Harizopoulos, S., Hachem, N., Helland, P.: The end of an architectural era (it's time for a complete rewrite). In: Proceedings of the 33rd International VLDB Conference, pp. 1150–1160 (2007)
17. Özcan, F., Tatbul, N., Abadi, D.J., Kornacker, M., Mohan, C., Ramasamy, K., Wiener, J.: Are we experiencing a big data bubble? In: Proceedings of the 2014 ACM SIGMOD International Conference on Management of Data, pp. 1407–1408 (2014)
18. Multi-model database – foundationdb @ONLINE (January 2015), https://foundationdb.com/
19. In-memory database, newsql and real-time analytics – voltdb @ONLINE (January 2015), http://voltdb.com/
20. Fischer, M.J., Lynch, N.A., Paterson, M.S.: Impossibility of distributed consensus with one faulty process. J. ACM 32, 374–382 (1985)

21. Thomson, A., Diamond, T., Weng, S.-C., Ren, K., Shao, P., Abadi, D.J.: Calvin: Fast Distributed Transactions for Partitioned Database Systems. In: Proc. of SIGMOD 2012, pp. 1–12. ACM (2012)

22. Sanz-Marco, V., Zolda, M., Kirner, R.: Efficient leader election for synchronous shared-memory systems. In: Proc. Int'l Workshop on Performance, Power and Predictability of Many-Core Embedded Systems (3PMCES 2014). Electronic Chips and Systems Design Initiative (ECSI) (March 2014)

23. Aguilera, M., Delporte-Gallet, C., Fauconnier, H., Toueg, S.: On implementing omega in systems with weak reliability and synchrony assumptions. Distributed Computing 21(4), 285–314 (2008)

24. Aguilera, M.K., Delporte-Gallet, C., Fauconnier, H., Toueg, S.: Communication-efficient leader election and consensus with limited link synchrony. In: Proceedings of the Twenty-Third Annual ACM Symposium on Principles of Distributed Computing, PODC 2004, pp. 328–337. ACM, New York (2004)

25. Larrea, M., Fernandez, A., Arevalo, S., Carlos, J., Carlos, J.: Optimal implementation of the weakest failure detector for solving consensus, pp. 52–59. IEEE Computer Society Press

26. Mostefaoui, A., Mourgaya, E., Raynal, M.: Asynchronous implementation of failure detectors. In: Proceedings of the 2003 International Conference on Dependable Systems and Networks, pp. 351–360 (June 2003)

Distributed Monitoring and Management of Exascale Systems in the Argo Project

Swann Perarnau[1](✉), Rajeev Thakur[1], Kamil Iskra[1], Ken Raffenetti[1],
Franck Cappello[1], Rinku Gupta[1], Pete Beckman[1], Marc Snir[1],
Henry Hoffmann[2], Martin Schulz[3], and Barry Rountree[3]

[1] Argonne National Laboratory, Lemont, IL 60439, USA
[2] University of Chicago, Chicago, IL 60637, USA
[3] Lawrence Livermore National Laboratory, Livermore, CA 94550, USA
schulzm@llnl.gov

Abstract. New computing technologies are expected to change the high-performance computing landscape dramatically. Future exascale systems will comprise hundreds of thousands of compute nodes linked by complex networks—resources that need to be actively monitored and controlled, at a scale difficult to manage from a central point as in previous systems.

In this context, we describe here on-going work in the Argo exascale software stack project to develop a distributed collection of services working together to track scientific applications across nodes, control the power budget of the system, and respond to eventual failures. Our solution leverages the idea of enclaves: a hierarchy of logical partitions of the system, representing groups of nodes sharing a common configuration, created to encapsulate user jobs as well as by the user inside its own job. These enclaves provide a second (and greater) level of control over portions of the system, can be tuned to manage specific scenarios, and have dedicated resources to do so.

1   Introduction

Disruptive new computing technology has already begun to change the scientific computing landscape. Hybrid CPUs, many-core systems, and low-power system-on-a-chip designs are being used in today's most powerful high-performance computing (HPC) systems. As these technology shifts continue and exascale machines emerge, the *Argo* research project aims to provide an operating system and runtime (OS/R) designed to support extreme-scale scientific computations. To this end, it seeks to efficiently leverage new chip and interconnect technologies while addressing the new modalities, programming environments, and workflows expected at exascale. At the heart of the project are four key innovations: dynamic reconfiguring of node resources in response to workload changes, allowance for massive concurrency, a hierarchical framework for management of nodes, and a cross-layer communication infrastructure that allows resource managers and optimizers to communicate efficiently across the platform. These innovations will result in an open-source prototype system that is expected to form the basis of production exascale systems deployed in the 2020 timeframe.

© IFIP International Federation for Information Processing 2015
A. Bessani and S. Bouchenak (Eds.): DAIS 2015, LNCS 9038, pp. 173–178, 2015.
DOI: 10.1007/978-3-319-19129-4_14

Argo is designed with a hierarchical approach. The system is organized in *enclaves*, a set of resources that share the same configuration and can be controlled as a whole. Enclaves can monitor their performance, respond to failures, and control power usage according to a budget. These enclaves form a hierarchy: the top enclave is acting over the whole system, while jobs are contained in their own enclave and the user can subdivide its job enclave further.

We describe here the early stages of an ongoing effort, as part of Argo, to design the services that will take care of creating, keeping track of, and destroying enclaves, as well as monitoring and controlling the resources and failures happening in those enclaves. Our design is influenced by two factors. First, we expect that future machines will differ significantly from current HPC systems in size, failure rate, and fine-grained access to resources. Second, we don't expect the Argo system to behave as commonly available distributed systems such as peer-to-peer or cloud infrastructures. Indeed, an HPC machine will still be composed of known, dedicated resources over which we have total control (as low level as necessary). As a result, we believe that several services typical of a distributed infrastructure can benefit from this unique setup and from being distributed across the hierarchy of enclaves.

In Section 2 we describe more fully the components of the Argo system. In Section 3 we detail typical services we identified as critical to Argo, while also representing distinct communication and control patterns that could benefit from our unique setup. In Section 4 we review related work, and in Section 4 we briefly discuss future work.

2   The Argo Machine: Architecture, Enclaves and Underlying Services

While predicting the exact architecture of future exascale systems is difficult, the Argo project bases its designs on general trends such as those highlighted in the Exascale Software Project Roadmap [1]. We expect the Argo machine to be composed of hundreds of thousands of compute nodes, with each node containing hundreds of cores. Furthermore, those nodes will be linked together by dedicated and highly efficient networks, integrating smart control and monitoring interfaces. We also expect that, in order to meet the U.S. DOE exascale budget limits, complex power management interfaces will be available at all levels of the machine.

The software stack designed by the Argo project to manage such a machine is divided into four key components. First, each compute node will use a customized operating system derived from Linux (*NodeOS*). Second, a runtime taking advantage of massive intranode parallelism (*Argobots*) will be available. Third, a global information bus or *backplane* will provide advanced communication services on top of the native network. In particular, a distributed key-value store and a pub-sub system will be available to other components. Fourth, the *GlobalOS*—the focus of this paper—will manage enclaves and their services.

As stated in Section 1, enclaves are logical groups of nodes sharing the same configuration. They are organized in a tree, whose root is the enclave containing all nodes. Inside an enclave, at least one node (*master*) hosts the services specific to this enclave. Masters communicate with each other to distribute control of the nodes in the system. We note that nodes are members of all enclaves above them in the hierarchy. In other words, a master node controls all nodes in its subtree in the hierarchy of enclaves, and not just the masters of its subenclaves. Enclaves cannot be created inside a compute node: they are logical constructs intended to manage only the distributed part of the Argo machine. Figure 1 gives an example of a hierarchy of four enclaves distributed across a system, with each enclave having its master replicated across several nodes.

This enclave concept is critical to the design of the distributed services managing the Argo machine. In particular, we organize responsibilities so that as much of the node management as possible is delegated to the deepest master in the hierarchy. Conversely, the higher in the hierarchy, the less the interaction between the master and nodes, and the more coarse-grained this interaction is. We give typical examples in the next section.

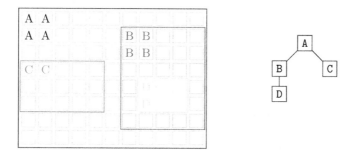

Fig. 1. Example of a hierarchy of 4 enclaves. On the left, the squares represent compute nodes, with the filled ones representing the master and its replica. On the right, the hierarchy of enclaves is represented as a tree.

3   Typical Services in the Argo Machine

Three services critical to GlobalOS can serve as examples of the different ways the enclave hierarchy is used in Argo.

3.1   Hierarchical Control Bus for Enclaves

The Argo system is used like any other HPC system: a user submits to the system a job comprising at least the number of nodes required, the time duration, the configuration (to be deployed across the job), and the script or application to run. In our infrastructure, each job is managed as an enclave, a direct child of the *root* enclave (which contains all nodes). Furthermore, the user can create enclaves inside the job, if he needs distinct parts of the allocated nodes to have different features or different configurations. This process distributes the responsibilities of node management between the masters at different levels of the hierarchy. The root master has the exclusive role of creating enclaves at its level, and does so only when receiving commands from the job scheduler. A master at the *job enclave* level might be responsible only for creating subenclaves; and so on. Similarly, since the user has control over all nodes in a job enclave, commands to reconfigure an enclave, a subtree of an enclave, or just one node might happen at different levels of the hierarchy.

Thus, the chain of command between the root master and a node can be seen as a bus, where commands flow from master to master, going deeper into the hierarchy, with each master affecting the process or injecting new commands until they reach a node. Some commands might be of higher priority (e.g., the root enclave asking for job termination) or be altered (e.g., a command that must span an entire enclave instead of just one node). Nevertheless, all enclave masters are responsible for the continuous working of their enclaves, from the moment the enclave management is delegated to them until the enclave exits (all nodes gracefully exit the enclave, including the master) or is destroyed (massive failure, forceful exit). We are designing this control bus on top of two mechanisms: a logical naming scheme that allows a message or command to be sent to different stages of the control bus (an enclave, a master, or a specific node) and a message broker dedicated to the control bus, present on each node, and forwarding messages across the bus in the right order.

The naming scheme is similar to paths in a filesystem: each enclave is a directory with the root enclave at the top, and nodes are files in those directories. A few special names also exist: '..' (parent enclave), '.' (closest enclave), and '*' (all enclaves/nodes). This naming scheme simplifies sending a command to a specific part of the system, even from a node having only partial knowledge of the hierarchy: it is enough to know the next master in the path. This knowledge is kept in the key-value store available in the Argo system, so that every node knows its own path and how to contact parent and children enclaves. As an example, a node in the enclave D will have the path /B/D/node.

The message broker infrastructure is also simple. A message broker runs on each node and uses the key-value store to route messages to the various masters on the bus. This broker also inspects each message to decide whether commands need to be triggered locally or whether the message needs to be altered or redirected. This design avoids specifying how those messages should be transported. Indeed, as several communication services are made available by the backplane, several communication channels might be available at the same time. For example, it might be more efficient to distribute a command across all nodes of an enclave by using a reliable publish-subscribe interface rather than using point-to-point communication. Such choices are being evaluated but might depend on the specific architecture our system is deployed on.

3.2   Distributed Power Management

Since we expect the size of an exascale machine to involve hundreds of thousands of compute nodes, controlling the total power consumption of the system is critical. Indeed, such systems represent tens of megawatts in consumption and a significant cost to any organization. Therefore, idle parts of the system or underutilized resources should be put in low-power modes as much as possible. To do so, we expect the architecture to provide meters distributed across the system to measure the current power usage and interfaces, similar to dynamic frequency scaling or Intel's RAPL [4] on each node. We therefore are designing a distributed power management service as part of GlobalOS.

This service comprises two components: a reader service, running on each node, that periodically reports power consumption to its enclave master and a power control service, installed on enclave masters, that distributes a global power budget across the enclave hierarchy. The power consumption reader design is straightforward. On each node, periodically the local measuring interface is used to gather information, which is then sent to the closest master. Each master then aggregates the data coming from its enclave and sends it to its parent, and so on. This information gathering is made possible by the publish-subscribe service of the backplane, and likewise for the aggregation. The power control service reacts to information coming from the consumption reader as well as global power budget limits set by the machine administrators. The exact algorithms used to distribute this power budget across the hierarchy will be derived from previous work [3,2].

3.3   Managing Failures as Exceptions

Given the expected size of an exascale machine, failures—in both hardware and software—will have a statistically greater chance of occurring than in previous systems. Consequently, all components of Argo are being designed with faults in mind. This effort includes replication of masters across the enclave hierarchy, for example.

While failure detection is a complex issue in itself, our focus here is on reactions to failures. We designed a service distributed across the enclave hierarchy that, when notified of failures, acts like an exception system: each master on the path between the failed component and the root enclave will receive the notification one by one, from the deepest in the hierarchy to the highest, and have a chance to act on it. If a master cannot act or resolve the failure, the parent master will take control, and so on.

The specific action a master takes will depend on the component that failed and on the recovery/reaction strategy active on the failure manager. We plan to design several strategies, ranging from restarting the component to destroying the enclave, that users will be able to configure inside their enclaves. We expect the root enclave to have the most complex strategy, with the additional role of notifying administrators in case of unrecoverable hardware failures, and having sole control of powering off and on nodes, for example.

4   Related Works and Conclusion

Similar projects on a new software stack for exascale systems have recently emerged, including the Hobbes project directed by Sandia National Laboratories in the United States and the post-K project directed by RIKEN in Japan. We are collaborating with them on the design of several components, and we expect these efforts to result in robust and versatile components to manage an entire machine. Recent cloud technologies, such as OpenStack, have also started to address the issues in orchestrating and monitoring distributed resources. These technologies are, however, targeted to systems with smaller numbers of compute nodes, no dedicated high-performance networks, and no static knowledge of the available hardware.

We are still in the design phase of our distributed framework for the provisioning, management, and monitoring of an exascale machine. Our goal is to build on the features of the future architecture and Argo's communication component, focusing on a hierarchical and lightweight solution that is tuned as issues become apparent as the project advances. We hope that in the coming year, with an integrated Argo prototype implemented, our research will move its focus to the study and design of efficient management strategies to be implemented into the various services of the GlobalOS.

Acknowledgement. This work was supported by the U.S. Dept. of Energy, Office of Science, Advanced Scientific Computing Research Program, under Contract DE-AC02-06CH11357. Part of this work was performed under the auspices of the U.S. Department of Energy by Lawrence Livermore National Laboratory under Contract DE-AC52-07NA27344 (LLNL-CONF-669278). The submitted manuscript has been created by UChicago Argonne, LLC, Operator of Argonne National Laboratory ("Argonne"). Argonne, a U.S. Department of Energy Office of Science laboratory, is operated under Contract No. DE-AC02-06CH11357. The U.S. Government retains for itself, and others acting on its behalf, a paid-up nonexclusive, irrevocable worldwide license in said article to reproduce, prepare derivative works, distribute copies to the public, and perform publicly and display publicly, by or on behalf of the Government.

References

1. Dongarra, J., Beckman, P., et al.: The International Exascale Software Project Roadmap. International Journal of High Performance Computing Applications 25(1), 3–60 (2011)
2. Ellsworth, D., Malony, A., Rountree, B., Schulz, M.: POW: system-wide dynamic reallocation of limited power in hpc. To appear in International ACM Symposium on High Performance Distributed Computing, HPDC 2015, Portland, OR, USA (2015)
3. Hoffmann, H., Maggio, M.: PCP: A generalized approach to optimizing performance under power constraints through resource management. In: International Conference on Autonomic Computing, ICAC 2014, Philadelphia, PA, USA (2014)
4. Rountree, B., Ahn, D.H., de Supinski, B.R., Lowenthal, D.K., Schulz, M.: Beyond DVFS: A first look at performance under a hardware-enforced power bound. In: International Parallel and Distributed Processing Symposium Workshops & PhD Forum, IPDPSW 2012, Shanghai, China (2012)

The Impact of Consistency on System Latency in Fault Tolerant Internet Computing

Olga Tarasyuk[1], Anatoliy Gorbenko[1], Alexander Romanovsky[2(✉)], Vyacheslav Kharchenko[1], and Vitalii Ruban[1]

[1] Department of Computer Systems and Networks,
National Aerospace University, Kharkiv, Ukraine
{O.Tarasyuk,A.Gorbenko}@csn.khai.edu, V.Kharchenko@khai.edu
[2] School of Computing Science, Newcastle University, Newcastle upon Tyne, UK
Alexander.Romanovsky@ncl.ac.uk

Abstract. The paper discusses our practical experience and theoretical results in investigating the impact of consistency on latency in distributed fault tolerant systems built over the Internet. Trade-offs between consistency, availability and latency are examined, as well as the role of the application timeout as the main determinant of the interplay between system availability and performance. The paper presents experimental results of measuring response time for replicated service-oriented systems that provide different consistency levels: ONE, ALL and QUORUM. These results clearly show that improvements in system consistency increase system latency. A set of novel analytical models is proposed that would enable quantified response time prediction depending on the level of consistency provided by a replicated system.

Keywords: Internet computing · Fault-tolerance · Consistency · Latency · Response time · Modelling

1 Introduction

Distributed computing has become an industrial trend, indispensable in dealing with enormous data growth. High availability requirements for many modern Internet applications require the use of system redundancy and data replication. Basic fault tolerant solutions such as *N*-modular, hot- and cold-spare redundancy usually assume a synchronous communication between replicas, which means that every message is delivered within a fixed and known amount of time [1]. This is a reasonable simplification for the local-area systems whose components are compactly located, for instance, within a single data centre.

This assumption does not appear to be relevant, however, for the wide-area systems, in which replicas are deployed over the Internet and their updates cannot be propagated immediately, which makes it difficult to guarantee consistency.

The Internet and, more generally, the wide-area networked systems are characterized by a high level of uncertainty, which makes it hard to guarantee that a client will receive a response from the service within a finite time. It has been previously shown

© IFIP International Federation for Information Processing 2015
A. Bessani and S. Bouchenak (Eds.): DAIS 2015, LNCS 9038, pp. 179–192, 2015.
DOI: 10.1007/978-3-319-19129-4_15

that there is a significant uncertainty of response time in service-oriented systems invoked over the Internet [2–4]. Besides, our experience and other studies [4–7] show that failures are a regular occurrence on the Internet, clouds and in scale-out data centre networks. When developers apply replication and other fault tolerant techniques in the Internet- and cloud-based systems, they need to understand the time overheads and be concerned about delays and their uncertainty.

In this paper we examine, both in experimental and theoretical terms, how different fault-tolerance solutions [8] implemented over the Internet affect system latency depending on the level of consistency provided. The paper discusses the trade-offs between consistency, availability and latency. Although these relations have been identified by the CAP theorem in qualitative terms [9, 10], it is still necessary to quantify how different fault-tolerant techniques affect system latency depending on the consistency level. The main contributions of the paper are probabilistic models that can predict the system response time depending on the chosen fault-tolerance technique and/or the selected consistency level, with the probabilistic behaviour of replicas as an input parameter.

The rest of the paper is organized as follows. In Section 2 we discuss the impact of the CAP theorem [9, 10] on distributed fault-tolerant systems and examine the trade-offs between system consistency, availability and latency. Section 3 summarises the results of experimental response time measurements for testbed fault-tolerant systems that have three replicas distributed over the Internet and support different consistency levels. The probabilistic models introduced in Section 4 define the relation between system response time and the consistency level provided. Section 5 evaluates the accuracy of the proposed analytical models by applying them in practice and comparing their results with our experimental data. Finally, some practical lessons learnt from our experimental and theoretical work are summarised in Section 6.

2   Understanding Trade-offs Between Consistency, Availability and Latency in Distributed Fault-Tolerant Systems

The CAP conjecture [9], which first appeared in 1998-1999, defines a trade-off between system availability, consistency and partition tolerance, stating that only two of the three properties can be preserved in distributed replicated systems at the same time. Gilbert and Lynch [10] view the CAP theorem as a particular case of a more general trade-off between consistency and availability in unreliable distributed systems which assume that updates are eventually propagated.

System partitioning, availability and latency are tightly connected. A replicated fault-tolerant system becomes partitioned when one of its parts does not respond due to arbitrary message loss, delay or replica failure, resulting in a timeout. System availability can be interpreted as a probability that each client request eventually receives a response.

In many real systems, however, a response that is too late (i.e. beyond the application timeout) is treated as a failure. High latency is an undesirable effect for many interactive web applications. In [13] the authors showed that if a response time increases by as little as 100 ms, it dramatically reduces the probability of the customer continuing to use the system.

Failure to receive responses from some of the replicas within the specified timeout causes partitioning of the replicated system. Thus, partitioning can be considered as a bound on the replica's response time. A slow network connection, a slow-responding replica or the wrong timeout settings can lead to an erroneus decision that the system has become partitioned. When the system detects a partition, it has to decide whether to return a possibly inconsistent response to a client or to send an exception message in reply, which undermines system availability.

The designers of the distributed fault-tolerant systems cannot prevent partitions which happen due to network failures, message losses, hacker attacks and components crashes and, hence, have to choose between availability and consistency. One of these two properties has to be sacrificed. If system developers decide to forfeit consistency they can also improve the system response time by returning the fastest response to the client without waiting for other replica responses until the timeout, though this would increase the probability of providing inconsistent results. Besides, timeout settings are also important. If the timeout is lower than the typical response time, a system is likely to enter the partition mode more often [11].

It is important to remember that none of these three properties is binary. For example, modern distributed database systems, e.g. Cassandra [14], can provide a discrete set of different consistency levels for each particular read or write request. The response time can theoretically vary between zero and infinity, although in practice it ranges between a minimal affordable time higher than zero and the application timeout. Availability varies between 0% and 100% as usual.

The architects of modern distributed database management systems and large-scale web applications such as Facebook, Twitter, etc. often decide to relax consistency requirements by introducing asynchronous data updates in order to achieve higher system availability and allow a longer response time. Yet the most promising approach is to balance these properties. For instance, the Cassandra NoSQL DDBS introduces a tunable replication factor and an adjustable consistency model so that a customer can choose a particular level of consistency to fit with the desired system latency.

The CAP theorem helps the developers to understand the system trade-offs between consistency and availability/latency [12]. Yet even though this theorem strongly suggests that better consistency undermines system availability and latency, developers do not have quantitative models to help them to estimate the system response time for the chosen consistency level and to achieve a precise trade-off between them.

Our interpretation of the CAP theorem and the trade-offs resulting from the CAP is depicted in Fig. 1. The application timeout can be considered as a bound between system availability and performance (in term of latency or response time) [15]. Thus, system designers should be able to set up timeouts according to the desired system response time, also keeping in mind the choice between consistency and availability.

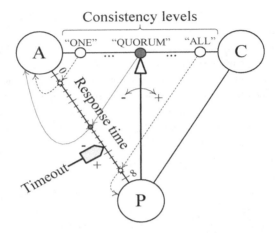

Fig. 1. The CAP trade-offs

In the following sections we discuss our practical experience on measuring latency of fault-tolerant service-oriented system depending on the provided consistency level and also introduce analytical models predicting system response time.

3   Experimental Investigation of the CAP Impact on Fault-Tolerant Service-Oriented Systems

3.1   Description of the Testbed Architecture

To investigate the CAP impact on fault-tolerant distributed systems we developed a testbed service-oriented system composed out of the three replicated web services (see Fig. 2). This is a typical setup employed in many fault-tolerant solutions.

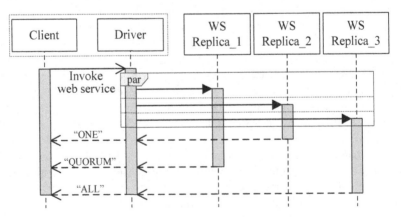

Fig. 2. Fault-tolerant service-oriented system

A testbed web service was written in Java and its replicas uploaded to Amazon Elastic Beanstalk and were deployed in the three different location domains: (i) US West (Oregon); (ii) South America (Sao Paulo) and Asia Pacific (Tokyo). Each web service replica performs a heavy-computational arithmetic calculation such as finding the n digit of Pi when n is a large number and returns the result to the driver. The driver is responsible for invoking each of the replicated web services, waiting for the web services to complete their execution and return response, and, finally, implementing a particular fault-tolerant scheme upon the obtained results.

AWS SDK for Java was used to connect web service replicas on Amazon EC2 from clients (driver) programming code that helps to take the complexity out of coding by providing Java APIs for AWS services.

In our study we investigated the three basic fault-tolerant patterns for web services [16] corresponding to different consistency levels (ONE, ALL, QUORUM). In all cases the driver simultaneously forwards client's request to all replicated web services. The consistency level determines the number of replicas which must return a response to the driver before it sends an adjudicated result to the client application:

- ONE (*hot-spare redundancy*) – when the FASTEST response is received the driver forwards it to the client. This is the weakest consistency level though it guarantees the minimal latency;
- ALL (*N-modular redundancy*) – the driver must wait until ALL replicas return their responses. In this case the response time is constrained by the slowest replica though the strongest consistency is provided;
- QUORUM – the driver must wait for the responses from a QUORUM of replica web services. It provides a compromise between the ONE and ALL options trading off latency versus consistency. The quorum is calculated as: (*amount_of_replicas* / 2) + 1, rounded down to an integer value. As far as in our experiments we use the replication factor of 3, the quorum is 2.

The driver also implements a timeout mechanism aimed to protect clients from endless waiting in case of network or web-services failures or cloud outages.

3.2   Response Time Measurement

The driver was implemented as part of the Java client software. The client software was run at a host in the Newcastle University (UK) corporate network. It invoked replica web services several thousand times in a loop using the driver as a proxy.

For the particular client's request we measured the response time of the each web service replica and also times when the driver produces responses corresponding to different consistency levels. The delay induced by the driver itself was negligible in our experiments.

The measurement results obtained for the first 100 invocations are presented in Figs. 3 and 4. Table 1 summarizes basic statistical characteristics of the measured data whereas probability density series (*pds*) of system and replicas response times are depicted in Figs. 5 and 6.

As expected, when the system is configured to provide consistency level ONE its latency in average is less than the average response time of the fastest replica. Average system latency in case it provides consistency level ALL is larger than the average response time of the slowest replica. System latency associated with consistency level QUORUM is in the middle.

However, our main observation is that it is hardly possible to make an accurate prediction of the average system latency corresponding to the certain consistency level when the only common statistical measures of replicas response time (i.e. minimal, maximal and average estimates and standard deviation) are known.

This finding resulting from our massive experiments and also confirmed by other researches [17] show that it is extremely difficult to predict the timing characteristics of various types of wide-area distributed systems, including fault-tolerant SOAs, distributed databases and file systems (e.g. Cassandra, GFS, HDFS), parallel processing systems (e.g. Hadoop Map-Reduce). The dynamic and changing nature of timing characteristics of such systems can be better captured by employing probability density functions.

In the next section we propose a probabilistic modelling approach that addresses this problem. It relies on using probability density functions (PDF) of replica response times to predict system latency at different consistency levels.

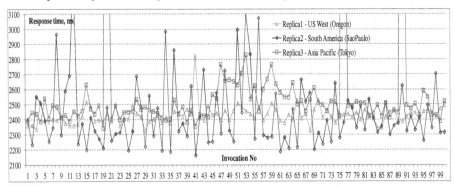

Fig. 3. Response time of different web service replicas

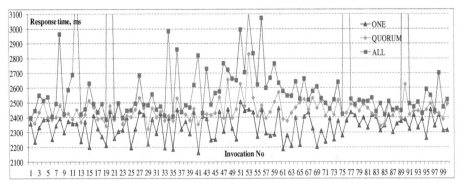

Fig. 4. System response time corresponding to different consistency levels

Table 1. Response time statistics

Response Time, ms	Replica1 (Oregon)	Replica2 (Sao Paulo)	Replica3 (Tokyo)	System consistency level		
				ONE	QUORUM	ALL
Minimal	2324	2164	2344	2164	2324	2386
Average	2428	2434	2588	2342	2449	2660
Maximal	2821	3371	5573	2509	2830	5573
Std. deviation	60	228	522	80	72	529

4   Probabilistic Models of System Response Time for Different Consistency Levels

We propose a set of probabilistic models that allow us to build a combined probability density function of system response time by taking into account provided consistency level and incorporating response time probability density functions for each replica.

When the system is configured to provide consistency level ALL, the probability of returning response to the client at time t is equal to the probability that one of the replicas (e.g. the first one) returns its response <u>exactly at time t</u>, i.e. $g_1(t)$ while two other replicas return their responses <u>not later than t</u> (by time t), i.e. $\int_0^t g_2(t) = G_2(t)$ and $\int_0^t g_3(t) = G_3(t)$.

So far as we have three replicas, all three possible combinations have to be accounted. As a result, the probability density function of the system response time for consistency level ALL can be defined as following:

$$f_{ALL}(t) = g_1(t)G_2(t)G_3(t) + g_2(t)G_1(t)G_3(t) + g_3(t)G_1(t)G_2(t). \quad (1)$$

where $g_1(t)$, $g_2(t)$ and $g_3(t)$ – are response time probability density functions of the first, second and third replicas respectively; $G_1(t)$, $G_2(t)$ and $G_3(t)$ – are response time cumulative distribution functions of the first, second and third replicas respectively.

When the system is configured to provide consistency level ONE, the probability of returning a response to the client at time t is equal to the probability that if only one of the replicas (e.g. the first one) returns its response <u>exactly at time t</u>, i.e. $g_1(t)$, while two other replicas return their responses <u>at the same time or later on</u>, i.e. $\int_t^\infty g_2(t) = 1 - G_2(t)$ and $\int_t^\infty g_3(t) = 1 - G_3(t)$.

Keeping in mind three possible combinations we can deduce the probability density function of the system response time for consistency level ALL as:

$$f_{ONE}(t) = g_1(t)\big(1 - G_2(t)\big)\big(1 - G_3(t)\big) + g_2(t)\big(1 - G_1(t)\big)\big(1 - G_3(t)\big) + \\ + g_3(t)\big(1 - G_1(t)\big)\big(1 - G_2(t)\big). \quad (2)$$

Deducing the response time probability density function for the QUORUM consistency level is based on a combination of the previous two cases.

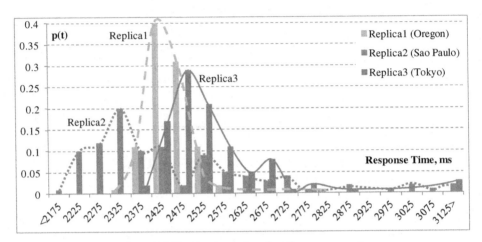

Fig. 5. Probability density series of replicas response times

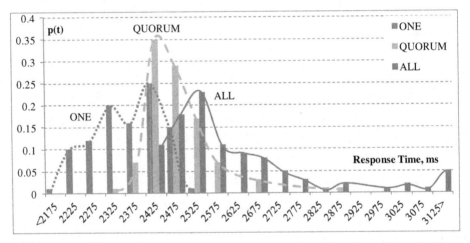

Fig. 6. Probability density series of system response time for different consistency levels

The probability of returning response to the client at time t is equal to the probability that one of the replicas returns its response exactly at time t; one of the two remained replicas returns its response by time t and another one responds at time t or later on. Taking into account all possible combinations the probability density function of the system response time for consistency level QUORUM can be deduced as:

$$f_{QUORUM}(t) = \left(g_1(t)G_2(t) + g_2(t)G_1(t)\right)\left(1 - G_3(t)\right) +$$
$$+ \left(g_1(t)G_3(t) + g_3(t)G_1(t)\right)\left(1 - G_2(t)\right) + \qquad (3)$$
$$+ \left(g_2(t)G_3(t) + g_3(t)G_2(t)\right)\left(1 - G_1(t)\right).$$

Using similar reasoning it is possible to deduce response time probability density functions of a system composed of n replicas:

$$f_{ALL}(t) = \sum_{i=1}^{n} \left(\frac{g_i(t)}{G_i(t)} \cdot \prod_{j=1}^{n} G_j(t) \right). \tag{4}$$

$$f_{ONE}(t) = \sum_{i=1}^{n} \left(\frac{g_i(t)}{1 - G_i(t)} \cdot \prod_{j=1}^{n} \left(1 - G_j(t) \right) \right). \tag{5}$$

It is extremely hard to build a general form of the probability density function of the system response time for consistency level QUORUM. However, the general reasoning is as following. The composed probability density function should be presented as a sum of m items, where m is a number of k-combinations of n (k is a number of replicas constituting a quorum). Each of the m items is a product of two factors. The first one defines the probability that a particular combination of k replicas return their responses by time t. Another factor defines the probability that the remaining $(n-k)$ replicas return their responses after t.

5   Models Validity

In this section we check the validity and accuracy of the proposed models by comparing their prediction with the experimental data presented in Section 3. This check includes the following four steps:

- finding out theoretical distribution laws that accurately approximate the measured replica response times;
- applying the proposed mathematical models (1), (2) and (3) to deduce probability density functions of the system response time for different consistency levels;
- estimating replica and system average response times using the theoretical probability distribution functions;
- comparing the theoretical and experimental values of replica and system average response times.

5.1   Finding Theoretical Distribution Laws of Replica Response Times

Theoretical distribution laws approximating replica response times can be found in a way described in [2]. It is based on performing a series of hypotheses checks in the Matlab numeric computing environment. The techniques of hypothesis testing consist of the two basic procedures. First, the values of distribution parameters are estimated by analysing an experimental sample. Second, the null hypothesis that experimental data has a particular distribution with certain parameters should be tested.

To perform hypothesis testing itself we used the `kstest` function: `[h, p] = kstest(t, cdf)`, conducting the Kolmogorov-Smirnov test to compare the distribution of t with the hypothesized distribution defined by matrix *cdf*.

The null hypothesis for the Kolmogorov-Smirnov test is that t has a distribution defined by *cdf*. The alternative hypothesis is that x does not have that distribution.

Result h is equal to '1' if we can reject the hypothesis, or '0' if we cannot. The function also returns the p-value which is the probability that x does not contradict the null hypothesis. We reject the hypothesis if the test is significant at the 5% level (if p-value is less than 0.05). The p-value returned by kstest was used to estimate the goodness-of-fit of the hypothesis. As a result of hypothesis testing we found out that the *Weibull* distribution fits well the response time of the first (Oregon) and the third (Tokyo) replicas. The response time of the second replica (Sao Paulo) can be accurately approximated by the *Gamma* distribution.

5.2   Deducing Probability Density Functions of the System Response Time

Mathcad has been used at the second stage of our investigation to deduce theoretical distributions of system response times for different consistency levels. It also allows to estimate average system latency and to plot probability density functions. Mathcad worksheet is shown in Fig. 7. It includes seven modelling steps.

At the 1st step we define abscissa axis t and its dimension in milliseconds. Secondly, we set up parameters of replicas response time distribution functions estimated in Matlab and also their shifts on the abscissa axis (i.e. minimal response time values).

At the 3rd and 4th steps the replica response time probability density functions $g_1(t)$, $g_2(t)$, $g_3(t)$ and the corresponding cumulative distribution functions $G_1(t)$, $G_2(t)$, $G_3(t)$ are defined using Mathcad library functions dweibull and dgamma.

At the 5th step we define probability density functions of the system response time corresponding to different consistency levels by combining replicas *pdf* and *cdf* according to the proposed equations (1), (2) and (3).

---

1 $\quad t := 2000, 2010 .. 3000$

2 $\quad$ a1 := 113.3578 $\qquad$ a2 := 1.5952 $\qquad$ a3 := 176.8796
$\quad$ b1 := 2.3041 $\qquad$ b2 := 164.1599 $\qquad$ b3 := 1.7467
$\quad$ min1 := 2324 $\qquad$ min2 := 2164 $\qquad$ min3 := 2344

3 $\quad g1(t) := \dfrac{1}{a1} \cdot \text{dweibull}\left[\dfrac{(t - min1)}{a1}, b1\right] \qquad g2(t) := \dfrac{1}{b2} \cdot \text{dgamma}\left[\dfrac{(t - min2)}{b2}, a2\right] \qquad g3(t) := \dfrac{1}{a3} \cdot \text{dweibull}\left[\dfrac{(t - min3)}{a3}, b3\right]$

4 $\quad G1(t) := \displaystyle\int_0^t g1(t)\,dt \qquad\qquad G2(t) := \displaystyle\int_0^t g2(t)\,dt \qquad\qquad G3(t) := \displaystyle\int_0^t g3(t)\,dt$

5 $\quad$ fALL(t) := g1(t)·G2(t)·G3(t) + g2(t)·G1(t)·G3(t) + g3(t)·G1(t)·G2(t)
$\quad$ fONE(t) := g1(t)·(1 − G2(t))·(1 − G3(t)) + g2(t)·(1 − G1(t))·(1 − G3(t)) + g3(t)·(1 − G1(t))·(1 − G2(t))
$\quad$ fQUORUM(t) := (g1(t)·G2(t)+g2(t)·G1(t))·(1−G3(t))+(g1(t)·G3(t)+g3(t)·G1(t))·(1−G2(t))+(g2(t)·G3(t)+g3(t)·G2(t))·(1−G1(t))

6 $\quad \displaystyle\int_0^{10000} t \cdot g1(t)\,dt = 2.424 \times 10^3 \qquad \int_0^{10000} t \cdot g2(t)\,dt = 2.426 \times 10^3 \qquad \int_0^{10000} t \cdot g3(t)\,dt = 2.502 \times 10^3$

7 $\quad \displaystyle\int_0^{10000} t \cdot fALL(t)\,dt = 2.567 \times 10^3 \qquad \int_0^{10000} t \cdot fONE(t)\,dt = 2.341 \times 10^3 \qquad \int_0^{10000} t \cdot fQUORUM(t)\,dt = 2.444 \times 10^3$

Fig. 7. Mathcad's worksheet

Probability distribution functions of replicas and system response times are shown in Figs. 8 and 9. The bulk of the values of probability density function $f_{ALL}(t)$ is shifted to the right on the abscissa axis as it was expected. The shapes of the $f_{ONE}(t)$ and $f_{QUORUM}(t)$ probability density functions are also in line with the reasonable expectations and experimentally obtained probability density series (see Fig. 6).

Finally, at steps 6 and 7 we estimate the system and replicas average response time by integrating their theoretical probability distribution functions.

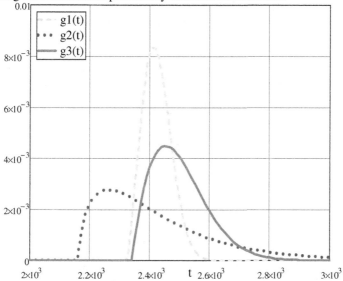

Fig. 8. Probability density functions of replicas response times

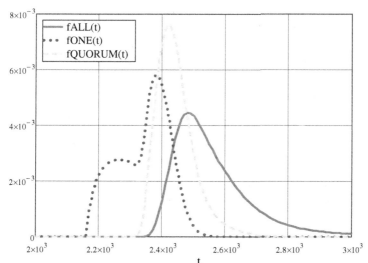

Fig. 9. Probability density functions of system response time for different consistency levels

5.3   Accuracy of Mathematical Modelling

Table 2 shows the deviation between the average values of the system and replicas response time estimated practically (see Table 1) and theoretically with the help of the obtained probability distribution functions. These results confirm the significant closeness between actual and modelled timing characteristics. To be sure that not only the average value can be accurately predicted we compare theoretical system probability density functions (see Fig. 9) and practically obtained probability density series (Fig. 6). With this purpose we estimated experimental and theoretical probabilities that system latency at different consistency levels is less than the specified time.

Table 2. Accuracy of mathematical modelling

	Replica1 (Oregon)	Replica2 (Sao Paulo)	Replica3 (Tokyo)	System consistency level		
				ONE	QUORUM	ALL
	Approximating theoretical distributions and their parameters					
distribution	Weibull	Gamma	Weibull			
alpha	113.3578	1.5952	176.8796			
beta	2.3041	164.1599	1.7467			
x-shift	2324	2164	2344			
	Average response time, ms					
measured	2428	2434	2588	2342	2449	2660
modelled	2424	2426	2502	2341	2444	2567
Deviation, %	0.18	0.34	3.32	0.03	0.19	3.51

Table 3. Deviation between theoretical system *pdf* and *pds* obtained experimentally

Time, ms	Probability that system latency is less than the specified time								
	ONE			QUORUM			ALL		
	pds	pdf	dev.,%	pds	pdf	dev.,%	pds	pdf	dev.,%
2175	0.01	0.009	10.00	0	0	-	0	0	-
2225	0.11	0.116	5.45	0	0	-	0	0	-
2275	0.23	0.252	9.57	0	0	-	0	0	-
2325	0.43	0.385	10.47	0.01	0	-	0	0	-
2375	0.59	0.596	1.02	0.08	0.097	21.25	0	0.003	-
2425	0.84	0.858	2.14	0.43	0.434	0.93	0.11	0.073	33.64
2475	0.99	0.975	1.52	0.72	0.752	4.44	0.29	0.263	9.31
2525	1	0.998	0.20	0.89	0.903	1.46	0.52	0.476	8.46
2575	1	1	0	0.96	0.961	0.10	0.63	0.643	2.06
2625	1	1	0	0.96	0.984	2.50	0.72	0.761	5.69
2675	1	1	0	0.99	0.994	0.40	0.8	0.841	5.13
2725	1	1	0	0.99	0.998	0.81	0.85	0.892	4.94
2775	1	1	0	0.99	0.999	0.91	0.88	0.924	5.00
2825	1	1	0	0.99	1	1.01	0.89	0.945	6.18
2875	1	1	0	1	1	0	0.91	0.959	5.38
2925	1	1	0	1	1	0	0.91	0.969	6.48
2975	1	1	0	1	1	0	0.92	0.977	6.20
3025	1	1	0	1	1	0	0.94	0.982	4.47
3075	1	1	0	1	1	0	0.95	0.987	3.89
Average deviation, %	2.12			2.25			7.12		

The results of this comparison (see Table 3) show a close approximation of the experimental data by the proposed analytical models, especially for the consistency levels ONE and QUORUM. The probabilistic model of the system response time for consistency level ALL gives slightly optimistic prediction, though the average deviation from the experimental data is only 7% – that is close enough.

6   Conclusion and Lessons Learnt

When employing fault-tolerance techniques over the Internet and clouds, engineers need to deal with delays, their uncertainty, timeouts, adjudication of asynchronous replies from replicas, and other specific issues involved in global distributed systems. The overall aim of this work was to study the impact of consistency on system latency in fault tolerant Internet computing.

Our experimental results clearly show that improving system consistency makes system latency worse. This finding confirms one of the generally accepted qualitative implications of the CAP theorem [9, 10]. However, so far system developers have not had any mathematical tools to help them to accurately predict the response time of large-scale replicated systems. While estimating the system worst-case execution time remains common practice for many applications (e.g. embedded computer systems, server fault-tolerance solutions, like STRATUS, etc.), this is no longer a viable solution for the wide-area service-oriented systems in which components can be distributed all over the Internet. In our previous works [2, 3] we demonstrated that extreme unpredictable delays exceeding the value of ten average response times can happen in such systems quite often. In this paper we have proposed a set of novel analytical models providing a *quantitative basis* for the system response time prediction depending on the consistency level provided for (or requested by) clients. The models allow us to derive the probability distribution function of the system response time which corresponds to a particular consistency level (ONE, ALL or QUORUM) by incorporating the probability density functions of the replica response times.

The validity of the proposed models has been verified against the experimental data reported in Section 3. It has been demonstrated that the proposed models ensure a significant level of accuracy in the system average response time prediction, especially in case of ONE and QUORUM consistency levels. The proposed models provide a mathematical basis for predicting latency of distributed fault and intrusion-tolerance techniques operating over the Internet. The models take into account the probabilistic uncertainty of replicas' response time and the required consistency level.

The practical application of our work is in allowing practitioners to predict system performance, and in offering them crucial support for the optimal timeout setup and for understanding the trade-off between system consistency and latency. Trading off system consistency against latency requires the knowledge of probability density functions (and parameter values) that accurately approximate replicas' response time. These probabilistic characteristics, which can be obtained by testing or during the trial usage, will need to be corrected at run-time or at tune-time to improve prediction accuracy. It would be possible to replace the response time probability density functions in the proposed models with probability density series. This would make it easier to use the models in practice.

Acknowledgements. We are grateful to Aad van Moorsel for his feedback on the earlier version of this work and Batyrkhan Omarov for his help with running some of the experiments. Alexander Romanovsky is partially supported by the EPSRC TRAMS-2 platform grant.

References

1. Lee, P.A., Anderson, T.: Fault Tolerance. Principles and Practice. Springer-Verlag (1990)
2. Gorbenko, A., et al.: Real Distribution of Response Time Instability in Service-Oriented Architecture. In: 29th IEEE Int'l Symp. Reliable Distributed Systems, pp. 92–99 (2010)
3. Gorbenko, A., et al.: Exploring Uncertainty of Delays as a Factor in End-to-End Cloud Response Time. In: 9th European Dependable Computing Conference, pp. 185–190 (2012)
4. Bakr, O., Keidar, I.: Evaluating the running time of a communication round over the internet. In: 21th Ann. ACM Symposium on Principles of Distributed Computing (PODC 2000), pp. 243–252 (2002)
5. Chen, Y., et al.: Measuring and Dealing with the Uncertainty of the SOA Solutions. In: Cardellini, V., et al. (eds.) Performance and Dependability in Service Computing: Concepts, Techniques and Research Directions, pp. 265–294. IGI Global (2011)
6. Potharaju, R., Jain, N.: When the Network Crumbles: An Empirical Study of Cloud Network Failures and their Impact on Services. In: 4th ACM Symposium on Cloud Computing, SoCC (2013)
7. Scott, C., Choffnes, D.R., Cunha, I., et al.: LIFEGUARD: practical repair of persistent route failures. In: ACM SIGCOMM 2012 Conference on Applications, Technologies, Architectures, and Protocols for Computer Communication, pp. 395–406 (2012)
8. Avizienis, A., Laprie, J.-C., Randell, B., Landwehr, C.: Basic Concepts and Taxonomy of Dependable and Secure Computing. IEEE Trans. on Dependable and Secure Computing 1(1), 11–33 (2004)
9. Brewer, E.: Towards Robust Distributed Systems. In: 19th Ann. ACM Symposium on Principles of Distributed Computing, PODC 2000, pp. 7–10 (2000)
10. Gilbert, S., Lynch, N.: Brewer's Conjecture and the Feasibility of Consistent, Available, Partition-Tolerant Web Services. ACM SIGACT News 33(2), 51–59 (2002)
11. Gorbenko, A., Romanovsky, A., Kharchenko, V., Tarasyuk, O.: Dependability of Service-Oriented Computing: Time-Probabilistic Failure Modelling. In: Avgeriou, P. (ed.) SERENE 2012. LNCS, vol. 7527, pp. 121–133. Springer, Heidelberg (2012)
12. Abadi, D.J.: Consistency Tradeoffs in Modern Distributed Database System Design. IEEE Computer 45(2), 37–42 (2012)
13. Brutlag, J.: Speed Matters for Google Web Search. Google (2009), http://services.google.com/fh/files/blogs/google_delayexp.pdf
14. Lakshman, A., Malik, P.: Cassandra: a decentralized structured storage system. ACM SIGOPS Operating Systems Review 44(2), 35–40 (2010)
15. Gorbenko, A., Romanovsky, A.: Time-Outing Internet Services. IEEE Security & Privacy 11(2), 68–71 (2013)
16. Gorbenko, A., Kharchenko, V., Romanovsky, A.: Using Inherent Service Redundancy and Diversity to Ensure Web Services Dependability. In: Butler, M., Jones, C., Romanovsky, A., Troubitsyna, E. (eds.) Methods, Models and Tools for Fault Tolerance. LNCS, vol. 5454, pp. 324–341. Springer, Heidelberg (2009)
17. Rao, J., Shekita, E.J., Tata, S.: Using Paxos to Build a Scalable, Consistent, and Highly Available Datastore. VLDB Endowment, 243–254 (2011)

A CRDT Supporting Selective Undo
for Collaborative Text Editing

Weihai Yu[1(✉)], Luc André[2,3,4], and Claudia-Lavinia Ignat[2,3,4]

[1] Department of Computer Science, UiT - The Arctic University of Norway,
Tromsø, Norway
[2] Inria, Villers-lès-Nancy, 54600, France
[3] Université de Lorraine, LORIA, UMR 7503, Vandoeuvre-lès-Nancy,
54506, France
[4] CNRS, LORIA, UMR 7503, Vandoeuvre-lès-Nancy, 54506, France

Abstract. Undo is an important feature of editors. However, even after over two decades of active research and development, support of undo for real-time collaborative editing is still very limited. We examine issues concerning undo in collaborative text editing and present an approach using a layered commutative replicated data type (CRDT). Our performance study shows that it provides sufficient responsiveness to the end users.

1 Introduction

Undo is a key feature of editors. In a single-user editor, a user can conveniently undo earlier editing operations in reverse chronological order. In a collaborative editor, however, users at different sites may generate operations concurrently. This means that a user cannot easily perceive a linear operation order. Some systems restrict what can be undone. For example, with Google Drive (https://drive.google.com), a user can only undo locally generated operations. User studies show that users indeed expect to be able to undo other users' operations when working on common tasks [1]. In the research community of collaborative editing, *selective undo* is widely regarded as an important feature [2–9]. With selective undo, a user can undo an earlier operation, regardless of when and where the operation was generated.

Current systems that support selective undo are subject to two main limitations. Firstly, they only support undo of operations on atomic objects (e.g. characters or unbreakable lines). In the case of string-wise operations such as copy-paste, find-replace or select-delete, users can typically only undo earlier operations character by character. Secondly, selective undo may lead to undesirable effects. For example, a user first inserts a misspelled word and then makes a correction. The correction depends on the first insertion of the word. It is undesirable to undo the insertion alone and leave the correction behind as a groundless modification.

In this paper we propose a novel approach to collaborative text editing that supports selective undo of string-wise operations. This is the first work that manages undesirable effects of undo.

© IFIP International Federation for Information Processing 2015
A. Bessani and S. Bouchenak (Eds.): DAIS 2015, LNCS 9038, pp. 193–206, 2015.
DOI: 10.1007/978-3-319-19129-4_16

2 Related Work

There are two general approaches to collaborative editing, based either on operation transformation (OT) [6, 7, 10] or on commutative replication data types (CRDT) [8, 9, 11–14]. With OT, a remote operation is transformed and integrated in the local site. The time complexity depends on the lengths of operation histories (linear at best). Furthermore, it is hard to design correct operation transformation functions [15]. One common way to relax certain required conditions for transformation functions is to restrict the order in which operations are transformed at all sites. Therefore OT approaches generally do not scale well and practically require the involvement of central servers. With CRDT, concurrent insertions are ordered based on the underlying data structure, so the time complexity may not depend on the lengths of operation histories. [16] reported that CRDT algorithms are better suited for large-scale distributed environments and outperform OT algorithms by orders of magnitudes.

Supporting string operations and selective undo requires obtaining at runtime relations among operations, such as whether a string is part of a larger insertion or whether an operation is an undo of another operation. Since strings might be split by subsequent operations and operations are executed concurrently, obtaining such relations can be complicated. Deriving such relations through operation transformation is particularly difficult. Currently, most related work can only apply undo to insertion and deletion of atomic objects [2–8]. To the best of our knowledge, only our previous work [9] supports selective undo of string operations. However, [9] does not account for possible undesirable effects of undo.

In this paper, we propose a novel CRDT that captures useful relations among operations. Our approach offers support for string-based undo and deals with undesirable effects of selective undo. Our current work is built on our previous work. The general view-model system structure is similar to the one described in [9]. The underlying scheme for character identifiers is similar to the one described in [11].

3 Undo Effects

Allowing undo of any operation without restriction might lead to undesirable effects.

Example 1. *The state after two insertions ins_1 (with string "this is hard") and ins_2 ("not ") is "this is not hard". Undoing ins_1 results in state "not ". If the text "is hard" is a single unit and the string "not " is part of it, then, without the text "is hard", the string "not " becomes groundless.*

When a user inserts a string *str* into an existing *unit string* str_0, str_0 is the *ground* of *str*. If str_0 had not existed, the user would not have inserted *str* and the existence of *str* is *groundless*.

The definition of unit strings depends on the types of documents. Without loss of generality, we define a unit string as being generated by a single operation, such as an insertion or the undo of a deletion. More specifically, if op_0 generates string str_0 and *ins* inserts string *str* into str_0, op_0 is the *ground operation* of *op* (or *op* is *built on* op_0)

and str_0 is the *ground string* of str. Furthermore, the built-on relation is transitive. That is, if op_2 is built on op_1 and op_1 is built on op_0, then op_2 is also built on op_0.

The effect of undoing an operation op should be as if op and all operations built on op had never occurred. More specifically, suppose $H^s = H_0 \cdot op \cdot H_1 \cdot undo(op) \cdot H_2$ is the history of operations at site s, where H_0 represents the sequence of operations executed before op, H_1 the sequence of operations after op and H_2 the sequence of operations after the undo of op. If we denote by $H^{\widetilde{op}}$ the sequence of operations as the result of removal from H of all operations built on op, then H^s and $H_0 \cdot H_1^{\widetilde{op}} \cdot H_2^{\widetilde{op}}$ should produce the same strings. Notice that op and $undo(op)$ may be generated from different sites. Also, although the operations in H_2 occur after the undo of op at site s, H_2 may still contain operations built on op, due to concurrent operations.

Our definition of ground operations might be too general to the user. In practice, the user may not agree that string str is built on str_0 (or str is useful outside the context of str_0). In such situations, the user should be able to decide which operations are not built on the operation being undone (or to manually select which groundless strings, detected by the editor, should remain after the undo). Thus, when a user tries to perform an undo that results in groundless strings, the editor should warn the user, so that the user is able to determine the final effect of the undo, or to simply give up the undo.

However, due to concurrent operations, a collaborative editor is not always able to warn the user of possible groundless strings in time. In Example 1, when a user at a remote site undoes ins_1 before ins_2 arrives, the undo does not cause any groundless string. In such cases, all sites should unanimously (without user intervention) eliminate the groundless string "not " when they receive both $undo(ins_1)$ and ins_2.

Example 2. *In Example 1, another site first executes ins_1 and then executes del_1 (" is hard") concurrently with ins_2. The string "not " inserted by ins_2 becomes groundless after a site executes both ins_2 and del_1.*

A concurrent deletion may also cause groundless strings. Notice that a deletion never causes groundless strings locally. Hence the sites should always unanimously eliminate groundless strings caused by remote deletions.

Our work ensures that there is no groundless effect of local undo (unless the user explicitly wants the effect) and there is no groundless effect of remote undo or deletion. Furthermore, it ensures the traditional correctness criteria convergence and intention preservation [6] as discussed in Section 6.

4 View and Model

With a collaborative editor, a document is concurrently updated from a number of peers at different sites. Every peer consists of a view of the document, a model, a log of operation history and several queues.

A peer concurrently receives local operations generated by the user and remote operations sent from other peers. Local operations take immediate effect in the view. The peer stores executed local operations and received remote operations in queues. During a synchronization cycle, it integrates the stored operations in the model and shows the effects of integrated remote operations in the view. The peer also records integrated operations in the log. Later, it broadcasts integrated local operations to other peers. At any time, the user may undo an operation selected from the log.

Every peer has a unique peer identifier *pid*. An operation originated at a peer has a peer update number *pun* that is incremented with every integrated local operation. Therefore, we can uniquely identify an operation with the pair (pid, pun). In what follows, we use op_{pun}^{pid} to denote an operation *op* identified with (pid, pun).

A view is mainly a string of characters. A user at a peer can insert or delete a substring at a position in the view, and undo an earlier integrated local or remote operation selected from the log.

A model materializes editing operations and relations among them. It consists of layers of linked nodes that encapsulate characters. Conceptually, characters have unique *identifiers* that are totally ordered (though not every identifier is explicitly represented in the model). For two characters c_l and c_r, if $c_l.id < c_r.id$, then c_l appears to the left of c_r. A character identifier is represented as a sequence of integers. For $c_l.id = p_0 \ldots p_{k-1} p_k^l \ldots$, $c_r.id = p_0 \ldots p_{k-1} p_k^r \ldots$ and $p_k^l < p_k^r$, the two identifiers start to differ at the $(k+1)$-th integer. Suppose we insert a string of characters $c_0 \ldots c_n$ between c_l and c_r. The identifier of character c_i $(0 \le i \le n)$ in the string is $p_0 \ldots p_{k-1} p_k p_{k+1} (p_{k+2} + i)$, where $p_k^l < p_k < p_k^r$ and p_{k+1} is a function of *pid*. If another peer inserts a string $c_0' \ldots c_m'$ at the same place and generates p_k', p_{k+1}' and p_{k+2}', the two strings are ordered according to p_k and p_k'. If $p_k = p_k'$, the two strings are then ordered according to p_{k+1} and p_{k+1}' (i.e. according to *pids*). We refer the interested readers to [11] for a more complete description of the generation of character identifiers.

Nodes at the lowest layer of a model represent insertions and contain inserted characters. Nodes at higher layers represent deletions. That is, a higher-layer node (outer node) deletes the characters in the lower-layer nodes (inner nodes) it contains.

A node contains the identifier cid_l of its leftmost character and cid_r of its rightmost character. The identifiers of the other characters (i.e. not at the edges of the node) are not explicitly represented in the model. An insertion node also contains a string *str* of characters.

Subsequent operations may split existing nodes. Nodes of the same operation share an *op* element as the operation's descriptor. The descriptor contains the identifier and type of the operation, a set $\mathscr{P}$ (for parents) of references to the descriptors of *op*'s ground operations and a set $\mathscr{C}$ (for children) of operations built on *op*. The descriptor also has an *undo* element that contains a set $\mathscr{U}$ of identifiers of its *undo* operations (there might be more than one, as multiple peers might concurrently undo the same operation). An *undo* element may itself have its own *undo* element (e.g. when the original operation is redone). Thus the *undo* elements of an operation form a chain. The operation is *effectively undone* if the length of the chain is an odd number.

An insertion is *self-visible* if it is not effectively undone. A deletion is *self-visible* if it is effectively undone. An operation is *visible* if it is self-visible and all its ground operations are visible. A character is *visible* if all operations on it are visible.

There are three types of links among nodes: *l-r* links maintain the left-right character order; op_l-op_r links connect nodes of the same operations; *i-o* links maintain the inner-outer relations. The outermost nodes and the nodes inside the same outer node are linked

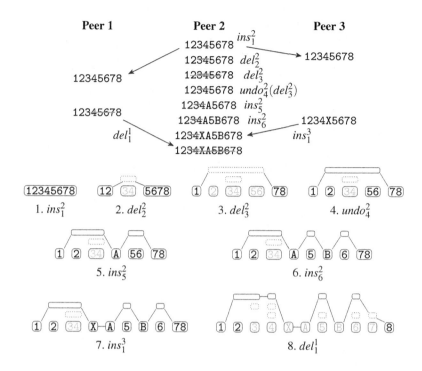

Fig. 1. Examples of model updates

with *l-r* links. When the view and the model are synchronized, the view equals to the concatenation of all visible characters of the outermost nodes through the *l-r* links.

Figure 1 shows an example with three peers. The upper part shows a number of operations generated at the peers. The lower part shows the model snapshots at Peer 2. Nodes of the same deletion are aligned horizontally. Nodes with dotted border are self-invisible. Characters in light gray are invisible. We describe how to update the model in the following section.

5   Operations and Undo

A user may execute the following normal view operations: (i) $ins(pos, str)$ inserts string *str* at position *pos*. (ii) $del(pos, len)$ deletes *len* characters right to position *pos*. In addition to the normal operations, the user can undo any operation selected from the log.

A peer stores executed normal view operations in a queue. It may aggregate consecutive operations, for instance, to form string operations from character operations. During a synchronization cycle, the peer turns view operations into model operations before integration.

To avoid traversing a large number of nodes for every local operation, a model maintains a *current position*, (v_{curr}, p_{curr}), where v_{curr} is the current node and p_{curr} is the offset to the left edge of v_{curr}. Because a user typically focuses on a small region at a time, the distances between consecutive operations are often short.

There are three normal model operations: (i) *move(m)* moves the current position a distance of *m* visible characters (leftwards when negative). (ii) *ins(str)* inserts string *str* at the current position. (iii) *del(len)* deletes *len* characters right to the current position.

A peer processes a local undo operation in the order opposite to normal operations. It first integrates the undo in the model and then synchronizes it to the view.

For each integrated local operation, a peer broadcasts a representation of the *model update* to remote peers. A node is uniquely identified by $(op.pid, op.pun, cid_l)$, where $(op.pid, op.pun)$ is the identifier of its operation and cid_l is the identifier of its leftmost character. The peer uses the identifiers of the involved nodes, offsets to the leftmost characters etc. to describe the update, so that remote peers can unambiguously locate the referent nodes and split boundaries. Each peer maintains a hash table of nodes using their identifiers, so locating a referent node takes near-constant time.

A model-view synchronization does the following tasks sequentially: (1) integrating local operations, (2) integrating remote operations, and (3) updating the view (with a *render* procedure). This ensures that, when a model integrates a local operation, there is no concurrent remote operation in the model.

Procedure. *localIns(pid, pun, str)*

---

1 $(v_l, v_r) \leftarrow split(nextVisible(v_{curr}, p_{curr}, 0))$
2 $v_{ins} \leftarrow Node(cidsBetween(v_l.cid_r, v_r.cid_l, pid, str.len), Op(pid, pun), str)$
3 $setInsGroundOps(v_{ins}.op, v_l, v_r)$
4 $insertBetween(v_{ins}, v_l, v_r)$
5 $v_{curr}, p_{curr} \leftarrow v_r, 0$

Procedure *localIns* integrates a local insertion. It places the new inserted string to the right of all invisible characters at the current position. Procedure *nextVisible(v, p, n)*, called from *localIns* (line 1) and *localDel* (lines 1 and 2), returns the position of the *n*-th visible character right to position (v, p). In Fig. 1-5, Peer 2 inserts "A" of ins_5^2 to the right of the invisible "34".

If the insertion position is inside an existing node, *localIns* splits the node (line 1). Procedure *split* returns either the new nodes after the split, or two existing nodes if the split position is at the edge of an existing node. It also splits the corresponding inner nodes, recursively down to an insertion node at the lowest layer. This way, it exposes the character identifiers at the position of the split. In Fig. 1-6, when inserting "B", Peer 2 splits the "56" nodes of both del_3^2 and ins_1^2.

Next, *localIns* creates a new insertion node (line 2). Procedure *cidsBetween* generates the character identifiers using the ones at the insertion position.

Procedure *setInsGroundOps* updates the $\mathscr{P}$ and $\mathscr{C}$ sets of the insertion and its ground operations (line 3). If v_l and v_r are of the same operation, then this operation is a ground operation of the new insertion. The procedure goes on with v_l's rightmost inner node and v_r's leftmost inner node, downward until the lowest layer. In Fig. 1-6, both del_3^2 and ins_1^2 are ground operations of ins_6^2.

Finally, *localIns* connects the new insertion node with the neighboring nodes (line 4) and moves the current position to the right end of the inserted string (line 5).

Procedure. *localDel(pid, pun, len)*

1 $(v_l, v_r) \leftarrow split(nextVisible(v_{curr}, p_{curr}, 0))$
2 $(v'_l, v'_r) \leftarrow split(nextVisible(v_r, 0, len))$
3 $v_{del} \leftarrow Node(v_r.cid_l, v'_l.cid_r, Op(pid, pun))$
4 $insertInners(v_{del}, [v_r..v'_l])$
5 $insertBetween(v_{del}, v_l, v'_r)$

Procedure *localDel* splits existing nodes at the deletion boundaries (lines 1 and 2), inserts a new node for the deletion at the outermost layer (lines 3 and 5) and associates to it the corresponding inner nodes (line 4). Notice that a deletion may contain invisible characters inside the deleted string. For example, del_3^2 in Fig. 1-3 contains "34".

A model integrates a remote update only when the update is *ready for integration*, i.e., when all nodes and elements which the update refers to exist in the model (possibly after some split). For example, ins_1^3 in Fig. 1 is ready for integration in models in which a node of ins_1^2 exists. The ready-for-integration condition is less strict than the general "happen-before" condition in the literature (such as [6]), because only the nodes and elements which the update *directly* refers to must exist in the model.

Procedure. *remoteIns(pid, pun, cid, str, 𝒢, v, p)*

1 $v_{ins} \leftarrow Node(cid, stringRightEndCid(cid, str.len), Op(pid, pun), str)$
2 $setGroundOps(v_{ins}.op, 𝒢)$
3 $(v_l, v_r) \leftarrow insNarrow(cid, split(v, p))$
4 $extendInsGroundOps(v_{ins}.op, v_l, v_r)$
5 $insertBetween(v_{ins}, top(v_l), top(v_r))$

A remote insertion specifies the inserted string *str*, the identifier of the leftmost character *cid*, ground operations 𝒢 of the insertion, and the insertion position (v, p). Procedure *remoteIns* re-generates the insertion node v_{ins} (line 1) and updates the 𝒫 and 𝒞 sets of $v_{ins}.op$ and operations in 𝒢 (line 2).

Next, *remoteIns* splits (if necessary) the nodes at the insertion position and narrows down the position among the concurrent insertions using character identifiers (line 3). In Fig. 1-7, there is already a concurrent insertion "A" at the position of ins_1^3. When the identifier of "X" is smaller than that of "A", Peer 2 inserts "X" between "4" and "A".

The procedure then updates the information about ground operations with respect to the concurrent operations (line 4): if the neighboring node v_l (or v_r) is a concurrent insertion, its ground operations become also the ground operations of the new insertion;

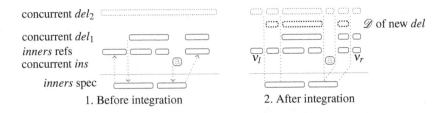

concurrent del_2

concurrent del_1
inners refs
concurrent ins
$\mathcal{D}$ of new del
v_l v_r

inners spec

1. Before integration   2. After integration

Fig. 2. Integrating a remote deletion

if a concurrent deletion contains both v_l and v_r, the deletion becomes a ground operation of the new insertion. The visibility of the remote insertion is therefore dependent on the visibility of the containing concurrent deletions. This addresses the issue illustrated in Example 2. In Fig. 1-7, del_3^2, which is a ground operation of ins_5^2 ("A"), becomes a ground operation of the new ins_1^3 ("X").

Finally, *remoteIns* connects the nodes at the outermost layer (line 5). In Fig. 1-7, the "X" node of ins_1^3 connects to "234" of del_3^2 and "A" of ins_5^2.

A remote deletion specifies the inner nodes of the deletion at the time of its creation. The referent inner nodes at the current peer may differ from the specified ones in two ways: (1) the remote peer might have split the inner nodes at deletion boundaries (as shown with the upward arrows in Fig. 2-1); (2) the current peer might have split the inner nodes when integrating concurrent operations (as shown with the downward arrows in Fig. 2-1). In the figure, del_1 is undone and the insertion of "a" *sees* the restored characters of del_1. del_2 sees both "a" and the restored characters of del_1.

Procedure. *remoteDel(pid, pun, inners)*

---

1 $(inners, v_l, v_r) \leftarrow prepareInners(inners)$
2 $del \leftarrow Op(pid, pun); \mathcal{D} \leftarrow makeDels(pid, pun, del, inners)$
3 **for** $v \in \mathcal{D}$ **do** $placeDel(v, overlappingDels(v))$
4 **for** v between $(v_l, v_r), v.op.type = ins \land \neg overlapping(v, \mathcal{D})$ **do**
5 $\quad \lfloor \quad setGroundOps(v.op, \{del\})$
6 $connectTopNodes(\mathcal{D})$

The *prepareInners* procedure (line 1 of Procedure *remoteDel*) uses the specified inner nodes to split the existing nodes at deletion boundaries and returns the new referent inner nodes and their left and right neighbors v_l and v_r (as shown in Fig. 2-2). The *makeDels* procedure (line 2) generates a set $\mathcal{D}$ of nodes for the remote deletion based on the referent inner nodes and concurrent operations. Procedure *placeDel* (line 3) places the generated deletion nodes against the nodes of the overlapping concurrent deletions. For example, a deletion with a larger *pid* is placed above a concurrent deletion with a smaller *pid*. The deletion becomes a ground operation of the concurrent insertions inside the *inners* nodes (lines 4 and 5). For the new deletion nodes at the outermost layer, *connectTopNodes* connects them with the neighboring nodes (line 6).

In Fig. 1-8, the del_1^1 update specifies a single inner node "4567" of ins_1^2. Procedure *prepareInners* splits the "34" nodes of ins_1^2, del_2^2 and del_3^2. Procedure *makeDels* generates the nodes for del_1^1. Procedure *placeDel* places the del_1^1 nodes below those of del_2^2 and del_3^2. del_1^1 becomes a ground operation of the concurrent insertions ins_5^2, ins_6^2 and ins_1^3, which makes characters "X", "A" and "B" invisible. Finally, Procedure *connectTopNodes* connects node "7" of del_1^1 with neighboring nodes "6" of del_3^2 and "8" of ins_1^2.

When a user tries to undo an operation and makes the operation invisible, any operation built on the undone operation becomes groundless (and therefore also invisible). In Fig. 1-7, undo of $undo_4^2$, or redo of del_3^2, would make the insertions ins_5^2, ins_6^2 and ins_1^3 (that are contained in $del_3^2.op.\mathscr{C}$) groundless. If there were other operations built on these insertions, they would also become groundless.

The user may selectively keep the effects of operations built on the operation being undone. In Fig. 1-7, if the user decides to redo del_3^2 and keep the visible effect of ins_6^2, the model then removes ins_6^2 from $del_3^2.op.\mathscr{C}$ and del_3^2 from $ins_6^2.op.\mathscr{P}$.

The execution of a local *undo* starts in the model, with the following steps: (1) integrate local and remote operations in the queues; (2) integrate the undo with the *undo* procedure; (3) move the current position to the edge of the undo; (4) synchronize the model with the view so that the user sees the effects of the undo.

Procedure. *undo(pid, pun, op)*

---

1   $push((pid, pun), op.undo.\mathscr{U})$

Procedure *undo* integrates both local and remote undo of an operation, which is either a normal operation or an undo of another operation. Procedure *undo* can receive either an *op* or an *undo* element as the argument of the *op* parameter. The procedure simply inserts the identifier of the undo into the corresponding $\mathscr{U}$ set.

For a remote undo, if there has been a concurrent identical undo and the $\mathscr{U}$ set was not empty, inserting a new identifier does not change the visibility of the operation and there is therefore no effect in the view. For a local undo, the real overhead is the move of the current position and the synchronization with the view.

6   Correctness

We consider two traditional correctness criteria, convergence and intention preservation, as defined in [6]. A formal proof is outside the scope of this paper.

Convergence requires that, all peers have the same view when they have integrated and synchronized the same set of operations. Our approach guarantees convergence by enforcing the following properties: (a) models of all peers have the same set of characters; (b) the characters have the same left-right order; (c) the characters have the same visibility.

Intention preservation requires that, for any operation *op*, (a) the effects of executing *op* at all peers are the same as the intention of *op*, and (b) the effect of executing *op* does not change the intention of independent operations.

Intention is not formally defined in [6] and is open to different interpretations. Generally, the *intention* of an operation is decided at the view of the originating peer. More specifically, an insertion is between two specific characters; a deletion removes a string of characters from the view; undo of an insertion removes the inserted characters from the view; undo of a deletion makes the removed characters re-appear in the view and the positions of the re-appeared characters must preserve the intentions of the corresponding insertions.

In our approach, there is also *induced intention* due to concurrent operations and selective undo. More specifically, the intention of an operation is preserved only when the intentions of all its ground operations are preserved. When the effect of an operation disappears (e.g. due to an undo or a deletion), the effects of all operations built on it should also disappear. The algorithms take care that every operation has the same induced intention at all peers.

Notice that undoing a deletion brings the deleted characters back in the view only when the insertions of the corresponding characters are not undone and the characters are not deleted by any concurrent overlapping deletion. That is, undoing a deletion does not change the intention of undoing any insertion or the intention of any other deletions. This is in contrast with related work that defines the effect of concurrent deletions of the same character as a single deletion: undoing a deletion thus changes the intention of all concurrent deletions of the same character. For example, in Fig. 1-8, if undoing del_1^1 makes the entire "4567" visible, the intentions of del_2^2 and del_3^2 are not preserved. On the other hand, concurrent undos of the same operation are regarded as a single undo, because they are always unambiguously defined on the same operation.

7   Performance

The response time of view operations is an important part of an editor's responsiveness to local user operations. Except selective undo, all view operations are executed completely in the view. Their performance therefore are nearly the same as a single-user editor. However, local view operations are executed only when system resources (CPU, memory etc.) are available, so responsiveness is dependent on the overall performance of the editor, including the more expensive model operations.

Table 1. Time complexity of procedures

split	$O(hn+l)$	move	$O(m)$
render	$O(m+rh)$	undo	$O(1)$
local *ins*	$O(s+hn+l)$	local *del*	$O(s+hn+l)$
remote *ins*	$O(k_i l + k_d + hn)$	remote *del*	$O(k_d(s+hn+l)+k_i)$

Table 1 summarizes the time complexity of the different procedures. In the table, parameter *m* is the distance of a move, i.e. the number of nodes at the outermost layer

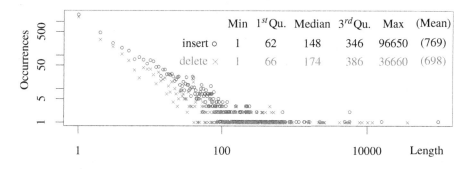

Fig. 3. Occurrences of operations with different lengths

a move traverses. l is the length of a character identifier. s is the span of an operation, i.e. the number of nodes between the leftmost and rightmost nodes of the operation, including those not belonging to the operation. h is the height of a node, i.e. the number of layers in the outer-inner structure. n is the number of a node's inner nodes. k_i is the number of concurrent conflicting insertions and k_d is the number of concurrent overlapping deletions. r is the size of the region to be rendered, i.e. the number of nodes in the region where new updates should be synchronized to the view.

We have implemented the core algorithms in Emacs Lisp, aiming at supporting collaborative editing in a widely used open-source editor. We ran two experiments for performance study. The first one is based on a trace of operations for editing a paper. This experiment can be considered to be representative for real-life editing sessions. It is nonetheless based on the trace of a single-user editor. The second experiment is based on generated operation traces that force a large number of conflicting concurrent operations. The measurement was taken under GNU Emacs 24.3.1 running in 32-bit Linux 3.14.2-ARCH on an old ThinkPad T61p (2007 model) with 2.2GHz Intel Core2 Duo CPU T7500 and 2GB RAM.

In the first experiment, we captured the trace of operations for editing a technical paper in a two-week period. The paper is based on the templates and even contents of other papers. Therefore the editing involves a number of copy, paste and deletion of relatively large text. This trace forms the view operations. We then aggregated and converted the view operations into model operations. Figure 3 shows the number of model operations and their lengths (numbers of characters) obtained from the trace.

We ran the trace with two peers. To make sure that operations are valid (i.e. with valid positions and lengths), the peers behave in the following way. For each operation, each peer generates and integrates a local operation, and sends the encoded representation of the update to the other peer. It then receives and integrates the identical update from the other peer, and undoes immediately the last identical operation of the second peer. Therefore, only the effects of the operations originated from the first peer remain. Finally, each peer sends the encoded representation of the undo to the other peer, and integrates the identical concurrent undo from the other peer.

Figure 4 shows the execution time of different procedures. The y-axis represents the execution time in milliseconds (ms). The x-axis represents the time at which the procedures are called.

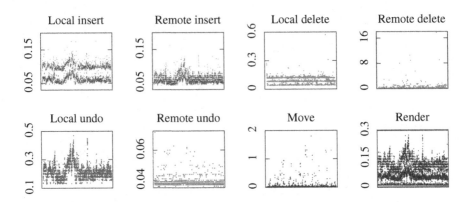

Fig. 4. Execution time (ms) of different procedures

The first important observation is that the execution time of all procedures stays pretty stable and is generally independent of the length of the operation history. This is mostly due to the use of hashing to locate nodes.

Integrating local and remote insertions takes around $0.05 \sim 0.1$ ms. Note that the sizes of inserted strings vary from one character to nearly 100K characters, but still the time for integration varies with very small margins. The reason is that character strings are mainly generated by view and networking procedures. Furthermore, string and buffer management in Emacs is efficient.

Integrating local and remote deletions takes around 0.2 ms. There are cases where integrating a local and remote deletion can take up to 0.6 ms and 17 ms respectively. In these cases, a deletion involves a relatively large number of nodes. That is, the s and n in Table 1 are relatively large.

Integrating a local undo takes around 0.2 ms. This includes checking for groundless strings, moving the current position to the undo, and synchronizing the view with the model. Integrating a remote undo takes only 0.04 ms.

Procedure *move* takes less than 0.2 ms the vast majority of times, because editing operations often focus on a small region for a period of time. Even in the occasions where the move distances are long, it takes less than 2 ms.

Procedure *render* takes around 0.1 ms. In the experiment, the model and view are synchronized after the integration of every remote update or local undo. Therefore, the execution time of Procedure *render* does not vary much. It should be pointed out that in the figure, the time of *render* is included in the integration of local undo but not in the other operations.

With respect to memory usage, at the peek, Emacs used an additional 10 MiB of main memory during the experiment. Totally, 20 MiB was allocated for the experiment, including the part that has been freed. This memory consumption is shared by two peers.

The first experiment simulates how the algorithms work with a real-life session. However, it does not reveal how they work when a document is simultaneously edited by a large number of users, because there are only two peers and conflicts of concurrent operations follow exactly the same patterns. In the second experiment, we study

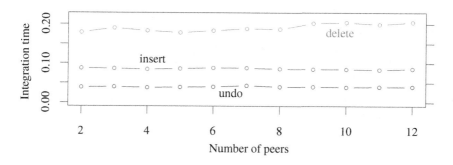

Fig. 5. Execution time (ms) with conflicting operations

the performance of our work when there are varying number of conflicting or overlapping concurrent operations. In what follows, we use conflicting operation to mean either conflicting insertions or overlapping insertions and deletions.

We generate the operations for N peers as follows. First, we generate a random position p in the view. Then for every peer, we generate a random operation at a random position near p. For the random operations, 50% of them are insertions, 30% are deletions and 20% are undo of an earlier operation that contains position p. An insertion inserts 10 characters. A deletion deletes 7 characters. They are at random positions between $p - 3$ and $p + 3$, inclusive. After all peers have integrated all local and remote operations, we generate a new random position p, and the same process continues. We run this process until the execution time stabilizes. We vary the number of peers N from 2 to 12. For a reasonably sized document, the number of users that simultaneously edit a very small region, is normally only a very small fraction of the total number of users. So we believe the experiment is sufficient for the most challenging situations in real-world scenarios.

Figure 5 shows the time for integrating remote updates. The time for integrating local operations is not shown, because when a local operation is integrated, there are no concurrent remote operations integrated in the model. The results indicate that the increase of the number of conflicts does not have observable effect on delay.

8   Conclusion

Selective undo has long been regarded as a desirable feature of collaborative editors. However, support for selective undo has remained for two decades at the "necessary first step", namely for character-only operations without any regard of possible undesirable effects. In this work, we proposed support for selective undo in collaborative editing, including support for string operations and management of possible undesirable undo effects. Key to our approach is a layered CRDT that materializes operation relations essential for string operations and selective undo. We analyzed the complexity of the algorithms and presented experimental results. The results indicate that the approach provides sufficient responsiveness to end users.

There are still open issues to be addressed before end users can finally use this work. Our next tasks include a GUI for selection of operations to be undone and management of undo effects, and session management that supports dynamic groups, combination of synchronous and asynchronous operations, network partition, and so on.

Acknowledgement. The authors are grateful for sabbatical support from UiT - The Arctic University of Norway and The Research Council of Norway. This work is partially funded by the french national research program STREAMS (ANR-10-SEGI-010).

References

1. Seifried, T., Rendl, C., Haller, M., Scott, S.D.: Regional undo/redo techniques for large interactive surfaces. In: CHI, pp. 2855–2864 (2012)
2. Ferrié, J., Vidot, N., Cart, M.: Concurrent undo operations in collaborative environments using operational transformation. In: CoopIS/DOA/ODBASE (1), pp. 155–173 (2004)
3. Prakash, A., Knister, M.J.: A framework for undoing actions in collaborative systems. ACM Trans. Comput.-Hum. Interact. 1(4), 295–330 (1994)
4. Ressel, M., Gunzenhäuser, R.: Reducing the problems of group undo. In: GROUP, pp. 131–139. ACM (1999)
5. Shao, B., Li, D., Gu, N.: An algorithm for selective undo of any operation in collaborative applications. In: GROUP, pp. 131–140. ACM (2010)
6. Sun, C., Jia, X., Zhang, Y., Yang, Y., Chen, D.: Achieving convergence, causality preservation, and intention preservation in real-time cooperative editing systems. ACM Trans. Comput.-Hum. Interact. 5(1), 63–108 (1998)
7. Sun, D., Sun, C.: Context-based operational transformation in distributed collaborative editing systems. IEEE Trans. Parallel Distrib. Syst. 20(10), 1454–1470 (2009)
8. Weiss, S., Urso, P., Molli, P.: Logoot-undo: Distributed collaborative editing system on P2P networks. IEEE Trans. Parallel Distrib. Syst. 21(8), 1162–1174 (2010)
9. Yu, W.: Supporting string-wise operations and selective undo for peer-to-peer group editing. In: GROUP. ACM (2014)
10. Ellis, C.A., Gibbs, S.J.: Concurrency control in groupware systems. In: SIGMOD, pp. 399–407. ACM (1989)
11. André, L., Martin, S., Oster, G., Ignat, C.-L.: Supporting adaptable granularity of changes for massive-scale collaborative editing. In: CollaborateCom. IEEE (2013)
12. Oster, G., Urso, P., Molli, P., Imine, A.: Data consistency for P2P collaborative editing. In: CSCW, pp. 259–268. ACM (2006)
13. Preguiça, N.M., Marquès, J.M., Shapiro, M., Letia, M.: A commutative replicated data type for cooperative editing. In: ICDCS, pp. 395–403. IEEE Computer Society (2009)
14. Roh, H.-G., Jeon, M., Kim, J., Lee, J.: Replicated abstract data types: Building blocks for collaborative applications. J. Parallel Distrib. Comput. 71(3), 354–368 (2011)
15. Imine, A., Molli, P., Oster, G., Rusinowitch, M.: Proving correctness of transformation functions functions in real-time groupware. In: ECSCW, pp. 277–293 (2003)
16. Ahmed-Nacer, M., Ignat, C.-L., Oster, G., Roh, H.-G., Urso, P.: Evaluating CRDTs for real-time document editing. In: DocEng, pp. 103–112. ACM (2011)

LiveCloudInspector: Towards Integrated IaaS Forensics in the Cloud

Julian Zach and Hans P. Reiser[✉]

University of Passau, Innstr. 43, 94032 Passau, Germany
julian.zach@t-online.de, hr@sec.uni-passau.de

Abstract. Cloud-based systems are becoming an increasingly attractive target for malicious attacks. In IaaS environments, malicious attacks on a cloud customer's virtual machine may affect the customer, who cannot use all diagnostic means that are available in dedicated in-house infrastructures, as well as the cloud provider, due to possible subsequent attacks against the cloud infrastructure and other co-hosted customers. This paper presents an integrated approach towards forensics and incident analysis in IaaS cloud environments. The proposed architecture enables the cloud provider to securely offer forensics services to its customers on a self-service platform. The architecture combines three important analysis techniques and provides significantly better investigation capabilities than existing systems: First, it supports host-based forensics based on virtual machine introspection. Second, it offers live remote capture of network traffic. Third, and most importantly, it provides hybrid combinations of the first two techniques, which enables enhanced analysis capabilities such as support for monitoring encrypted communication.

1 Introduction

1.1 Motivation

The increasing shift of resources towards the cloud makes it necessary to deal with new IT security challenges. As more and more resources are out-sourced into the cloud, these will be a more likely target of malicious activities. Traditional mechanisms for investigating such incidents are, to large extent, insufficient.

A basic problem is the separation between cloud provider and cloud user. In an Infrastructure-as-a-Service (IaaS) cloud, the cloud customer is responsible for all software layers within a virtual machine, but in case of a security incident, the customer cannot apply traditional investigation approaches and tools that require direct access to the physical hardware. On the other hand, the cloud provider has no knowledge about internals of the customer's virtual machines and thus is also in a weak position for an in-depth investigation. A second important challenge is multi-tenancy. Significant efficiency benefits of cloud computing stem from the shared use of resources by multiple customers. A fundamental requirement of cloud infrastructures is the strict separation between multiple tenants using shared physical hardware. An investigation of one customer must not affect the availability, integrity or confidentiality of resources used by other customers.

© IFIP International Federation for Information Processing 2015
A. Bessani and S. Bouchenak (Eds.): DAIS 2015, LNCS 9038, pp. 207–220, 2015.
DOI: 10.1007/978-3-319-19129-4_17

1.2   Problem Statement

It is straight-forward to use existing post-incident investigation tools that analyse static main memory snapshots or analyse log files created during system execution in an IaaS cloud environment. Main memory snapshots can efficiently be created from within active virtual machines, and log files can be obtained from the system within the virtual machine as well as from the cloud management system. A fundamental limitations of these approaches, however, is that they enable only static a-posteriori analysis. What is currently missing are appropriate methods for direct *live* investigations on a running system.

In this paper we propose a novel, integrated architecture for live IaaS forensics. The architecture enables the cloud provider to offer forensics services to customers via a secure interface. The architecture, which we implemented in the LiveCloudInspector prototype, makes three important contributions:

- It enables remote host forensics based on virtual machine introspection (VMI) with a self-service interface for customers;
- It enables efficient, transparent remote network forensics in IaaS cloud infrastructures;
- It offers novel analysis capabilities that yield additional insight by combining host and network forensics.

The combined analysis makes important contributions to enhancing the investigation process. Specifically, it enables correlating recorded network traffic with running processes, indicating exactly to which process data has been sent to or received from; it supports dedicated network monitoring of selected processes; and it supports transparent monitoring of encrypted network traffic using VMI-based session key extraction.

This paper is structured as follows: In the next section, we discuss related work. In Section 3, we summarize the network monitoring and virtual-machine introspection mechanisms our work builds upon. Section 4 presents our architecture. Section 5 describes and evaluates our prototype implementation. Finally, we present our conclusions in Section 6.

2   Related Work

The problem of incident investigation in cloud computing environments has gained some attention only in the recent years. Birk et al. [2] state that the ability to perform forensic investigations in the cloud is of high relevance, but seldomly discussed. The authors argue that guidelines and best practices for investigations in the cloud are rare, often outdated, or non-existent. Similarly, Taylor et al. [12] conclude that "currently there do not appear to be any published guidelines that specifically address the conduct of computer forensic investigations of cloud computing systems."

Dykstra and Sherman [3] tried to deploy existing forensics tools such as Guidance EnCase in an IaaS cloud to acquire forensic data remotely over the Internet.

The paper provides an excellent discussion of the limitations of such an approach. In particular, it argues why data acquired that way might not be trustworthy.

Martini and Choo [7] describe a conceptual framework for collecting forensic data from a cloud environment. The paper includes an extensive discussion of related work on digital forensics and cloud forensics on a broader scope than we include here as well as a high-level description of a conceptual framework. To our knowledge, no practical implementation of that framework exists so far.

In practice, the mechanism with most widespread support by existing cloud providers is the export of virtual machine snapshots[1]. Such virtual machine snapshots contain data of the virtual disk, but not live data such as the main memory. They can only be used for off-line forensic investigations. Some providers implement additional features such as Amazon Cloud Watch[2], which provides basic run-time monitoring features that collect various metrics about run-time behaviour, and Amazon Cloud Trail[3], which records AWS API calls and delivers log-files to the customer.

FROST (Forensic OpenStack Tool) [4] has recently been presented as a forensic toolkit within the OpenStack platform. FROST collects data at the cloud provider and host operating system level und makes it available to the customer by additional API methods. These methods allow downloading API logs, firewall logs and retrieving disk images. Similar to our approach, it advocates the idea of integrating forensics tools and interfaces into a cloud platform management infrastructure. What differentiates our work from FROST are enhanced mechanisms for data acquisition and analysis, specifically supporting *live* analysis.

Gebhardt et al. [6] implemented a network forensics tool for the cloud that extends the OpenNebula management platform. This tools allows recording network traffic on demand and delivering network traffic dumps to the customer for further investigation. The LiveCloudInspector includes a very similar approach for network monitoring, but as a main contributions adds additional data acquisition and analysis methods.

Our framework enhances these existing approaches by implementing both network and host forensics based on dynamic run-time introspection in a single integrated platform. The combination of network monitoring with host introspection yields better insights and enables useful additional mechanisms such as automated correlation of network traffic with running processes and automated decryption of encrypted TLS channels based on secret-key extraction.

3   Background

3.1   Virtual Machine Introspection

Virtual machine introspection (VMI) is an established technology in which the virtual machine monitor (VMM) transparently inspects internal data of a running virtual machine. The VMM has full control of all resources of the VM (such

---

[1] http://aws.amazon.com/ec2/vm-import/ [validated on 2014-09-20]

[2] http://aws.amazon.com/cloudwatch [validated on 2014-09-20]

[3] http://aws.amazon.com/cloudtrail [validated on 2014-09-20]

as main memory, hard disks, and network devices), and thus is in a position for accessing all of them.

Our prototype implementation builds upon the state-of-the-art introspection library LibVMI[4], which supports both Xen and KVM hypervisors. LibVMI requires some knowledge about the OS running within the VM to interpret VM memory correctly. In this paper, we assume that such information exists a priori and can be provided statically to LibVMI. This should, for example, be the case, if the user wants to investigate its own virtual machines. In situations in which such information is not available, our system could be combined with approaches that automatically bridge this semantic gap, such as Insight-VMI [10].

The first goal of our proposed architecture is to enable remote acquisition of memory snapshots using VMI in an IaaS cloud-computing environment.

3.2   High-Level Memory Analysis

While LibVMI offers some low-level API for transparently obtaining data from a running VM, it frequently is desirable to derive more high-level information. Several existing tools such as F-Response[5] and VAD tools[6] support such analysis on the basis of a static main memory snapshot. In our prototype, we use the Volatility framework[7], which can also be combined with live VMI. Volatility has a modular architecture and, for example, includes modules that based on a target system's main memory content enumerate all processes (*pslist*), existing network connections (*connscan*), open files (*filescan*) and registry entries (*hivelist*), or extract sections of main memory of individual processes (*memdump*).

The second goal of our proposed architecture is to enable secure remote use of this tool in a public cloud environment.

3.3   Network Monitoring Background

According to Garfinkel [5], tools for network forensics operate either host-based (such as *Wireshark*[8]) or network-wide (such as NIKSUN NetDetector). They either capture all network packets and store them for later analysis (*"catch-it-as-you-can"*) or analyse packets directly after reception and store only information produced by that analysis for later further processing (*"stop-look-and-listen"*).

Our third goal is to enable remote packet sniffing in a cloud environment, which means that we aim at designing a service that captures all network packets of a virtual machine and stores them for later analysis by the client. For such a host-based catch-it-as-you-can service, we additionally consider continuous monitoring of virtual machines that are migrated and VMI-assisted filtering of recorded traffic.

---

[4] https://code.google.com/p/vmitools/ [validated 2014-09-20]
[5] https://www.f-response.com/ [validated 2014-10-20]
[6] http://vadtools.sourceforge.net [validated 2014-10-20]
[7] http://www.volatilityfoundation.org [validated 2014-09-20]
[8] https://www.wireshark.org [validated 2014-09-20]

3.4   TLS Decryption Background

Analysis tools such as Wireshark contain protocol dissectors for hundreds of different protocols. Dissectors are able to automatically interpret and display protocol details. Wireshark is able to dissect TLS traffic, and if provided with the RSA private key, it can decrypt messages used for exchanging the RSA-encrypted session key (*RSA key exchange*). After obtaining the session key, all subsequent TLS traffic can easily be decrypted.

Shamir et al. [11] have shown that RSA private keys can be located in main memory dumps based on algebraic properties. Such approach could be used for our system, but only with significant limitations: It works only for incoming connections (otherwise, the session key is sent to the remote host, encrypted with the remote host's public key, and the corresponding private key of the remote host cannot be retrieved locally), and it does not work with other key exchange mechanisms that offer forward secrecy, such as Diffie Hellman and ECDH.

Our goal is to reuse as much as possible of the Wireshark TLS dissector, but enhance it with VMI mechanisms that retrieve the *session key* from main memory. We want to be able to monitor all TLS traffic, both incoming and outgoing, and independent of the key exchange mechanisms used.

4   Design and Architecture

Our main goal is to design a secure system that enables cloud users and authorized third parties to perform investigations on some target VMs as a self service (i.e., without manual support by the cloud provider). In this section, we first present the role model of our approach and the high-level design, followed by a detailed description of workflows for simple and complex analysis tasks.

4.1   Role Model

Various roles can be differentiated in an IaaS cloud. Figure 1 illustrates the roles that we consider. Our design makes the assumption that the cloud provider itself (including its staff) is trustworthy. We do not consider malicious insiders (such as a malicious administrator of the cloud provider). Such cases might be tackled with trusted cloud computing techniques, for example such as presented by Rocha et al. [9], but this is beyond the scope of the present paper. We consider the following attacks against our architecture:

- Unauthorized malicious third parties that try to attack the forensics system from outside;
- Users and external investigators that are authorized to investigate virtual machines of a specific user, but exploit the forensics system to gain access to or harm other users, violating the separation of tenants;
- Attackers that deploy (as a user) their own virtual machines within the cloud infrastructure and use those as a starting point for attacks against the forensics system.

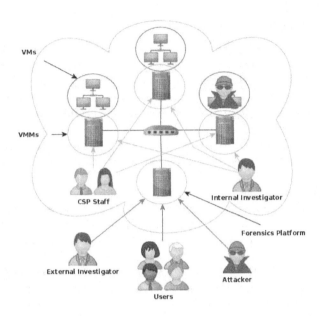

Fig. 1. Trusted and untrusted roles in the LiveCloudInspector architecture: The cloud service provider (CSP) including its staff is trusted, while all other parties (external investigators, users, VMs hosted by the CSP) are untrusted

4.2   Design

Figure 2 shows an overview of the architecture of LiveCloudInspector. It distinguishes between two parts of the forensics system. First, a dedicated *forensics platform* implements all supported workflows as well as the public service interface. Workflows are included for low-level direct main memory dumps of virtual machines, for selected memory forensic operations, and for network forensics. The workflow implementations interact with corresponding counterparts that are deployed as a *forensic remote service* on all cloud hosts.

Our design does not integrate the forensics mechanisms deeply into a cloud management platform such as OpenStack[9] or OpenNebula[10]. Instead we aim at proposing a *portable* architecture that can, with little effort, be reused on multiple cloud platforms or different versions of the same platform.

Nevertheless, there are two dependencies on the cloud management system. First, we do not want to have a separate user management system. Instead, LiveCloudInspector will use a platform-specific adaptor to interact with the cloud management system for user authentication and authorization. Second, we depend on the cloud management system for locating the physical host of target virtual machines and for tracking them on migration operations.

---

[9] http://www.openstack.org [validated 2014-09-20]
[10] http://opennebula.org [validated 2014-09-20]

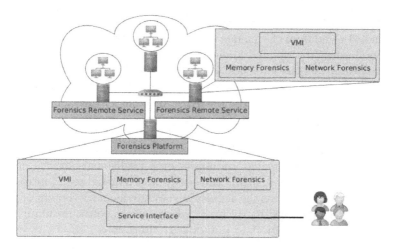

Fig. 2. The LiveCloudInspector architecture adds two components to a cloud environment: A dedicated *Forensics Platform* and decentralized *Forensics Remote Services* deployed on all cloud hosts

The *service interface* of the forensics platform is the public, remotely accessible interface for users and external investigators. After checking the authorization of a client to access the forensics platform via the cloud management system, it accepts commands for *VMI*, *memory forensics* or *network forensics*, retrieves the location of a virtual machine from the platform's management layer, and finally remotely interacts with the corresponding *forensic remote service*.

In the following, we first discuss the details of all *simple workflows*, which are workflows for either recording network traffic or for VMI-based host forensics, followed by a discussion of *complex workflows*, which use a combination of host introspection and network monitoring in order to derive more in-depth insights.

4.3 Simple Workflows

Remote Main Memory Dump. is the first workflow and enables remote snapshots of the *main memory* of a virtual machine. Note that this is fundamentally different from the usual *disk* snapshot generation supported by several cloud providers. Often, relevant artefacts of problems or malicious activities manifest themselves only in main memory, and not on persistent disk storage.

In this workflow, a cloud user or an authorized investigator requests a memory dump at the LiveCloudInspector platform. The platform checks user authentication and authorization and, if access to the specified VM is granted, retrieves the physical location of the VM from the cloud management platform and requests a memory dump from the forensics remote service at the physical host. Finally, the memory dump is made available for download for the cloud user or investigator.

The advantage of this workflow is that the investigator can use any tool of his/her choice to analyse the memory dump. Under the assumption of a trustworthy cloud infrastructure and forensics service, a digital signature attached to the memory dump by the forensics remote service can guarantee the validity of the snapshot. The disadvantage of this workflow is the cost for transferring the memory dump (potentially several gigabytes for large VM instances). A further limitation of the approach is that information in CPU registers or main memory cache is not recorded in the main memory dump.

It should be noted that in fact main memory forensics in a virtual machine is much easier than main memory forensics on a traditional physical host. The main memory of a virtual machine can easily be extracted using introspection tools such as libVMI, whereas the acquisition of main memory content of physical machines requires dedicated hardware or, alternatively, software running on the host that potentially is subject to (unnoticed) alterations.

Remote Memory Forensics enables remote execution of more complex forensics analysis of VM memory. The data source is the same as in the first workflow (i.e., the main memory of a target virtual machine), but instead of transferring the whole memory dump to the investigator, the analysis is performed directly at the target host. For this purpose, such analysis capabilities are enabled directly as a service. In our prototype implementation, we offer remote execution of *Volatility* commands. Volatility supports many high-level diagnostic operations, as briefly discussed in Section 3, and is able to directly interact with VM memory using libVMI.

The advantage of this workflow is that the memory snapshots do not need to be transferred to the investigator. The main disadvantage is that only those remote forensics tools and operations are supported that have been implemented in the forensics platform. We do not support the execution of arbitrary code selected by the user, because this might raise a lot of security questions.

Network Forensics yields additional information for the analysis of anomalous occurrences and intrusions by observing communication patterns. For example, some malware might be periodically communicating with a command-and-control server. Observing network traffic using physical access to the network is an established approach in forensics. In a public IaaS cloud, the investigator has, in most if not all cases, no direct access to physical hosts. Instead, a mechanism for remote acquisition of network traffic is required.

Multi-tenancy potentially raises additional challenges for such remote acquisition, depending on how multi-tenancy is handled by the network infrastructure used by the cloud provider. If each customer (or each VM) has its own, separate virtual network, the traffic of this virtual network can be used for investigation. If multiple tenants share the same local network, additional filtering needs to be applied to the recorded traffic in order to assure strict separation of tenants.

The network monitoring part of the LiveCloudInspector approach is based on previous work by Gebhardt et al. [6]. Unlike the previous work, which integrated the forensics service deeply into OpenNebula, our focus was put on minimizing

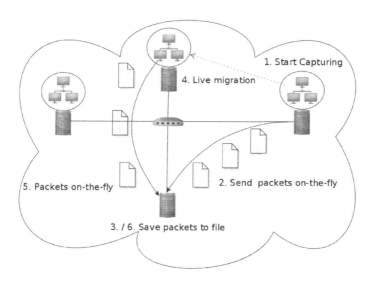

Fig. 3. This image illustrates the high-level interactions between forensics platform (bottom host) and forensics remote service (all other hosts) during VM migration

the dependency on the cloud management system. This makes LiveCloudInspector portable to other cloud management infrastructures.

The basic network capture service implements the recording of network traffic on request by the user. The traffic capture is remotely initiated by remote interaction between forensics platform and forensics remote service. In order to avoid storage overhead on the physical host where the traffic is recorded and also in order to minimize the delay between recording and analysis, each recorded packet is directly sent from the forensics remote service to the forensics platform, where it is made available for download to the investigator.

Virtual Machine Migration is handled by an extension of the network forensics workflow. A cloud management platform may perform live VM migration for purposes such as load balancing or maintenance operations. Many VM managers support not only cold migration (shutting down a VM and relaunching it on a different host), but also hot (live) migration (moving the VM to a different host without shut-down or interruption of client connections).

The LiveCloudInspector supports appropriate coordination mechanisms for handling continuous network capturing during VM migration, as illustrated by Figure 3. For this purpose, it is necessary to receive pre-migration and post-migration events from the cloud management platform, which enable a coordinated activation of traffic acquisition at the migration target and deactivation at the migration source after finishing the migration. Traffic from both the old and the new location are collected by the Forensics Platform and presented to the investigator as a single network capture.

4.4   Complex Workflows

One of the most significant advantages of a hybrid network and host forensics approach is that data of both sources can be combined, which yields several benefits.

Process-Specific Network Monitoring for a single process running within a virtual machine is a first example of a complex workflow. A problem of remote network forensics is that potentially large amounts of recorded data (the whole traffic of a virtual machine) need to be transferred to the investigator.

The LiveCloudInspector allows the investigator to filter the recorded traffic according to running processes within the VM. In order to achieve this, information (IP address and TCP/UDP port numbers) from the captured network is correlated with data about network connections and processes acquired by virtual-machine memory introspection. While this is similar to network forensics workflow, it has the big advantage of requiring less data to be transferred to the investigator.

Correlating Process Names with Network Traffic is a workflow that can be used for monitoring all network communication and correlating each connection with information about the communicating process on the local machine. This might yield only little benefit for incoming connections towards the virtual machine, as usually the target process will be uniquely identified by the destination port and target ports other than the intended services will likely be blocked by a firewall.

Information about corresponding processes can be of valuable benefit for outgoing connections (i.e., originating at the virtual machine under investigation). In this cases, local port numbers usually do not reveal any information about the process the connection originates from.

Monitoring Encrypted TLS Communication is a possibly even more interesting benefit of the combination of host and network forensics. The basic idea is that the session key of a TLS session can directly be extracted using virtual-machine introspection, and then later be used to decrypt all encrypted TLS communication.

The TLS decrypter of LiveCloudInspector can be activated by the network monitor. If a TLS connection is detected, we need to wait for the right point in time for starting the key search. The session key has been calculated by the TLS implementation after the initial TLS handshake has finished and encryption is started using a *ChangeCipherSpec* message. At this point in time, a main memory snapshot of the communicating process within the VM is created and the search for the session key is started concurrent to continuously recording the encrypted traffic.

5   Implementation and Evaluation

5.1   Implementation

We have implemented the proposed architecture in the LiveCloudInspector prototype.

This prototype is designed for working with the OpenNebula cloud management infrastructure. We tried to avoid strong dependency on a specific cloud management product, so we expect that it is easy to port our prototype to other systems. The user interface of LiveCloudInspector is not integrated internally into OpenNebula, but instead a separate web-based interface was created. For this purpose, a front-end running as Java Server Pages on an Apache Tomcat application server were implemented. The front end enables the user to activate several backends for low-level VMI access, for high-level memory introspection, and for network forensics.

The user interface interacts with OpenNebula for authenticating users. The authorization to access virtual machines via LiveCloudInspector is thus not handled with a separate user management system, instead the internal user management of OpenNebula is used. For this purposes we implemented a *Custom Realm* for Tomcat[11] that forwards a user authentication request to OpenNebula authentication core.

A forensics remote service implemented in Java is executed on each cloud host. This service offers a remote interface for interaction with the forensics server. We used SIMON Remote[12] for implementing calls from the server to the remote service, as it is easier to deploy than standard Java RMI. The remote service uses TLS with additional client authentication to make sure that only the forensics server can interact with the remote service.

Our current prototype for the TLS decryption assumes that the session key is directly stored in main memory as a byte array. So far, we successfully validated our key extractor with OpenSSL, JSSE, GnuTLS and Microsoft Schannel implementations. We directly use the decryption functionality of the Wireshark TLS dissector, and thus our implementation works with all TLS ciphers supported by Wireshark.

5.2   Rootkit Case Study

As a first use case we considered a virtual machine infected by the Linux rootkit KBeast. This rootkit is installed as a kernel module and implements features such as key logging and a remote backdoor. The rootkit takes various measures for hiding itself from the user. For example, it hides itself from commands listing the loaded kernel modules (such as *lsmod*), it hides the backdoor process from the process list, and hides network connections of the backdoor from tools such as *netstat*. It is, thus, difficult to detect the rootkit by tools running *within* the virtual machine.

---

[11] http://tomcat.apache.org/tomcat-7.0-doc/realm-howto.html [validated 2014-10-20]
[12] http://dev.root1.de/projects/simon [validated 2014-10-20]

Using our LiveCloudInspector prototype, we were able to remotely execute volatility functions, e.g., to extract information about kernel modules, network connections, and process lists via VM introspection. As the rootkit is not able to manipulate the information extracted using VMI, we were immediately able to distinguish between an infected and a correct virtual machine.

5.3 Security Evaluation

Our IaaS forensics architecture aims at enhancing the security of cloud computing by enhancing the capabilities for incident analysis, but it also represents an additional component that increases the system's complexity and attack surface and possibly causes additional security risks. We therefore discuss protection mechanisms included in our architecture against the threads described in Section 4.1.

Unauthorized malicious third parties that try to attack the forensics system from outside can interact with the service interface of the forensics platform. Our prototype implements client authentication by delegation to the OpenNebula platform. Assuming a correct implementation of the authorization system in the forensics platform, only users that can access the cloud management platform can access the forensics platform.

Clients that are valid users and thus successfully authenticate to the forensics platform might try to acquire information about other users, violating the strict separation of tenants. In our system, for both network and host forensics, OpenNebula's VM-ID is used to identify the target virtual machine. For all operations, OpenNebula is contacted for all access to that VM-ID, and OpenNebula checks the user's authorization. Only users that are authorized to access a virtual machine via the OpenNebula API are allowed to access it via the forensics platform.

User input is also used in the interaction between the forensics platform's backends and the forensic remote services. In particular, for remote memory forensics, the user has a lot of control over arguments passed to the Volatility tool. Careful input validation is necessary in order to avoid possible injection attacks at this interface.

The *Forensic Remote Service* can also be a target of malicious attacks, originating either from outside or from a virtual machine within the cloud infrastructure. Besides blocking such interaction at the network level using firewall rules we additionally implemented two-way authentication between the *Forensics Platform* and *Forensics Remote Services*, making this kind of attack infeasible.

5.4 Limitations

A frequently discussed limitation of introspection-based tools for malware analysis is split-personality malware. Examples such as RedPill and variants [8] show that it is easy for malware to detect whether it is running in a virtualized environment and thus could behave differently than in a production environment.

This issue is not a problem for our approach, as we apply VMI directly in the production environment.

What is a potential problem are attempts to subvert VMI, as shown for example by DKSM [1]. Our current prototype implementation is based on LibVMI, which relies on the assumption that the provided kernel system map corresponds to the actual kernel in the VM. If the layout of kernel data structures is altered by malware within the virtual machine, VMI can possibly produce wrong data. This is not a direct limitation of our architecture itself, but is an implication of the introspection mechanism in use, and the investigator using our system needs to be aware of this potential problem. The development of more robust introspection solutions that are not vulnerable to such attacks will help to remedy this limitation.

Our monitoring approach for encrypted communication works for traffic that uses standard implementations of TLS. We assume that session keys are stored in main memory (which all popular implementations of TLS that we are aware of do), and that traffic is encrypted according to the specification of TLS. This is most likely true for all software intentionally running within the virtual machine (this is under full control of the user of the VM). Often, even malware uses standard TLS for communication on command-and-control channels, but this could easily be replaced by some other proprietary encryption mechanisms. Our prototype will not be able to decrypt such connections that use encryption methods different to standard TLS.

6 Conclusions

In this paper, we have presented the design and implementation of LiveCloudInspector. LiveCloudInspector enables forensics as a service in public cloud environments. The architecture combines, in a single system, three mechanisms that support the analysis of security incidents:

- It enables transparent live host forensics based on virtual-machine introspection. This feature includes both the possibility of acquiring low-level memory snapshots and the possibility of analysing the running system with high-level Volatility commands.
- It enables remote network forensics by implementing a live network traffic capture mechanism. This mechanism makes sure that captured data is filtered correctly in a multi-tenant environment, and it also supports virtual machine migration during the capture process.
- It combines network monitoring with VMI-based host analysis. This yields interesting new analysis capabilities, such as directly monitoring traffic of specific processes, correlating information about processes with network traffic, and secret key extracting for monitoring encrypted TLS communication. The session key extraction works for both incoming and outgoing connections, it even supports channels established with perfect forward secrecy (i.e., Diffie-Helman based session key establishment), and unlike interception-based approaches it is fully transparent for the communication endpoints.

With these contributions, our architecture enhances the possibilities for investigating security incidents in infrastructure-as-a-service cloud environments.

Acknowledgments. The research leading to these results was supported by the "Bavarian State Ministry of Education, Science and the Arts" as part of the FORSEC research association.

References

1. Bahram, S., Jiang, X., Wang, Z., Grace, M., Li, J., Srinivasan, D., Rhee, J., Xu, D.: DKSM: Subverting virtual machine introspection for fun and profit. In: 29th IEEE Symposium on Reliable Distributed Systems (SRDS), pp. 82–91 (October 2010)
2. Birk, D., Wegener, C.: Technical issues of forensic investigations in cloud computing environments. In: Proceedings of the 2011 Sixth IEEE International Workshop on Systematic Approaches to Digital Forensic Engineering, SADFE 2011, pp. 1–10. IEEE Computer Society, Washington, DC (2011)
3. Dykstra, J., Sherman, A.T.: Acquiring forensic evidence from infrastructure-as-a-service cloud computing: Exploring and evaluating tools, trust, and techniques. Digital Investigation 9, 90–98 (2012)
4. Dykstra, J., Sherman, A.T.: Design and implementation of FROST: Digital forensic tools for the OpenStack cloud computing platform. Digit. Investig. 10, 87–95 (2013)
5. Garfinkel, S.: Network forensics: Tapping the internet, http://www.oreillynet.com/pub/a/network/2002/04/26/nettap.html (April 01, 2015)
6. Gebhardt, T., Reiser, H.P.: Network forensics for cloud computing. In: Dowling, J., Taïani, F. (eds.) DAIS 2013. LNCS, vol. 7891, pp. 29–42. Springer, Heidelberg (2013)
7. Martini, B., Choo, K.R.: An integrated conceptual digital forensic framework for cloud computing. Digital Investigation 9(2), 71–80 (2012)
8. Paleari, R., Martignoni, L., Roglia, G.F., Bruschi, D.: A fistful of red-pills: How to automatically generate procedures to detect cpu emulators. In: Proceedings of the 3rd USENIX Conference on Offensive Technologies, WOOT 2009. USENIX Association, Berkeley (2009)
9. Rocha, F., Abreu, S., Correia, M.: The final frontier: Confidentiality and privacy in the cloud. Computer 44(9), 44–50 (2011)
10. Schneider, C., Pfoh, J., Eckert, C.: A universal semantic bridge for virtual machine introspection. In: Jajodia, S., Mazumdar, C. (eds.) ICISS 2011. LNCS, vol. 7093, pp. 370–373. Springer, Heidelberg (2011)
11. Shamir, A., van Someren, N.: Playing "hide and seek" with stored keys. In: Franklin, M.K. (ed.) FC 1999. LNCS, vol. 1648, pp. 118–124. Springer, Heidelberg (1999)
12. Taylor, M., Haggerty, J., Gresty, D., Lamb, D.: Forensic investigation of cloud computing systems. Netw. Secur. 2011(3), 4–10 (2011)

Author Index

Printed in the United States
By Bookmasters